MADRESFIELD

One home, one family,
one thousand years

Jane Mulvagh

BLACK SWAN

TRANSWORLD PUBLISHERS
61–63 Uxbridge Road, London W5 5SA
A Random House Group Company
www.rbooks.co.uk

MADRESFIELD
A BLACK SWAN BOOK: 9780552772389

First published in Great Britain
in 2008 by Doubleday
a division of Transworld Publishers
Black Swan edition published 2009

Addresses for Random House Group Ltd companies outside the UK
can be found at: www.randomhouse.co.uk
The Random House Group Ltd Reg. No. 954009

The Random House Group Limited supports The Forest Stewardship Council
(FSC), the leading international forest certification organisation. All our titles
that are printed on Greenpeace approved FSC certified paper carry the FSC logo.
Our paper procurement policy can be found at www.rbooks.co.uk/environment

Typeset in 11/15pt Giovanni Book by
Falcon Oast Graphic Art Ltd.
Printed in the UK by CPI Cox & Wyman, Reading, RG1 8EX.

2 4 6 8 10 9 7 5 3 1

To Constance and Margot
and in loving memory of Peter Paul Mulvagh

Wakefield Tower, Rowena and Salisbury NFL   Eric Whitfield

There is nothing as unique in English architecture as the house ... no nation is more committed to its development, because no nation has identified itself more with the house.

Hermann Muthesius

CONTENTS

THE
Lygon
FAMILY HISTORY

A Simplified Version Showing the Male Lineage and Principal Characters

Robert de Braci
active 1196
Dug the moat

Robert de Braci *m* Maud de Warenne
active 1316

Sir Robert de Braci
active 1328
Huntsman and warrior

Joan de Braci *m* Thomas Lygon
active 1423   of Kidderminster
Great-granddaughter
of Sir Robert

Thomas Lygon *m* Anne Gifford
active 1435
Commission de Wallis
et Fossatis

Lord Beauchamp of Powick
m Elizabeth Stafford

Anne Beauchamp *m* **Richard Lygon**
active 1490   1439–1512

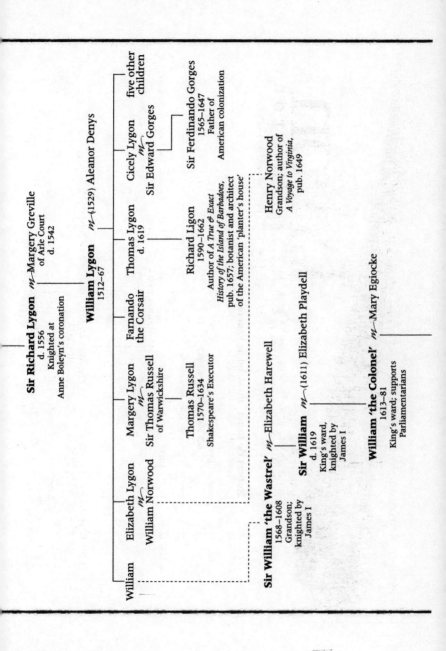

Sir Richard Lygon *m* Margery Greville
d. 1556   of Arle Court
Knighted at   d. 1542
Anne Boleyn's coronation

William Lygon *m* (1529) Aleanor Denys
1512–67

Elizabeth Lygon   Margery Lygon   William   Farnando   Thomas Lygon   Cicely Lygon   five other
m   *m*   the Corsair   d. 1619   *m*   children
William Norwood   Sir Thomas Russell   Sir Edward Gorges
                   of Warwickshire

                   Thomas Russell   Richard Ligon   Sir Ferdinando Gorges
                   1570–1634   1590–1662   1565–1647
                   Shakespeare's Executor   Author of *A True & Exact*   Father of
                                                   History of the Island of Barbadoes,   American colonization
                                                   pub. 1657; botanist and architect
                                                   of the American 'planter's house'

                                                   Henry Norwood
                                                   Grandson; author of
                                                   A Voyage to Virginia,
                                                   pub. 1649

Sir William 'the Wastrel' *m* Elizabeth Harewell
1568–1608
Grandson;
knighted by
James I

                   Sir William *m* (1611) Elizabeth Playdell
                   d. 1619
                   King's ward,
                   knighted by
                   James I

                   William 'the Colonel' *m* Mary Egiocke
                   1613–81
                   King's ward; supports
                   Parliamentarians

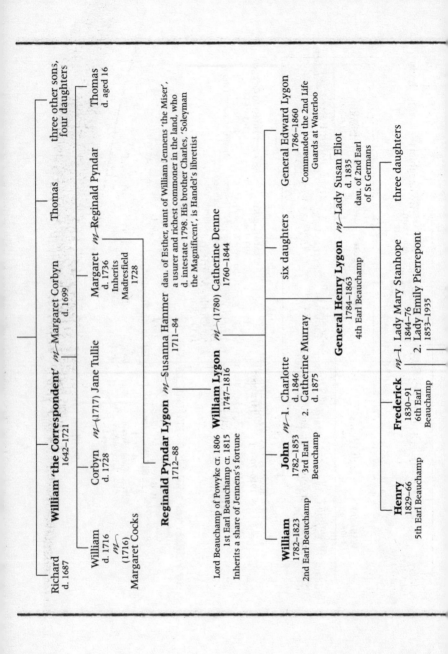

Richard
d. 1687

William 'the Correspondent' *m*—Margaret Corbyn
1642–1721   d. 1699

Thomas

three other sons,
four daughters

William
d. 1716
m
(1716)
Margaret Cocks

Corbyn
d. 1728
m—(1717) Jane Tullie

Margaret
d. 1736
Inherits
Madresfield
1728
m—Reginald Pyndar

Thomas
d. aged 16

Reginald Pyndar Lygon *m*—Susanna Hanmer
1712–88   1711–84

William Lygon
1747–1816
m—(1780) Catherine Denne
1760–1844

dau. of Esther, aunt of William Jennens 'the Miser',
a usurer and richest commoner in the land, who
d. intestate 1798. His brother Charles, 'Soleyman
the Magnificent', is Handel's librettist

Lord Beauchamp of Powyke *cr.* 1806
1st Earl Beauchamp *cr.* 1815
Inherits a share of Jennens's fortune

William
1782–1823
2nd Earl Beauchamp

John
1782–1853
3rd Earl
Beauchamp
m—1. Charlotte
           d. 1846
       2. Catherine Murray
           d. 1875

six daughters

General Henry Lygon
1784–1863
4th Earl Beauchamp

General Edward Lygon
1786–1860
Commanded the 2nd Life
Guards at Waterloo
m—Lady Susan Eliot
       d. 1835
       dau. of 2nd Earl
       of St Germans

three daughters

Henry
1829–66
5th Earl Beauchamp

Frederick
1830–91
6th Earl
Beauchamp
m—1. Lady Mary Stanhope
           1844–76
       2. Lady Emily Pierrepont
           1853–1935

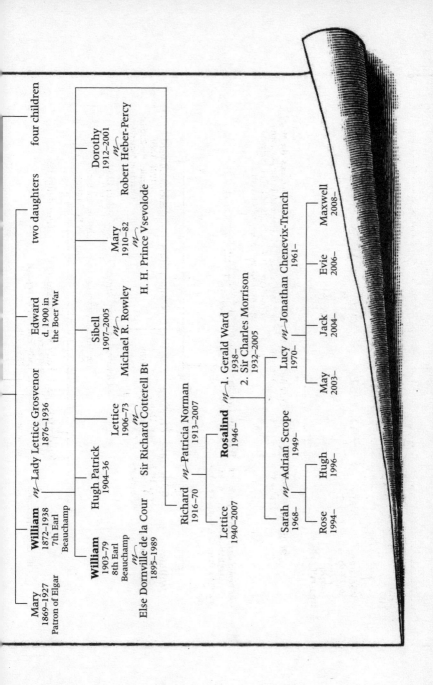

Mary
1869–1927
Patron of Elgar

William
1872–1938
7th Earl
Beauchamp
m Lady Lettice Grosvenor
1876–1936

Edward
d. 1900 in
the Boer War

two daughters

four children

William
1903–79
8th Earl
Beauchamp
m
Else Dornville de la Cour
1895–1989

Hugh Patrick
1904–36

Lettice
1906–73
m
Sir Richard Cotterell Bt

Sibell
1907–2005
m
Michael R. Rowley

Mary
1910–82
m
H. H. Prince Vsevolode

Dorothy
1912–2001
m
Robert Heber-Percy

Richard *m* Patricia Norman
1916–70   1913–2007

Lettice
1940–2007

Rosalind *m* 1. Gerald Ward
1946–   1938–
              2. Sir Charles Morrison
                 1932–2005

Sarah *m* Adrian Scrope
1968–   1949–

Lucy *m* Jonathan Chenevix-Trench
1970–   1961–

Rose
1994–

Hugh
1996–

May
2003–

Jack
2004–

Evie
2006–

Maxwell
2008–

BRIDESHEAD RE-REVISITED

The summit of Clent Hill, just a few miles west of Birmingham, is scarcely one thousand feet above sea level, but the view from the top surpasses that which may be had from many a higher elevation. In one direction is Birmingham itself, and what used in an earlier time to be known as the Black Country. But to the west, a completely different vista opens out across the Severn Valley, extending from the Clee Hills via the Malverns to the Cotswolds and Bredon, which encompasses Shropshire, Herefordshire, Worcestershire and Gloucestershire, and offers distant glimpses of the Welsh Marches beyond. It is an unforgettable panorama, by turns wide, grand and spectacular, yet also touchingly vulnerable, intimate and domestic – a bird's eye view of a self-enclosed world that at different times and in different idioms has been evoked and celebrated by P. G. Wodehouse in his comic saga of pigs, Lord Emsworth and Blandings Castle, by Stanley

Baldwin in his homespun speeches projecting rural, Christian, Tory values, by Edward Elgar whose 'Enigma' Variations paid homage to some of his Severnside friends and acquaintances, and by Francis Brett Young in his bestselling inter-war novels.

Despite its proximity to the Midlands, this is in some ways a region remarkably untouched by heavy industry or disfigured by urban sprawl – a world of moated manor houses and homely rectories, of village churches and war memorials. It remains very inward-looking in its perspectives and conservative in its culture; it is self-consciously English, and it does not seem to change all that much. One reason for this sense of reposeful permanence is that for much of their history, the counties bordering the River Severn were dominated by the gentry and squirearchy, rather than by great magnates or Whig grandees. (The Dukes of Beaufort at Badminton and the Earls of Dudley at Witley Court were very much the exceptions who proved the rule.) As Francis Brett Young put it in one of his novels, 'No title or abundant wealth has ever come their way; no brilliant blossom has ever adorned their family tree; its sole virtue consists in its astonishing permanence.' Warming to his theme, he went on: 'Wars may redden the land, revolution may change its face and dynasties may divide it,' but the local county families 'still go on; they are so near to the soil, their roots stretch so far down, that mere accidents such as these are powerless to move them.'

Brett Young's words might seem to apply, for many

centuries of their near-millennium-long history, to the Lygon family and their romantic house, Madresfield Court, which stands in this landscape to the west of the River Severn and to the east of the Malvern Hills, and to whose then châtelaine he dedicated one of his novels. Across those thousand years, their moated manor has never been bought and has never been sold (though it has several times passed through the female line), and for much of their history, successive generations of owners kept a relatively low profile, confining themselves to involvement in local affairs, to representing the county at Westminster, and to the standard activities and recreations of their class. Yet as this fascinating book makes plain, such remarkable continuity across the centuries is not quite what it seems, as the Beauchamps were followed by the de Bracis, and it was not until the fifteenth century that the Lygons appeared on the scene. *Their* male line died out in turn in the eighteenth century, and the family name was only perpetuated because Reginald Pyndar, who married Margaret Lygon, changed his name to hers. The complex and intriguing descent of the Madresfield house and estate is expertly unravelled in the pages that follow.

Only in the early nineteenth century did a title and more abundant wealth come the family's way. The Lygons were transformed into the Earls Beauchamp (in an act of ancestral homage to the earlier dynasty); Madresfield was embellished and extended (and provided with both a library and a chapel); and the sixth earl was a significant churchman (he helped found Keble College, Oxford) and politician (he held office in the governments of Disraeli and Salisbury). But it was not until the time of the seventh Earl Beauchamp that the family and their house became more generally known beyond the confines of Worcestershire. During the 1890s and 1900s, the earl himself was a civic worthy, imperial proconsul and (turning his back on his family's traditional Toryism) Liberal Cabinet minister. His sister, Lady Mary Lygon, was a friend and patron of Elgar, and he portrayed her in the thirteenth of his 'Enigma' Variations. There was also a terrible scandal, as the seventh earl's career eventually crashed into ruins. Meanwhile, Evelyn Waugh was a regular and appreciative visitor to Madresfield, and he would later immortalize both the family and their house in *Brideshead Revisited*.

For many people who have watched the television adaptation of Waugh's lush evocation of Catholic angst, aristocratic self-indulgence and patrician decline, Brideshead means Castle Howard in Yorkshire, where so much of the series was actually filmed. Yet despite – indeed, because of – its many and manifold splendours, Castle Howard is not like Waugh's Brideshead at all. It is a Whig extravaganza, a Vanbrugh stage set, a palazzo fortissimo: all drums and trumpets, marble and monuments, columns and cupolas, triumphal arches, man-made landscapes, artificial lakes, long vistas and big skies. Brideshead, by contrast, is understated, out of the way, emerging from the countryside rather than dominating it, and thus it was, and thus it is, with the model that was Madresfield. Jane Mulvagh's book brings both the place and its occupants to life, with a fine eye for telling detail, architectural and personal. She rightly gives as much attention to the house as to the people who have lived in it, and by artfully interconnecting the family and their mansion across the centuries, she chronicles what is, indeed, a remarkable story of 'astonishing permanence', which also enables us to see Waugh and his work in a wholly new light. Truly, historically and authentically, this book is *Brideshead Re-Revisited*.

David Cannadine

Acknowledgements

Five people were central to the writing of this book and without them it would not have been possible. Firstly, Rosalind Morrison who opened her home and the unique Muniment Room at Madresfield to me and was a constant support; Professor David Cannadine, who suggested this project and 'supervised' me all the way; Edmondo di Robilant who introduced me to Rosalind Morrison; Dr Rowena E. Archer, an inspirational guide through medieval England; and Angelica von Hase whose research and editorial eye were fastidious.

George Ramsden, James Stourton, Peter Straus, Oonagh Wohanka, Mike Shaw, Lucy Lethbridge, Celia Lyttelton and Selina Hastings read the manuscript and offered invaluable advice for which I thank them. I would also like to thank Patrick Janson-Smith, a keen supporter of the project, Marianne Velmans for her editorial guidance and kindly patience, Michèle David for her fine editing, and Sheila Lee and all the staff at Doubleday. Greta Payne and Mavis Corbin of the Barbados Museum and Historical Society; Pauline Sidell, the archivist of the Grocers' Company of the City of London; Dr Philip Mansell; David Gilmour; Sophie Slade, the curator of the Charles Dickens Museum,

London; Robert Gray; Bryan Maggs; Mark Getty; Dr Jerrold Northrop Moore; David Hart, the silversmith; the late Lord Deedes; the late Diana, Lady Mosley; the archivist Janet Sinclair; Dr Tania Rose; and Desmond Guinness: all lent their expert advice and I am grateful to them all.

Many hours were spent with the late Lady Sibell Rowley who was forthright, humorous and downright honest. I loved our many exchanges over 'picnic' lunches in her cottage.

Nic Barlow took the arresting photographs for this book and was a joy to work with: quick-witted, inventive and alert to Madresfield's unique *genius loci*.

The London Library, the Kensington Public Library, the college libraries of King's, Cambridge, and Keble, Oxford, and the Elgar Birthplace Museum, Worcestershire, provided invaluable sources and their staff, and Tony Smith and Kirsty Anderson at G. Heywood Hill bookshop, all contributed to this book.

My thanks also go to the staff at Madresfield, Colin Lee, Lin Lamore and Jane Facer.

Finally, with loyalty and love my husband Anthony Bourne and our two daughters have lived with *Madresfield*. Thank you.

PROLOGUE

*I had been there before; first with Sebastian more than
twenty years ago on a cloudless day in June, when the
ditches were creamy with meadowsweet and the air heavy
with all the scents of summer.*

'What a place to live in!' I said.

*'You must see the garden front and the fountain.' He
leaned forward and put the car into gear. 'It's where my
family live'; and even then, rapt in the vision, I felt,
momentarily, an ominous chill at the words he used –
not, 'that is my house', but 'it's where my family live'.*

Evelyn Waugh, *Brideshead Revisited*

The house upon which Evelyn Waugh based
Brideshead was Madresfield Court in
Worcestershire, the home of the Lygons for nearly one
thousand years. Madresfield, sitting on its Anglo-Saxon
foundations, slowly accreting, generation by

generation, its inimitable character, appealed to Waugh's medieval heart. He would have thrilled to the knowledge that the Lygons' family home has never been bought or sold. Instead, from the eleventh century to today it has been passed down through twenty-eight generations by direct descent, on three occasions through women. 'I loved buildings that grew silently with the centuries, catching and keeping the best of each generation,' one of his characters explains.

Charles Ryder, the novel's narrator, had befriended Sebastian Flyte at Oxford. Waugh met Hugh Lygon (pronounced *liggon*) there in 1922 and theirs became an enduring and intense friendship, cut short by Hugh's premature death in 1936. He came to know and to love Madresfield when one of Hugh's four sisters, Dorothy, first invited him to stay for Christmas in 1931. Arriving by train, he was picked up at Malvern Link railway station and driven the three miles to Madresfield. From the moment the car entered the estate along the Gloucester Drive, which runs straight for exactly one mile, he would have seen in the distance, set against the Malvern Hills, the great old house. As they proceeded up the drive, passing through hoar-frosted meadows set with mistletoe-bearing oaks, the architecturally piecemeal details of the house would have emerged, one by one, from out of the mists which rise from its wide medieval moat; first, the spire of the wooden tower, then, in succession, the 'Jacobean' barley-twist and 'quilted' brick chimneys, the Tudor crow-steps, the neo-Gothic gables, corbels and gargoyles and finally the patchwork of mullioned windows.

Madresfield is approached up one of four tree-lined avenues – oak, Lombardy poplar, lime and cedar – and presents its oldest and barest face to the visitor. This is not a suave house. No Doric columns rise up to dwarf a man. The celluloid image of a baroque 'Brideshead' is misleading and could not be further from the real Madresfield. Instead, it is a very English dwelling, a moated manor house, erected as a retreat from the world rather than a Continental showpiece to impress it.

In times of trouble, politician Viscount Halifax advised his fellow countrymen to 'look to your moat!' and Madresfield is girdled with a deep one. When the house and moat were first built, a single bridge offered the only entrance. Today, as the visitor steps across this bridge, the reflection of the Tudor brickwork is distorted in the watery wake of the ducks below. To the right, curious to see who is entering, four dogs invariably peer through the heraldic stained glass of the twenty-foot-wide bay window that hangs over the moat, above which crow-stepped gables rise. Indifferent to symmetry, none of the roof-scapes tally. On each summit a 'fluttering' ironwork banner bearing the letter 'B' reminds the visitor that he is entering the home of the Earls Beauchamp, the title granted to the Lygon family in 1815. Their motto, *Fortuna mea est in bello campo*, is a Latin translation of Psalm 16, verse 6: 'The lines are fallen unto me in pleasant places; yea I have a goodly heritage.' And indeed they have. It is also a pun on their choice of title, *bello campo* becoming *beau champ*.

The entrance passage under the Tudor arch is flanked by a pair of guards' rooms. A bicycle is propped against the wall just as C. R. Ashbee, the Arts and Crafts architect and designer, would have left the bone-shaker on which he pedalled from the Cotswolds one hundred years ago to work on the house. Twelfth-century oak outer doors facing the bridge lead via the entrance passage to inner doors dating from the reign of Henry VIII. Neither pair has handles or locks on the outside. This house has never been left unoccupied.

The first impression on entering Madresfield today is one of a working home. The visitor will not be bowled over by its grandeur. There is no need for him to tilt his head back to gaze at a frescoed ceiling high above or to marvel at vaguely recognizable old masters hanging in gilt frames. The ceilings are relatively low, the rugs have seen much use, and the only paintings displayed in the hall are small watercolours of the house and its park by an accomplished ancestor. Perhaps a dry-cleaning ticket and a catalogue for spring bulbs are tucked under a bronze bust of the seventh earl. A wicker basket of fundraising flyers for Worcester Cathedral sits on the oak gate-leg table. A number of dog baskets and two dozen pairs of comfortable shoes and rubber boots are lined up against the oak-panelled wall.

Madresfield's core was built before the Georgian preference for a rational floor plan for domestic architecture and lack of funds prohibited major changes until relatively recently. Instead, this architectural hybrid contains a hotchpotch of styles, the accretions of each generation, seemingly oblivious to the changing fashions and influences from abroad.

To the right lies the great Library, giving on to a Smoking Room that evokes the easy comforts of an antiquarian's sitting room. Returning to the Entrance Hall, the Ante-room beyond it contains marble busts and Gobelin tapestries hint at a formality to come. Beyond again, two sets of double doors open on to the Saloon, which is furnished with French *ancien régime* furniture and ancestral portraits. In pride of place hangs a likeness of William Jennens, the richest commoner in the land when he died in 1798. His connection with the family had a transforming effect on their lives. Another pair of doors leads to what must surely be the climax: the Drawing Room. A thirty-foot-high ceiling is suspended over a spectacular room, sixty feet by forty, aired by two bay windows; one looks out on to the park and Bredon Hill beyond, the other on to the stone-paved Moat Garden planted with lavender. Here was delivered an ultimatum from King George V, which would have tragic consequences.

There are no enfilades in Madresfield. Instead, the visitor tumbles unexpectedly – like Alice – from a small room to a huge one and then on to a tiny one. Turning from the Drawing Room, he enters what is probably the largest room in which he has ever stood: the Staircase Hall. Nearly three storeys high, it is crowned with a trio of glass cupolas through which sunlight pours down on to seemingly endless parquet. A black ebony staircase and gallery cleave to the walls on three sides and the newel posts are surmounted by carved swans and bears, supporters taken from the family crest. These grave sentinels stand above several hundred barley-sugar-twist banisters cut from rock crystal. Madresfield's façade never suggested such scale. More double doors open on to the Great Hall, the Tudor heart of this great manor house. Up under the hammerbeam roof sits a Musicians' Gallery from where a small door leads into the first floor Long Gallery, which runs the length of the house and was used to promenade in when the weather was inclement.

In the middle of the nineteenth century the medieval core of Madresfield was wrapped on three sides by a neo-Gothic extension which resulted in a vast house of 160 rooms covering two acres. The interiors are scruffy here, smart over there, and suggest a robust family home which has grown quietly over a millennium. How else could one explain a portrait of Queen Elizabeth I hanging opposite a pair of Australian boomerangs? The Lygons have never resorted to hiring the 'good' taste of decorators. Instead the sumptuous sits next to the threadbare and the heraldic rests easily alongside the modern. Above all, it has remained rooted in country life – literally remote from court life and the metropolis – and consequently, its landscape, its setting, its park are as fundamental to the whole as the building. Nature is not left at the door but welcomed in to flourish as oak-leaf carvings on bookcases, apple blossom sprigs bursting from Chinese vases and an idealized conjunction of the year's flowers in an English glade painted on to the Chapel frescoes.

It is not the great treasures but the unexpected juxtapositions that catch the eye: an English slipware plate between a pair of Laura Ashley lamps; the Georgian marble fireplace set with William Morris tiles; a plastic soda-water bottle and roll of kitchen towel sitting at the foot of a porphyry bust of Marcus Aurelius, in case a dog defiles the old parquet; the 'Holbein' (attributed with some optimism) hanging over a limewood trilby hat and gloves recently carved by a Lygon; two sofas, one covered with a sixties elephant cord, the other with an Arts and Crafts linen flanked by a pair of chairs made by Louis XIV's *ébéniste*, André-Charles Boulle.

The written word, more than decorative objects, is accorded the greatest respect at Madresfield. Not only does the house hold muniments dating back to the Middle Ages, but the Library contains over twelve thousand volumes including medieval manuscripts. Piles of books tracing the arc of the Englishman's imagination sit on side tables and many have a particular relevance to a Lygon to whom they may have been dedicated or by whom they were inspired, be it Malory's *Le Morte D'Arthur*, Sir Walter Scott's *Ivanhoe*, John Keble's *The Christian Year*, Charles Dickens's *Bleak House*, Macaulay's poems, Charlotte M. Yonge's *The Heir of Redclyffe*, the score for Elgar's 'Enigma' Variations,

Hilaire Belloc's *Cautionary Tales*, Francis Brett Young's *Portrait of Clare* or Evelyn Waugh's *Brideshead Revisited*. The size of the house is suggested by the fact that the books are stamped 'Please return to the Smoking Room' or 'the Library' rather than just 'Madresfield'. (One of the library stacks is carved with the admonition 'Thou shalt not steal'.) The very masonry and wood-work of the building pay homage to the written word. Homilies are moulded into the neo-Jacobean plaster-work; stanzas of Shelley's poetry are carved in three-foot-high letters into the cornices; a word-square of *Fredricus Fecit* ('Made by Frederick', the sixth earl) is chiselled into a stone fireplace; a bronze sundial in the topiary garden is cast with 'That day is wasted on which we have not laughed'. George Romney's portrait of the great historian Edward Gibbon hangs in pride of place above the fireplace in the Drawing Room.

The Lygons' ancestors, the de Bracis, settled here soon after the *Domesday Book* was compiled in 1086 and built a wattle-and-daub manor house surrounded by a deep ditch. Few landed families have survived the vicissitudes of so many centuries: plague, civil war, profligacy, agricultural recession, insurance debts – and even fewer have resisted the simple temptation to sell up and seek their fortune elsewhere. It is a remarkable continuity. Today, Madresfield is lived in by Rosalind Morrison (*née* Lygon), niece of William Lygon, the eighth and last Earl Beauchamp.

In a millennium which has seen the pace of human life accelerate and a steady increase in both migration and the dissemination of information about people's affairs, a family that has remained still and private is worthy of note. As a rule the Lygons have kept their heads down and their feet firmly on English soil. And today, in our age of constant motion, it is intriguing to explore a family which continues to be rooted in its homeland.

The history of the house is interwoven with the history of England. Over the centuries, the Lygons have welcomed painters, writers, prime ministers, theologians, royals and rebels to their home and it has left its mark on these visitors. Had Farnando Lygon and his co-conspirators' plot succeeded in 1556, Mary Tudor would have lost the throne. An exceptionally large and contested inheritance, eventually resolved in the Lygons' favour, provided one of the main inspirations for Charles Dickens's *Bleak House*. Sir Edward Elgar dedicated music to his muse, Lady Mary Lygon. To further the cause of the Oxford Movement, Frederick, the sixth earl, founded Keble College, Oxford, in memory of the Victorian poet and Tractarian John Keble. The seventh earl, a Liberal Cabinet minister, made a stand against the Great War and championed the rights of the conscientious objector.

The Lygons' story is not just one of survival but also of social and economic ascent, from minor squirearchy to the companions of kings, a steady rise which can be traced in Madresfield's Muniment Room. The relatively unknown muniments still stored in the house are perhaps the Lygons' most valuable asset. Their earliest document is a land charter from Henry I, the Conqueror's son, dated 1121. The archive includes letters from statesmen, monarchs and artists; settlements made on or by medieval wives; loans, wills and love letters. Papers cast new light on the commercial opportunities of Stuart London; on royal family life as observed by various Lygons in attendance; on the bitterness surrounding the Oxford Movement; on Asquith's Cabinet in the hours before Britain declared war on Germany in 1914 and on other matters of national significance.

In the 1930s, the Lygons were riven by a scandal and in a protective sweep all the relevant papers were destroyed – or so it seemed until a fire broke out on Boxing Day 2006 in another house just fifteen miles away. Out of the charred remains the firemen pulled some diaries. The complete story could now be told.

Madresfield stands in a rural backwater, which partly explains its survival. An old and particular Englishness lingers in the West Midlands, an Englishness once captured in different ways by four of its sons: Langland, Shakespeare, Elgar and Housman. Gloucestershire, Worcestershire, Herefordshire: their names suggest a progression into remoteness. Here lies a quieter England of orchards, hop yards and mistletoe-bearing trees. Its half-timbered buildings conjure up an older England that is simpler than the noble cupolas and spires of Oxford and the honey-coloured manor houses of the Cotswolds on its eastern border. The Severn and Teme Rivers meander through this low, misty landscape which stretches from the edge of the Cotswolds to the foot of those 'blue remembered hills', the Malverns.

A poor transport infrastructure has left west Worcestershire relatively inaccessible. It is one of England's smallest counties, just thirty-five miles long and thirty miles wide. As you journey into it from the east, across the fertile plain known as the Vale of Evesham, the Malvern Hills, 'those curious bubblings up' as William Cobbett called them in the nineteenth century, gradually come into view, undulating for eight and a half miles across the horizon. For centuries they gave travellers their bearings and guided the Lygons home. These, the oldest hills in England, form the ridge along which the poet William Langland wandered in the fourteenth century and wrote *Piers Plowman*. Six centuries later, lying on his deathbed, Sir Edward Elgar struggled to whistle the first movement of his Cello Concerto and, turning to his friend, the violinist William Reed, he said, 'Billy, if ever you're walking on the Malvern Hills and hear that, don't be frightened. It's only me.' From their peak, at 1,395 feet, he could have seen across half a dozen counties. In their lee, and on the western side of the River Severn, stands Madresfield.

Families and habits thrive in a timeless fashion in this region that has not attracted grandees or supported large estates but has sheltered a conservative squirearchy, passionate ruralists and those wishing to remain far from the crowd. Three hundred years ago when the essayist Addison wanted to find a typical Englishman for his journal *The Spectator*, he invented Sir Roger de Coverley of Worcestershire. On his rural rides in the 1820s, William Cobbett noted 'there is no *visible* misery . . . and I cannot take my leave of this country without observing that I do not recollect to have seen one miserable object in it.'

Often, Madresfield is shrouded in summer mists or winter fogs that rise from the encircling waters. The name of this arrestingly romantic home is derived from the Old English *maeðeresfeld* for 'Mower's Field'; men settled on this field in Anglo-Saxon times, perhaps earlier. Far from the convulsions of power, the Lygons' home has retained something of pre-industrial Albion. Each generation, by tethering itself to country matters, has had more in common with the villager than the courtier.

This is a story not just of a house but also of a landscape. It begins with a plot of land, a plot into which a ditch was dug to defend a home. Over nine centuries later, that ditch saved the Lygon home. Thus, in a millennium, the tale has described one great circle.

To sit inside this old house today is to be enveloped in an ancient and secure stillness. There is hardly a sound save for, on windy days, a rattling pane. Cocooned by the wooden panelling, protected by the deep moat beyond, the smells of Madresfield heighten the sense of place: beeswax polish; mock-orange blossom in a copper planter on the oak trestle; the sweet mustiness of a draught blown across a Lowlands tapestry; smoke coiling up from logs burning in the grate. Looking out from one of the mullioned windows across the flat and richly wooded park towards the Malvern Hills to the south, it is easy to imagine that this had always been a desirable place to settle.

Chapter One

THE NURSERY WINDOW

The view looking out from the Lygon Nursery at Madresfield in which Evelyn Waugh wrote is less romantic and inviting. It is curtailed and thus free from distractions. Five sash windows, barred for children's safety, face west, over the twenty-foot-wide moat but no further than the dense yew hedge beyond. This is the servants' side of the house where the hedges grow taller to screen their work from family and guests. The restricted view was helpful to Waugh, who needed to concentrate and to write his way out of debt. There was little else during that New Year of 1932 to deflect him from his recollections of Africa, which he was fashioning here at the Nursery table into two books: the satirical novel *Black Mischief*, and the travel book *Remote People*. As Waugh described the heat of Ethiopia, he occasionally looked out at the balls of mistletoe hanging high in the lime trees beyond and the winter-flowering viburnum fringing the brick moat below and his senses were brought back to the frost of England.

Up on the second floor, tucked away from the throng of the house, the Nursery floor is neat, uncluttered and painted a clean and soothing magnolia. The children's world remains undisturbed today. Framed illustrations by Kate Greenaway and others of the Holy Family and Little Red Riding Hood hang either side of the white-washed shelves on which Nanny placed the humble mementos of her charges' first travels and achievements: a little milk jug from Piancavallo; a wooden model of a Swiss chalet; a snap of a medieval German town hall; a tarnished silver sports trophy; a set of frosted Bakelite eggcups. In one corner stands 'Lygon House', the dolls' house. This vignette of a children's world lingered in Waugh's memory to be used over a decade later in a fictional nursery belonging to the Flytes in *Brideshead Revisited*. Concentrating on the job at hand, he sat here, that January in 1932, on one of the seven rush-seated, straight-backed chairs, each distinguished by its own child's name, colour and flower. One, in periwinkle-blue with garlands of forget-me-nots, reads 'Hugh Patrick'; another, of pale green with snowdrops, reads 'Mary'; the dove-grey one with orange blossom belonged to 'Dorothy'.

Lady Dorothy Lygon was only nineteen when Evelyn Waugh first came to Madresfield at Christmas 1931. She remembers him writing 'slowly and reluctantly a great deal of *Black Mischief* while staying with us, groaning loudly as he shut himself away . . . for a few hours every day' in their old Day Nursery. He dedicated the novel to

Lady Mary Lygon (Maimie), by William Acton. It was said that her beauty was such that it once caused the band to stop playing when she entered a ballroom.

her and her sister Mary. The Lygon sisters, only two years apart in age, cut very different figures. Mary, like her older brother Hugh, had classically symmetrical features and was a beauty. This sexually confident blonde rode hard, played hard and was soon drawn into a fast set. Plain Dorothy, with her chubby cheeks and bottle-bottom spectacles, quick intelligence and loyal and tender heart, was her sister's devoted companion. These accomplished horsewomen, who signed themselves in visitors' books 'Sporting Hostess' and 'ADC to Sporting Hostess' respectively, were inseparable.

Too often Waugh was disturbed by the sisters rushing down the linoleum-floored corridor and bursting through the swing door to drag him out for a ride or just to sit and chatter while they embroidered chair-covers. Their conversation was low-brow, their affection uncomplicated. To these relatively innocent debutantes, this well-travelled guest was an avuncular and amusing novelty and he shared with them the absurdities of the outside, grown-up world. In return, Waugh relaxed amidst the sisters' silliness, mimicry and informality, and delighted in their childlike world of games, secret language and gentle teasing. They became his adoring audience.

A month earlier, on 20 November 1931, Waugh had been thrilled with Dorothy's invitation to come to Madresfield for Christmas and replied in the arch parlance of the fashionable set:

Dearest Lady Dorothy, It would just be too lovely for any words to join in your Christmas cheer. Deevy, in fact hot stuff. Oh, but you can't really mean it. Oh you are an awful tease! I'm just going up to town to replenish my wardrobe for the occasion because my country tailor-made has sprung a leak. It has been patched with tweed of a very curious colour and its seat looks now not unlike Cleopatra's breasts [he draws two circles with holes] . . . But the prospect of coming to Madresfield relieves all my gloom and HOW.

Though Waugh later considered Dorothy one of his closest friends, he had initially met her two older brothers, William, Viscount Elmley – the courtesy title for the Beauchamp heir – and Hugh, up at Oxford in 1922. When he had arrived at Hertford College he had briefly gravitated towards some scholarly Wykehamists and experimented with two intense homosexual friendships, one with Richard Pares and the other with Alastair Graham. But by his second term, Waugh had been led by Terence Greenidge through 'that low door in the wall' into the pleasure garden of aristocratic privilege, rarefied tastes and conscientious hedonism, later recalled in *Brideshead Revisited*. Here, indulging his 'preference for the well-born' in this male playground from which women were largely absent, he had found the Lygons and their set and forged abiding friendships. Together with Greenidge, a childlike and lovable prankster and Tractarian in Waugh's college, who later became a novelist, he had drunk late into the night

The Hon. Hugh Lygon, c. 1929. Evelyn Waugh met him at Oxford and showed a great tendresse for him. He described him as 'just missing the happiness he sought, without ambition, unhappy in love, a man of great sweetness'.

along with the travel writer Robert Byron, the writer and aesthete Harold Acton, Henry Yorke (also known as the fashionable novelist Henry Green), Frank, later Lord, Pakenham, the politician and social reformer, the film producer John Sutro, the writer Patrick Balfour (later Lord Kinross) and the soldier and politician Hubert Duggan. They were members of the Hypocrites' Club, so called because their motto, in Greek, was the opening line of Pindar's Olympian Odes, 'Water is best'. Viscount Elmley was its president and stipulated that 'members may prance but not dance'. Waugh had examined his new playmates and found himself enjoying his status among them.

While Elmley was too conscious of his own high rank in society to offer true companionship, Waugh had from the beginning shown a *tendresse* for the dreaminess of Hugh, the beautiful and seemingly eternal boy 'always just missing the happiness he sought, without ambition, unhappy in love, a man of great sweetness'. Waugh and Hugh had intended to share rooms in Merton Street the following term but Waugh was sent down from Oxford. Their friendship was to deepen later with travel.

To Waugh's set, an interest in domestic architecture was almost a cult. Madresfield, sitting on its Anglo-Saxon foundations, slowly enriching, generation by generation, its inimitable character, appealed to Waugh's sense of provenance. Under its hammerbeamed roofs, he could revel in its Gothic and Arts and Crafts interiors. At Oxford he had written an essay entitled 'The

Pre-Raphaelite Brotherhood, 1847–1854', a precursor to his first book, a biography of Dante Gabriel Rossetti. Both pieces of writing displayed his love of the medieval, his interest in William Morris and John Ruskin. To Waugh, Pre-Raphaelite and Gothic art resonated with European culture and provided the vital link between pre-Reformation England and Rome, the church to which he had recently turned.

The blind hedonism of his set, however, had begun, by the end of the twenties, to disgust Waugh. In the preface to *Vile Bodies*, published in 1930, he makes a reference to a 'sharp disturbance in my private life'. That 'disturbance' was divorce from his wife of only one year, Evelyn Gardner, daughter of Lord Burghclere, who was known as 'She-Evelyn'. She had cuckolded him with a mutual friend. 'How he howled with despair,' Acton later recalled. Waugh turned to Olivia Plunket Greene and then Teresa Jungman but, both being Catholic converts, they found an excuse to spurn this divorcee. Waugh briefly sought consolation in the arms of female prostitutes, but for the spiritual sustenance that he craved he turned to the doctrinal certainties of the Catholic Church and the temporal comforts of the Lygons. He fell in love with the whole family and their home, Madresfield.

Upon the break-up of his marriage, Waugh emerged from an amoral vortex to seek a moral code by which he could resist temptation and, he hoped, find peace of mind. The world had become 'unintelligible and unendurable without God'. He began to take instruction from Father Martin D'Arcy at Farm Street in Mayfair, whose challenging mind prepared Waugh for his conversion. He was received into the Church one year before his first visit to Madresfield. Though the Lygons were not Catholics, they were steeped in the seriousness and devotion of Anglo-Catholicism. Waugh would have known that the Lygons' grandfather, Frederick, the sixth earl, had played an important role in the Oxford Movement and had himself been tempted by Catholicism. The Chapel was the setting for their religious observance and the Library housed one of the greatest Christian book collections in England. Was Waugh's conversion to England's 'Old Religion' consolidated by the pre-Reformation liturgical texts in this rich library? Since he considered his was a rational rather than an emotional conversion and, according to D'Arcy, he 'never spoke of experiences or feelings', preferring exact doctrines, he could not have ignored such an exceptional resource at a time when his busy mind was wrestling with questions of faith.

Between 1928 and 1937, Waugh roamed the world, taking three major trips which provided the settings for his books. Being itinerant, he owned 'no possessions which could not conveniently go on a porter's barrow'. When he returned to England, since the ordinariness of his father's suburban house in Golders Green held little attraction for him now – he walked to Hampstead to ensure a smarter postmark on his letters – he would either stay at the Savile Club in London, retire to a country inn to write, or join house parties, particularly

Evelyn Waugh was a frequent visitor to Madresfield, and his signature is repeatedly found in the visitors' book. He struck up an avuncular friendship with the two youngest Lygon sisters, Maimie (Mary) and Coote (Dorothy).

at Madresfield. From that first visit late in 1931, it became his bolt-hole, his 'paraclete'. In their parents' absence, the younger Lygons, particularly the three unmarried daughters – Mary, Sibell and Dorothy – colonized Madresfield with their friends. In upper-class circles, it became known as virtually the only place in England where one could go and play unsupervised. Vaguely chaperoned by Miss Byron, their one-time governess, the social life at 'Mad' was no longer run by their strict parents and louche characters like Waugh were included precisely because the young had the run of the house. In spite of their parents' absence, domestic standards were exactingly upheld in accordance with Lord Beauchamp's instructions from abroad. The children continued to be waited upon by nineteen servants. Their father – being always a stickler for uniform and ceremony – insisted that his butlers and footmen continue to be dressed in a precise livery of black tailcoats buttoned in real silver and the grooms formally tailored in black worsted with a funereal black silk top hat sporting a large black cockade.

The ritual of Madresfield, like the ritual of the Catholic Church, was relished by Waugh. Naturally, he was quartered in the 'Bachelor Wing' on the first floor in the Victorian part of the house and enjoyed the constant stream of fellow guests. The red morocco-bound visitors' book for this period is a roll call of a slice of contemporary society: the society beauties Diana Fellowes, Princess Natalie Paley, Doris, Lady Castlerosse and Phillis de Janzé (*née* Boyd, who replaced the first 'i' in her Christian name with a racier 'y' from one year's entry to the next); the society photographer Cecil Beaton; the composer and aesthete Lord Berners and his boyfriend Robert Heber-Percy; the writers Robert Byron, John Sutro, Nancy Mitford and Alan Pryce-Jones; Winston Churchill's son Randolph and Barbara McCorquodale (later Barbara Cartland), who had Elmley, the Madresfield heir, in her sights. Waugh penned his first entry in the visitors' book for 4–6 January 1932 and three weeks later he returned with Hubert Duggan, the homosexual Scottish aristocrat and aesthete Hamish St Clair Erskine and Teresa 'Baby' Jungman, with whom he was hopelessly in love. In 1932 alone, Waugh stayed on several occasions amounting to nearly seven weeks. 'Mad' quickly became his home from home, a refuge, providing emotional and spiritual convalescence, quietude and fun.

Madresfield also provided him with an escape from the rivalries of literary London, the deprivations of the Dark Continent and the tarnished glamour of 'Metroland', which he parodied in *Decline and Fall*. Its comforts were on a grand scale and, since he liked 'the best which he couldn't really finance', it was also a relief from the bills of high living.

Within a short while Waugh was calling the sisters by the family pet names: Mary was Maimie and Dorothy was Coote, though Sibell was always Sibell. Coote's name arose from a mistake. Her siblings considered her to be so secretive that whenever they sang the hymn

'God moves in a mysterious way' they were reminded of *her* mysterious ways. 'We thought the hymn had been written by a Mrs Coote but it turned out not to be,' recalled Sibell. In fact it was by Cowper. It is typical that these devoutly brought-up children should use a religious reference as an in-joke and no less typical that they 'got it wrong!' Sibell laughed. Nevertheless, the name stuck, although Coote kept its origin a secret until she died. Eager to stay in touch while travelling, Waugh started an almost weekly correspondence with Maimie and Coote. These letters reveal the growing familiarity between the mature writer and these playful, aristocratic debutantes that was remarkably candid for the times and their circumstances, though at no time did either woman have a sexual affair with him. Addressing Maimie affectionately as 'Blondie' and Dorothy as 'Pollen' or 'Little Pol', he signed himself with the mock-Masonic sobriquet 'Boaz' and drew Masonic symbols, such as swastikas and pentangles, all over the letters. These were possibly a dig at Elmley, whom Waugh now dismissed as a bloated prig, and who in 1925 had been initiated into the Grand Lodge, a secret society that the Church of Rome considered immoral. Waugh and the Lygon sisters' correspondence is peppered with in-jokes and abbreviations as he played to their feigned and real innocence, often signing himself off with 'MLFF' [Much love from Frisky].

In 1932 he wrote to the two of them from the Savile Club in London:

Oh how I indeed care to live in your Liberty Hall but the trouble about poor Bo is that he is a lazy bugger and if he was in a home with you crazy girls he would just sit about and chatter and get d.d. [dead drunk] and ride a horse and have a heavenly time but would he write his book? No, and must he? By God he must. So you see, but listen. How would it be for me to stay in some minor farm in your neighbourhood and then any time I had written 5,000 words I could have a reward and walk to your lovely home and have heavenly tea party with you.

The following year, on 1 January 1933, from the Georgetown Club in British Guiana he reported:

It is only five weeks since I left Madresfield. Now I am four thousand miles away and oh what a changed world. Instead of the swishing meadows of Worcestershire and the noble line of the Malvern Hills that I love so dearly, I look out upon limitless swamp broken only by primeval forest, desert and mountain.

He missed their badinage, adding, 'I suppose I will not be able to understand any Madresfield jokes by the time I get home.'

With familiarity came bawdiness. The smutty gossip and his descriptions of sexual encounters or the sexual appetites of fellow travellers written to the sisters were enlivened with the imaginary and childish interjections of a Tommy McDougal, the attractive local master of foxhounds, whom Waugh had dismissed as a fool. So, for example: 'Well, I am living with the bright young Yorkes. Last night I saw a terribly drunk man with a prostitute. WOTS A POSTATUTE PLESE? Ask your little playfellow Dorothea, she will show you, Tommy.'

Waugh's frankness about having to make money would have interested the Lygon girls who, in their father's absence, while living in the lap of luxury, were always short of pin-money and reduced (as Sibell put it) to accepting 'hand-me-down stockings from Doris Castlerosse'. Keen to supplement their purses, Coote placed advertisements in journals which read 'Woman wants work' and took jobs as Girl Friday, typist and general factotum. Sibell, meanwhile, briefly worked as a receptionist in a Bond Street hairdresser's run by Violet Cripps, an erstwhile wife of her uncle, Bend'or, the Duke of Westminster. However, she preferred hunting to working, sighing that 'the time is coming when there will be no idleness in Mayfair. We shall all work.' Sibell also tried her hand at writing, contributing to the society pages of *Harper's Bazaar*, and through these we can glance at the private world of laughter, flirtation and idleness that the sisters created at Madresfield during the early thirties. Her articles were accompanied by photographs of girls ankle-deep in dogs and dressed in striped cardigans, lisle stockings and lace-up gillie shoes, fashionably slouching against Roman busts on the Caesars' Lawn while their men cavorted across the Moat Courtyard sporting Oxford bags and sleeveless Fair Isles. Their guests gathered to ride, hunt, go racing and, on cold evenings, to sit by the fire and play games of mimicry and general foolery.

Diana Mosley retained a vivid memory of Waugh and understood his importance in the Lygon circle: 'Wherever Evelyn was he made it exceptional – brilliant company! His malicious wit, his quickness on the uptake . . . he was an incredibly clever man who saw the fun in everything and made life wonderful.' Unlike Diana, or her sisters, however, Sibell regarded their habitual guest as 'rather tiresome and terribly rude', especially to Miss Jagger, a local spinster who lived with the family but was not part of the London social scene. She was gentle and devoted to the Lygons and they, in turn, adored her, which infuriated Waugh. 'He kicked her in the ankles, on purpose – pure jealousy – because we liked her so much. We even had a word for "to help" – "to Jagger". He was always copying our nick-names and vocabulary.' Sibell often had run-ins with him. 'He didn't like me very much because I wouldn't become a Catholic,' she recalls. He was also furious when she became a close friend of Monsignor Ronald Knox, one of the most famous Catholic priests in England. Waugh idolized Knox and later wrote his biography. Venting his fury, he would chastise Sibell: 'You've got no business having a Roman Catholic to stay!' but she simply dismissed it as, again, 'pure jealousy'. On one occasion, Waugh, in imitation of the abbreviated entries made by two peers in the visitors' book, signed himself simply 'Waugh'. 'When were *you* ennobled?' the waspish Sibell asked.

Sibell had little time for his social ambitions and, as an accomplished horsewoman, watched with wry amusement as the tubby urban-dweller took to the saddle at the local riding academy under the strict instruction of Captain Jack Hance. Determined to adopt upper-class pastimes, such as hunting, and needing to be able to ride on planned travels, Waugh bravely struggled to overcome his equestrian limitations. Signing himself 'the famous man-about-town', he wrote yet again to 'Poll' and 'Blondie' that the reason he had not joined them hunting hare on a horse in the rain was that 'my little bicycle was lame'.

Throughout these years, Waugh remained close to Hugh Lygon and their friendship was both tested and strengthened by an unlikely adventure. It is hard to imagine Waugh, whose physique and mannerisms call to mind a stocky cleric, roped to the tall Botticellian beauty Hugh as they pulled a sledge across the frozen tundra. However, in August 1934 that is exactly the situation in which they found themselves. Members of the Oxford University Arctic Expedition had set out to map the north-east territory of Norway inside the Arctic Circle and Waugh, at a loose end that summer and having unexpectedly run into Hugh outside his club in St James's, agreed to accompany him on what he imagined would be high jinks in the snow. They were following in a long tradition of the English gentleman who, in an attempt to escape from the tidy certainties of civilization, is drawn to intractable landscapes.

Having stocked up with bottles of '60%', the only

liquor available from a meagre store at Tromsø on the Norwegian coast, they boarded a primitive sealing boat with the expedition's leader, Alexander Glen. They set sail into the heavy seas and the grey, round-the-clock daylight of the Arctic summer, 'which proved to be as cold as an English February, no worse', Waugh recalled in his account of the journey. Playing piquet, knocking back 60% and managing their nausea for three days, they were then set down on a shingle beach from where they were to continue the journey in the raw twilight on foot across Spitzbergen.

The three men hauled a sledge, a boat, a tent recently used on Everest and six weeks' supply of margarine and pemmican (dried reindeer fat and albumen) up on to dry land. As the terrain was a nesting ground for tern, their progress was impeded by eggs and fledglings underfoot and squadrons of female terns stooping from above to peck at the crowns of their balaclavas. They set off through icy white fog, each man carrying thirty or forty pounds of provisions on his back, towards the moraine of a glacier which they intended to climb, passing through a mosquito-ridden valley of mud and sharp flinty stones. Finally, they reached the ice over which they had anticipated effortlessly sliding their sledge to base camp, only to find an unexpected thaw had created a mosaic of frozen ridges, ice gravel and other obstacles. Glen tethered his companions to one another and then to the sledge like human huskies and from the back he steered the vehicle this way and that through the impossible terrain. Despite twelve hours' heaving at a stretch, they progressed just five miles a day. An alternative plan was needed. They headed for a trapper's cabin on the coastline which lay the far side of a wide and shallow river. When they got there, the exhausted trio found a hovel 'the size of a *wagon-lit* and extremely dirty'.

The following day Hugh and Glen set off to scout the area while Waugh was the homemaker, sweeping the floors before he collapsed into the only bed to sleep. As Hugh and Glen attempted to recross the river they had forded the previous day, they found it in full spate, transformed in one night into an almost impassable torrent. Hugh, an amateur heavyweight boxer, managed to get across but his companion could not and the noise of the rushing water became so deafening that the two men could not hear one another. With Hugh now unable to come back over, Glen signalled that he would return with Waugh to rescue him. Rousing Waugh, Glen brought him to the edge of the river. They roped themselves together and both plunged in. The torrent rushed down upon them bearing boulders and blocks of ice. On reaching Hugh, they tossed him some twine but inevitably it snapped. 'Hugh and I were swept down, tumbling over and over. I had time to form the clear impression that we were both done for . . . Hugh was struck by a small iceberg midstream.' Somehow they dragged themselves to safety and they crawled back exhausted to the hut, rubbed one another down with sand to restore circulation and sank into a twenty-four-hour sleep. Four days later, despite Hugh's badly damaged knee, they made for home. On his return to England in September, Waugh wrote to his school friend, later a Labour politician, Tom Driberg: 'Just back from Spitzbergen which was hell – a fiasco very narrowly retrieved from disaster.' Having subsisted for several weeks on pemmican and margarine, he wrote to the Lygon sisters, pressing them to see him while he was still thin and almost handsome and urged them to 'tell Hughie to hurry up and have Catholic lessons'.

The mind of Waugh the writer, as well as his spirituality, was stimulated at Madresfield. He observed the details of its architecture and the characteristics of its inhabitants. In the words of his friend and later biographer Christopher Sykes, he discovered 'la vie de château at Madresfield'. The first manifestation of the Lygons in his writing appeared in 1930 in *Vile Bodies* in which he recreated the following scene from a time before he had met the sisters. It was probably recounted to him by Hugh. One evening, after a dance, Maimie and Sibell returned to the Lygons' London residence in Belgrave Square, Halkin House, at one a.m., but could not get in because the footman had fallen asleep. In those days, ladies did not carry money and would not have had a key to their parents' front door. Stranded in Belgravia dressed in white Norman Hartnell gowns, they decided that the only solution was to walk round to the only other local family they knew: the Baldwins, at Number 10 Downing Street. They remembered that the Prime Minister had a doorman, a footman and a policeman, one of whom was sure to help them. The disgruntled servant at Number 10 refused to admit them until he had roused the Prime Minister to vouch for them. Fortunately, despite their political differences, Earl Beauchamp and Stanley Baldwin were old friends. The following morning Baldwin telephoned Beauchamp and asked him to send round a lady's maid with a change of clothes and a carriage. 'Balderdash and poppycock!' retorted the earl and insisted instead that his daughters leave the Prime Minister's official residence in broad daylight and in full evening dress and walk home.

Madresfield, the house, appeared in 'English Gothic', the third chapter of *A Handful of Dust*, Waugh's novel published four years later. This chapter describes Tony Last's ancestral home, Hetton Abbey, rebuilt in 1864 in a style his aunt considered to 'have been adapted by Mr Pecksniff from one of his pupils' designs for an orphanage. But there was not a glazed brick or encaustic tile that was not dear to Tony's heart.' He continues:

The general aspect and atmosphere of the place; the line of its battlements against the sky; the central clock tower where quarterly chimes disturb all but the heaviest sleepers; the ecclesiastical gloom of the great hall, its ceiling groined and painted in diapers of red and gold, supported on shafts of polished granite with vine-wreathed capitals, half-lit by day through lancet windows of armorial stained glass, at night by a vast gasolier of brass and wrought iron, wired now and fitted with twenty electric bulbs . . .

Read this and you are standing in the Lygons' home. A first edition of *A Handful of Dust* sits on a shelf in the Smoking Room at Madresfield. The inscription inside, written in Waugh's small, emphatic handwriting, reads: 'To Hughie, to whom it should have been dedicated, from Evelyn, September 3rd, 1934' – just days after their return from Spitzbergen.

Waugh not only drank in the medievalism of Madresfield, he also savoured his encounters with the aristocracy, studying their habits and developing 'perfect pitch' in describing their jargon. He was fascinated to learn that his friend's father, the seventh earl, considered it middle class not to decant champagne into jugs. How effectively nicknames and idiosyncratic jargon could exclude an outsider. How scruffily dressed the aristocrat could be at home. With his ear for dialogue and his eye for mannerisms, Waugh absorbed them well enough to be able to reproduce them faultlessly – even reverentially – in his novels.

The Nursery set in this ancient house, where Waugh had written large parts of his two Abyssinian books, abided in his memory as a place of inspiration and as a safe haven that recalled his mother and his nurse, Lucy Hodges. Harold Acton noticed how the writer was drawn to childhood, his flat in Canonbury Square which he shared briefly with She-Evelyn being 'rather like a nursery, really'.

A decade later, in his imagination, Waugh would return to the Lygon Nursery. During 1944, while on sick leave from wartime service, the novelist conflated his own and the Lygons' nurseries, rooms where he had felt secure and loved, as part of the inspiration for his most successful novel, his 'attempt to trace the workings of the divine purpose in a pagan world', his paean to a lost England, the deeply nostalgic *Brideshead Revisited: The Sacred and Profane Memories of Captain Charles Ryder*. Numerous details in the novel recall Madresfield and the Lygons. Charles Ryder's first steps into Sebastian Flyte's enchanted world are a vital moment of initiation which Waugh conjures up with precision and symbolism. As Charles cautiously opens the door to Sebastian's Oxford college rooms, he sees him 'alone . . . peeling a plover's egg taken from a large nest of moss in the centre of his table'. Sebastian's refined and leisured world is immediately conjured in this single tableau. Waugh knew that these eggs, manna from a nobleman's estate, were a springtime delicacy enjoyed almost exclusively by the landed classes. In the book, Lady Marchmain had had them sent down from their country seat to please her son. The plovers obligingly laid early for her.

The black and white broad-winged birds, also known as lapwings, or peewits because of their distinctive calls, lay their eggs precariously in open ploughed fields rather than up high in nests. Sibell, who until her recent death was the only surviving Lygon of Waugh's generation, remembers the ritual of plover's eggs in her childhood.

We were always sent out to look for them. They laid in the park quite a lot and the great thing was *not* to tread on them because they looked exactly like the earth. Princess Louise Augusta loved them and once, when she came to stay, Mother realized that there weren't any left so she had the bantams' eggs painted olive green with black spots. They have a very fragile shell and any fool could have seen they were not plover's eggs. The princess was furious!

To Waugh, these little eggs, like Proust's Madeleine biscuits, were freighted with nostalgia for a vanished Arcadia. Coaxing details from his memory, like a master gardener allowing a pear to blet, he picked the story before he was ready to write, allowed it to ripen during months of loneliness and longing for home in an unstable world, and then presented it to his reader at the ideal moment for consumption: when luxury – even plenty – was a distant and romantic memory. Though, in years to come, he would be embarrassed by *Brideshead*'s lush language, its preoccupation with sweetmeats, vintage wines, opulent interiors and unabashed richness, to the war-weary reader, constrained by rationing, its luxurious descriptions had a similar escapist appeal as Dior's nostalgic Edwardian 'New Look' of 1947 or the mouth-watering recipes in Elizabeth David's *Mediterranean Food* published in 1950. In *Brideshead Revisited* Waugh had given his reader a glimpse of the white hart in a dark wood.

In Part One, 'Et in Arcadia Ego', Charles seeks refuge from the uncertainties of adult life. He steps through 'a low door in a wall' and for a while, by Sebastian's side, he escapes life's complexities. Sebastian, like Waugh, was in love with his own childhood and as Hugh Lygon was to Evelyn Waugh, so Sebastian was to Charles in the novel. The beautiful Sebastian carried a teddy bear called Aloysius under his arm wherever he went. The idea for a Brideshead bear was given to Waugh by his friend the poet John Betjeman, who was known to carry a bear called Archie. In acknowledgement of his indebtedness, Waugh allowed him to name the bear. Betjeman chose Aloysius, after Aloysius Gonzaga, the patron saint of youth, who had given his name to the first Roman Catholic church Betjeman had entered as a preparatory school boy at the Dragon School. This local church, the main Catholic Church in Oxford, was emphatically and therefore temptingly out of bounds. The sweetness and purity of the nursery recurs as a motif throughout Charles and Sebastian's undergraduate love affair. Recalling those Oxford days, Charles tells us:

> It seemed as though I was being given a brief spell of what I had never known, a happy childhood, and though its toys were silk shirts and liqueurs and cigars and its naughtiness high in the catalogue of grave sins, there was something of nursery freshness about us that fell little short of the joy of innocence.

In the physical absence of their father and emotional absence of their mother, the fictional Nanny Hawkins became the figure to whom the young Flytes returned for womb-like comfort. She serves as an unchanging landmark in Sebastian's childhood and an essential reference point just as, in the absence of their parents, the Lygons' nanny was a permanent fixture in their own lives.

Despite Waugh's disclaimer on the title page that 'I am not I: thou art not he or she: they are not they', there can be little doubt that the fictional Flytes are, in great part, a composite of the Lygons. Their extraordinary family difficulties were 'suggested to Evelyn' and find strong echoes in this novel. It is his tribute to them. Just prior to the publication of *Brideshead Revisited*, Waugh wrote to Coote about the new novel which he considered to be his *magnum opus*. 'I am writing a very beautiful book, to bring tears, about very rich, beautiful, high-born people who live in palaces and have no troubles except what they make themselves and those are mainly the demons sex and drink which after all are easy to bear as troubles go nowadays.' He goes on to explain to her, in what reads like a veiled apology, that it was 'all about a family whose father lives abroad, as it might be Boom [Lord Beauchamp] – but it's not Boom', he tried to assure her. '. . . and a younger son: people will say he's like Hughie, but you'll see he's not really Hughie – and there's a house as it might be Mad, but it isn't really Mad.' The resonances are just too many and too exact for such a disclaimer to ring true. Indeed, towards the end of his life when Waugh was interviewed for the BBC by fellow novelist Elizabeth Jane Howard, he conceded that the fiction writer invents very few characters.

In the original manuscript, the head of the Flyte family is, like the Lygons', an earl, but Waugh later promoted him to marquess, a rank that Frederick Lygon, the sixth Earl Beauchamp, had coveted but failed to obtain. Like William, the seventh earl (Waugh's friends' father), Lord Marchmain is in exile and in disgrace – sexual disgrace, for leaving Lady Marchmain to go and live with his mistress in Venice. '"No one knows papa. He's a social leper. Hadn't you heard?"' Sebastian asks Charles. At the beginning of the novel Charles's cousin Jasper warns him to '"Beware of the Anglo-Catholics – they're all sodomites with unpleasant accents."' Both absent fathers relish high culture – Marchmain being 'as appreciative of porphyry as Boom'. The scenes of Charles and Sebastian discussing Bellini with Marchmain in Venice recall Elmley, Hugh and Robert Byron's grand tour with Lord Beauchamp during their Easter vacation of 1924. There are other parallels between the Flytes and the Lygons. Like the fictional family, the Lygons encountered financial difficulties between the wars necessitating the sale of eight thousand acres in 1919 and two Rembrandts in the twenties. Husband and wife were estranged. Lady Marchmain, like her real-life model, Lady Beauchamp, was pious and narrow-minded and her religious fervour alienated rather than united her family. In the novel, Lord Marchmain's heir, Lord Brideshead ('Bridey') chose to marry an older widow who could not bear him children. His two sisters did not have children either and consequently the Marchmain line died out. The pompous Elmley, later the eighth earl, also married an older widow; they too were childless and so the Beauchamp title became extinct. On 11 November 1940 Waugh wrote to his second wife Laura that Elmley 'sits at Madresfield in the crypt of the chapel in a bombproof waistcoat'. Details in the novel recall Elmley's absurdity, such as his stamp and cigarette-card collecting, which became Bridey's match-box collecting. Waugh often cast older brothers as unpleasant figures of fun in his stories. It was a form of fraternal revenge. He had always been ill at ease with his own brother, Alec, whom he believed to be more admired and loved by their father.

'Obviously, Evelyn invented Lord Marchmain,' Diana Mosley concedes, 'but he took the circumstances though I'm sure he never actually met Lord Beauchamp.' He never did. In public, Waugh may have adamantly denied that his *Brideshead* characters were taken from real life, partly out of respect for the Lygons but more importantly as he wished the story to be read as a product of his imagination and not as a biography of friends. However, in private – according to Lady Mosley – he confided that the real-life Lady Marchmain was 'the sister of a prominent Duke', as was Lady Beauchamp. Sebastian and Hugh shared an epicene beauty and, despite their apparent great fortune and charm, both were doomed to be unhappy in love, hopelessly melancholy, damned by drink and to die young. While Sebastian was a composite – part Alastair Graham, Waugh's lover at Oxford, part Hugh Lygon and part imagined youth – Coote understandably could not ignore the resonances with her own family and, recalling her dead brother, she mournfully replied to Waugh's letter, 'Sebastian gives me such pangs.' Laura Waugh described Coote as 'the nicest of all your friends' and throughout her life, Coote, a kind and loyal woman, fiercely defended Waugh's creative integrity and refused to accept the suggestion that *Brideshead* was the Lygon story. Coote's niece, Rosalind Morrison, on the other hand, recalls her father Dickie giving her as a teenager a copy of the novel. When she picked up several family resemblances, he explained that it had, indeed, been based on them. It was Waugh's encomium to the Lygons and showed how their home, Madresfield, was engraved on his heart.

Chapter Two

THE DITCH

A great part of Madresfield's appeal for Evelyn Waugh lay in its antiquity: it was etched into the English landscape in Anglo-Saxon times and was settled by the Lygons' Norman forefathers over nine hundred years ago. Once the family had settled in a 'mower's field' in the lee of the hills, Robert de Braci, their ancestor, was keen to defend it. He began by digging a ditch.

In the late autumn of 1196 three serious-looking men – Robert de Braci, his son William and their bailiff – all wrapped in woollen cloaks against the foul November weather, stood on a bank of mud watching two serfs digging below them. This was the first opportunity since the harvest to start work on this pressing task. One of the men, dressed in a sodden hemp tunic and hose which hung down over his patched shoes, his leather jerkin discarded, rested his mattock on his shoulder. The other serf, hooded, continued working barefoot.

The scars left on the landscape leave clues to Robert's preoccupations. He needed to dig a ditch to mark his boundary and to redirect water for subsistence and protection. It may also have provided a defensive position in which to crouch during battle or a mass grave for interring bodies after plague or war. Anxious to define and to defend the extent of his land and mindful that it was uncertainly held in post-Conquest England, Robert felt it imperative to finish the work. He was surrounded by powerful landowners. Richard the Lionheart's hunting grounds ran two miles to the south at Malvern Chase; the Abbot of Westminster's lay to the north; and those belonging to Sir William Beauchamp stretched out to the west. Beyond that lay Malvern Priory, whose foundation charter of 1121 is the oldest document in the Madresfield Muniments. Among the witnesses to this charter was Walter Beauchamp, King Henry I's steward. It was through his wife Emmeline, daughter of the notorious Worcestershire sheriff, Urse d'Abitot, that Madresfield passed to the Lygons. Two medieval women – Joan de Braci and Anne Beauchamp – secured this desirable estate for the Lygons through their marriages.

Since earliest times Madresfield had been remote. None of the great Roman roads ran through the region and for centuries much of the county of Worcestershire was covered in dense forest and undrained river valleys. It was in an uncharted and unreclaimed fragment of one of these great Worcestershire forests, lying three miles from the banks of the River Severn between

Powick and Great Malvern in Pershore Hundred, that the original Anglo-Saxon settlement was made. These primeval woods provided shelter for wild boar which was hunted by the king and his courtiers, and after the Conquest, William I enclosed sixty-eight forests with ditches and banks. Laws against poaching, even from Anglo-Saxon times, were stringent. Thus, the *Anglo-Saxon Chronicle* informs us that:

> *Whoever killed a hart or hind*
> *Shall be made blind.*
> *He preserved the harts and boars*
> *And loved the stags as if he was their father.*

The Conqueror's eldest son, William Rufus, hanged poachers caught on Crown land, while his younger son and subsequent successor, Henry I, 'gelded and gouged' them.

Urse d'Abitot, Walter Beauchamp's father-in-law, had been granted forty 'hides' of land in Worcestershire by the Conqueror. As sheriff, he was known to be troublesome to the local convent of St Mary and dispossessed the monks of several of their manors; his son Richard was accused of murder, leaving the sheriff's daughter, Emmeline, as sole heiress, and Madresfield, her *maritagium*, came to her Beauchamp husband. According to the Pipe Rolls (Exchequer accounts of royal income, arranged by county) of 1192, 'Metheresfeld' was then leased to Robert de Braci for an annual payment of half a knight's fee. A *maritagium* was a dowry often in the form of land given by a father to his daughter upon her marriage which reverted to her family if the grantees left no children. A knight's fee was a grant of land made by a landowner in return for military service and one knight's fee obliged the tenant to forty days' service per annum. De Braci was therefore not a freeholder but a tenant of these lands.

At the time when Robert de Braci was digging the ditch, England was so sparsely populated that Worcestershire had no more than ten people per square mile. Pioneers painstakingly reclaimed the land – strip by strip, acre by acre – hacking down virgin forest. The only sign of habitation would have been a breeze-blown trail of smoke rising through the oak and ash canopy from a hearth. Since the oldest part of Madresfield rests on Anglo-Saxon foundations, we can assume that it had been regarded for some time as a habitable site. Perhaps it lay in a mown field that had once been a clearing in the forest, in view of the probable derivation of the name from the Anglo-Saxon for 'Mown' or 'Mower's Field'. It is difficult to determine when the present moat was dug but, like the ditch, it would have been a significant and laborious project undertaken not to lend dignity to the property but to provide much needed protection against raiders. The workforce may not have been drawn from Robert's serfs but from teams of itinerant Welsh dikers who specialized in such labour. If there were swans on Robert's moat they were not a decorative flourish; by feeding on the aquatic plants they kept the moat-water flowing freely from the spring one mile to the south.

By the thirteenth century, the de Braci family had clearly achieved some standing since they began to seal their deeds with their own coat of arms. Their heraldic shield, which appears as early as the reign of Henry III, comprised *gules, a fess or, and two mullets in chief argent*: a red shield with a horizontal gold band in the centre and a silver band at the top studded with two silver spurs. Their seal is attached to numerous surviving documents, the earliest dated 1385, stored in Madresfield's Muniment Room under the house. This chilly room, fifteen feet square, is a windowless cell approached down dank steps that trace the curvature of the moat. Behind a thick iron door its walls are lined with aluminium shelves on which stand grey cardboard boxes containing over eight thousand documents, including the charter granted by Henry I, letters, deeds, apprentices' contracts, menus, staff accounts and wages, diaries, scrapbooks, indentures, architects' plans and estate maps. They include two hundred medieval deeds and quit claims, marriage settlements, wills, inventories, fines, apprenticeship agreements and court accounts, which are written on parchment typically the size of a man's two palms held side by side. Some are so brittle that they creak when unfolded despite being as soft as down to the touch. Like pearls, they benefit from human touch, which yields oils that 'feed' the hide. Written by scribes in Latin in the early years and then in the English vernacular, they are still precisely legible; the 'signatures' take the form of coin-sized wax seals which hang like the charms on a bracelet from folded strips of vellum. One edge of some of the inscribed medieval contracts is cut with an indented line which married exactly with the 'copy' document given to the other party. In some cases, the edge of these 'indentures' is decorated with flowers or beasts, which, once rejoined, offered further proof of authenticity. The traces of medieval administration left in documents primarily concern land: its ownership, leasing, boundaries, reclamation and inheritance. Ninety per cent of Madresfield's records refer to lands held and lands leased, providing us with a picture of the legal intricacies and the economy of the estate in the earliest days.

In modern terms, the de Bracis would be described as gentlemen, though the rank of gentleman was not legally recognized until the fifteenth century. Accorded by common repute rather than by statute, it was an imprecise term implying that the holder claimed 'gentle', even knightly, ancestry, earned his living by renting freely held lands to others rather than by menial labour and possibly held office in the militia, in the administration or in a nobleman's household. The de Bracis farmed perhaps three or four hundred acres and would have retained half a dozen servants. As contented Worcestershire landowners they tended to marry their neighbours and served on local commissions. They represented Worcester in Parliament from 1299, when a Rogerus de Braci is mentioned in that of Edward I. (For sixty-five years and in eight Parliaments successive Roberts de Braci – father following son –

were returned for the city.) They were clearly prospering.

By 1316 another Robert de Braci, married to Maud de Warenne, held three knight's fees of land in Warmendon, Madresfield and Leigh. The following year he settled these manors on their grandson, yet another Robert, probably on the occasion of his marriage.

The young Robert was knighted and by 1328 is described as being Keeper of the manor of Hanley and the chase of Malvern. He was a keen huntsman. Despite his office and consequent responsibilities, royal documents for the reign of Edward III record that in June 1333 Robert and his brother Richard were accused of hunting in Malvern Chase in defiance of the king's forest law. This charge not only tells us that he was mischievous, even reckless, but also that the family could afford to keep fine horses for the chase, as well as carthorses to work the land, and that they enjoyed the pastimes of 'gentlemen'. The following year, the brothers were caught hunting in the bishop's park at Blockley and in 1347 were charged with trespassing, again in Malvern Chase, this time in the company of the parson of Madresfield, whose clerical living was in de Braci's gift. Sir Robert did not see his disregard for the law as incompatible with his higher status.

Did he serve his king at Crécy in 1346? Was he one of the thousands of Englishmen at the long siege of Calais in 1347? It's highly likely. Certainly he served as a justice of the peace and on county commissions despite his illegal activities. Sir Robert would have been well equipped for campaigns abroad with his king because the accounts of Hanley Castle record that already in 1327 he had three sets of plate armour – two sets made in Flanders – four padded tunics, four light helmets, four pairs of plate gloves, a helmet with visor, three coats of chain mail, twenty-two crossbows – three of which were broken – and myriad other weapons. There is an addendum to these accounts: a gift that included a number of 'small items' such as three pairs of 'quern-stones', 135 panes of lead, two iron door bars, perhaps used to secure doors at Madresfield, and 'a bucket for drawing water'.

Through the next two years, Sir Robert's family witnessed the greatest calamity of the later Middle Ages: the Black Death. It spread across Europe, via Italy, from the east and arrived in England in 1348. The island's seclusion was compromised because of continual contact with the Continent by merchants, tradesmen, couriers and soldiers travelling back and forth during the Hundred Years' War. Recurrent epidemics probably halved the population. Huge tracts of land lay empty, animals untended, farms unclaimed, houses abandoned, gardens overgrown and bodies unburied for want of survivors to dig and fill mass graves. The progress of the plague depicts the geography of medieval trade. It entered Worcestershire along trading routes from the port of Bristol and reached its peak in the county in June 1349. The de Bracis, however, survived and we find Robertus de Braci, *miles*, or soldier, returned to Parliament for the city of Worcester in 1360–1. Whether their settlement was sufficiently isolated or they cautiously avoided contact with strangers, it is impossible to know. Nevertheless, their community may have been transformed in a similar way to that recorded by the king's escheator at Hartlebury, near Kidderminster, twenty-five miles north-east of Madresfield: tenants could not be got at any price, mills lay abandoned, forges idle, and pigeon houses in ruins, even the very birds had fled.

Along with other survivors, the de Bracis would have exploited the opportunity following the abandonment of lands. The social instability arising from what contemporaries called the 'Great Mortality' paved the way for the Peasants' Revolt of 1381 when serfs – realizing that the dearth of able-bodied men had inflated labour costs – began to challenge the feudal demands placed upon them. They could now sell their labour to the highest payer and expand their own landholdings, establishing themselves as free men. The leaders of the revolt were spurred on by the Lollard cleric John Ball, who was dubbed by the French chronicler Froissart 'the mad priest of Kent'. The rebels' notions of equality were neatly captured by Ball's couplet:

> *When Adam delved and Eve span*
> *Who was then the gentleman?*

Such social instability raised concerns about status and lineage which were encapsulated by coats of arms. Although in 1385 the de Braci coat of arms seems to have been established, the same year saw a great debate between Sir Richard Scrope and Sir Robert Grosvenor over the right to bear the coat of arms *azure a bend' or*: a blue shield with diagonal gold band. Geoffrey Chaucer was called to give evidence on Scrope's behalf before the Court of Chivalry. Did the arms under contention belong, or should they belong, to Scrope? he was asked. Chaucer replied that in France he had seen both Sir Henry le Scrope armed as a banneret in the same arms, and Sir Richard Scrope armed in the whole arms. He insisted that the arms were known to be those of the Scrope family from a time 'beyond the memory of man' and were commonly seen on their banners and in glass windows. Had he ever heard of a challenge being made by Grosvenor or by any of his ancestors? No. He did recall passing along Friday Street in London on one occasion when he spotted a new signboard with these arms and asked what lodging had hung out the Scrope arms. A man replied that they were not Scrope arms but those 'painted and placed here by a knight of the county of Chester whom men call Sir Robert Grosvenor'. One can imagine the withering manner in which Chaucer advised the court this was the first time he had ever heard anyone speak of a Sir Robert Grosvenor or of someone even bearing the name of Grosvenor. Although Scrope won the case, the Grosvenors to this day use Bend'or as a name for sons. Although the de Bracis played no part in this dispute their Lygon successors were to confront the Grosvenor sensitivity at the loss of the case many centuries later.

During these turbulent years of the late fourteenth

century, an erstwhile pupil of the Great Priory at
Malvern called William Langland wandered over
the Malvern Hills, which dominate the view from the
front of the house at Madresfield as they undulate for
over eight miles across the horizon. Along the way he
stopped to write poems and songs which he sold for a
living. He tells us that he lay down in these hills, 'under
a broad bank by a brook's side . . . and . . . fell into a
sleep for it sounded so merry', and, upon waking, he
wrote *Piers Plowman*. This long Christian allegory and
social satire describes the dreaming hero, a ploughman,
who encounters God in the form of the Tower of Truth,
the devil in the form of a dungeon and 'a fair field full
of folk', representing mankind. It has been suggested
that Langland, like Ball, was a sympathizer of the new
Lollard heresy, and his poem was often quoted by Ball
and others striving for social reform. Contemporary
inventories for Madresfield do not record ownership of
any books and we cannot be sure that members of the
de Braci family could read. Much later, however, one of
Robert's descendants added to the Library a copy of
Langland's poem along with Chaucer's *Canterbury Tales*
and Froissart's *Chronicles*.

In this strictly hierarchical world, a man could rise in
rank through service, marriage or war. Sir Robert de
Braci's grandson, William, had an only daughter, Joan.
William de Braci chose Thomas Lygon as a husband for
his daughter, settling the manor of Warmendon on the
couple in 1423. Marriage, particularly for landowners,
was a business affair in which bloodline and property

mattered more than attraction or feelings. Young Lygon, from Kidderminster, had a Norman name but it seems that he was neither a significant landowner nor a holder of office. The absence of early Lygon deeds in the Madresfield archive suggests he may even have been of a lower rank than minor gentry since it was customary for a gentle family to retain its documents, and he does not appear in the records of local government. Is the de Braci family tree incomplete? When Joan was promised to Thomas Lygon perhaps she was not the heir but had a brother or brothers who subsequently predeceased her. Whatever the explanation, it was a fortunate outcome for Thomas since the handsome estate of Madresfield did in the end come to his family through Joan. Her father William was surely dead when her mother, Isabel, handed Madresfield to her grandson, Thomas and Joan's son, another William, reserving for her own use the two-chimneyed gatehouse with the upper and lower chambers. This wording Isabel used gives us a glimpse of how the house looked in the mid-fifteenth century. A gatehouse was the common construction of those seeking to mark their place in the world.

Hundreds of Worcestershire oaks were felled to erect the timber-framed manor house to which Thomas and his family eventually moved. The building was completed with wattle-and-daub – such structures were surprisingly durable. Romanticizing the late medieval period as 'a hand-made world throughout', the twentieth-century artist and master carver Eric Gill might have been describing Joan and Thomas's moated home. It was also relatively empty. Their two principal rooms, the Great Hall and their chamber, may well have been 'carpeted' in rushes and lit with candles, made in the larder, and rushnips: dried rushes dipped in melted animal fat. They were burned at both ends – hence the expression. The household dined together in the Great Hall sitting at trestle tables and on benches made by estate joiners. Ambient noise in such a large and resonant room would have been considerable and, if their pockets could stretch to such a luxury, the Lygons might have hung an Arras or Flanders tapestry. The only pieces of furniture in their chamber, which served as both a retiring room and a bedroom, might have been a bed and, at the foot of it, a chest to store clothes and the family muniments, a truckle bed for one of their sons William and Thomas, or a servant, as well as a jointed stool or two and perhaps a small table. If there was a chair this would have been a luxury enjoyed by Thomas, as the head of the household. Their bed, dressed with a straw or rush mattress and fustians – blankets – might typically have been hung with warm fabrics such as buckram or worsted wool. These might have been the work of local Benedictine monks, making up a tester at its head, a canopy above and curtains and cushions around them – all lending warmth and comfort as well as absorbing sound. There was little privacy in a medieval home and so discreet conversations took place inside the bed – a makeshift office – to which, for example, the bailiff would be summoned;

or, if Joan felt the need to remonstrate with Thomas, a 'curtain lecture' would have been given to him from inside the bed.

To mask the household smells, Joan would have prepared rose- or marjoram-water in the summer and caprifoil-water, an infusion of honeysuckle and other woodbine, in the winter to sprinkle about their home. Sprigs of herbs would also have burned in the open fire.

The Lygons lived together with their kith and kin in a small community which was highly coloured, though relatively quiet. Medieval man rarely heard a sound louder than sixty decibels: a crying animal, a barking dog, a shouting man, a pealing church bell, or the sawing, grinding, spinning or hammering of a tool being worked in a courtyard or a clearing beyond the house; or wind howling through the oaks in a storm. But while their serfs were limited to wearing drab, natural tones of wool and hemp lifted only by the blue hue extracted from woad, the Lygons could mark their rank with richer dyes: 'sanguine', a blood-red, 'murrey' from the mulberry, orange, rose and 'tawny', a mottled yellowy-brown; and with furs. Colour, particularly intense colour, distinguished a man or woman of rank, as did fur, and once local artisans and yeomen could afford to add squirrel linings to their clothing, the Lygons would have sought scarcer pelts such as marten.

Thomas was appointed the king's escheator in the shire. As an heiress, Joan also had power and responsibility. Though English common law subordinated her to Thomas, on becoming a widow she returned to the status known as *femme sole*, accorded to maidens over twenty-one. This meant she held personal rights on a par with a man and could hold land in her own name, make a will or contract and sue or be sued. These rights passed from her to her husband only for the duration of their marriage. If they had a child, and Joan died, then according to 'the courtesy of England' her lands too passed to her husband until his death. If, however, Joan survived Thomas then she could enjoy her dower: that is, one-third of his land as well as any they had been granted jointly or subsequently acquired together. These she retained even if she remarried. Consequently, a landed widow was powerful and might be sought after.

Ladies of the manor, such as Joan, were advised by the French writer Christine de Pisan to be 'wise and sound administrators and manage their affairs well' not only in their husband's absence – perhaps necessitated by war, business or court commitments – but also with a sense of common purpose side by side with him in their 'complementary and overlapping roles'. Christine recommended mastering the details of tenure and feudal law for the manorial court, which a wife continued to convene in her husband's absence, the management of the estates, the supervision of the bailiff and the running of their household.

In this 'hand-made world', Joan had to feed and clothe some two dozen people, and supervise the harvest and the stocking of the stewes. She had to oversee the preparation of the food: baking, curing, brewing; the crafting of furniture; the purchase of essential items unavailable on the estate: salt and spices, certain cloths and tanned leather; the cleanliness and upkeep of the house and the care and health of their children. The family might have owned a Book of Hours, a layman's prayer book scripted in Latin on to parchment. Much later such a book, one amongst many at one time owned by the Scropes, was added to the Madresfield Library by Frederick Lygon, the sixth Earl Beauchamp. Not only would a medieval family have referred to it for their devotions up to eight times a day, but Joan might have used it to teach William and Thomas to read and to learn their prayers by tallow light. These prayer books were so valued that they were singled out in wills and passed down, typically through women, as part of the family's inheritance.

In order to meet the religious obligation of avoiding meat on Wednesdays, Fridays and throughout Lent, a medieval family had either to find a source of fish or restrict its diet to vegetables, fruits and cereals on these days. Despite living a long way from the coast, the Lygons could eat fish such as pike, bream, roach and lamprey, stocked in the two stewes that had been excavated in their grounds beyond the moat. The expense of digging and maintaining these was considerable. In 1294, for example, the expense of just cleaning Westminster Abbey's pools at Knowle was £7 14s. 11d., the equivalent of a skilled labourer's wage for two years. In the prologue to the *Canterbury Tales*,

Chaucer conveyed the Franklin's standing – even pretensions – by informing the reader that he had 'many a bream and many a luce in stuwe'. At certain times of the year, perhaps the Lygons also sent their men with lanterns and nets down to the banks of the nearby River Severn in search of 'white gold': the transparent, glittering elvers or 'glass eels' which are annually carried up the river on a tide that sweeps in across the Atlantic from the Sargasso Sea. The great river was also source of a salmon or two. In October they harvested nature's 'sweets' – the tiny brown pear-shaped berries, or chequers, of the wild service trees – and hung them on strings above the hearth. The children waited for them to ripen before plucking them down to savour their sweet, exotic flavour of apricot tinged with tamarind. The adults brewed them into a fiery liqueur. These delicacies, along with game, preserved meats and poultry, would have impressed any guest who dined in Madresfield's Great Hall.

Joan and Thomas's heir, William, married Elizabeth Arundell but died without issue in 1448. Their second son, Thomas, married Anne Gifford who brought the manor of Bradwell to the Lygons. Young Thomas became a man of consequence and was held in some respect in the shire. In 1476 the king appointed him sheriff and he served on the commission 'De Wallis et Fossatis' (for walls and ditches), an important body which settled boundary disputes and maintained ditches and dikes. A document of 1471 suggests that he had an illegitimate child William, who in Worcestershire dialect would have been called a 'husbud', as well as a legitimate heir, Richard (1439–1512).

A deed dated 25 April 1459 shows us that there were dealings between Thomas Lygon and his powerful neighbour Richard Beauchamp concerning the release of some lands. This Beauchamp was a scion of one of the most eminent Norman families to be granted lands by the Conqueror – leading members had included William de Beauchamp, the first Earl of Warwick, and Sir Walter de Beauchamp, a crusader and Steward of the Household of Edward I. The marriage of a Beauchamp to Emmeline D'Abitot brought the Beauchamps into the county. As with the de Bracis and the Lygons, their rank and power increased, though on a grander scale, through a series of marriages to heiresses. The mother of Henry VII, for example, could claim Beauchamp blood.

Richard Beauchamp's father, John, was ennobled as Lord Beauchamp of Powick in 1447 and died in 1475. He chose a muzzled bear and a collared and coroneted swan as supporters for his coat of arms. The bear stood as testament to his being a kinsman of the Earls of Warwick; the swan pinned his political colours to the mast as it was the badge of the House of Lancaster. During this politically charged time and during the vicissitudes of the Wars of the Roses, Lord Beauchamp was a staunch supporter of the Lancastrian king, Henry VI. (It is not known which side the Lygons supported but since the Beauchamps were supporters of the House of Lancaster it seems very likely that the Lygons – keen to ally themselves with this great family – followed suit.)

The fact that Beauchamp became Treasurer of England in 1450 bears testimony to the importance of this nobleman. After two years' service he departed with a reward of four hundred pounds for his service during this 'moost troublouseust season'. In 1446/7 his son Richard married Elizabeth Stafford, the daughter of Humphrey Stafford, and they had three daughters but no son. As co-heiresses these girls would have been regarded as extremely desirable catches. Richard, who was to become the second Lord Beauchamp of Powick, and Thomas Lygon both served as MPs for Worcestershire in the parliament of 1472–5. Perhaps they met en route to the capital or in Parliament itself. Perhaps it was thanks to Thomas Lygon's interaction with him – as a trusted lawyer or steward – that Beauchamp gave his blessing to Thomas's heir, Richard, a relatively modest squire, marrying his second daughter, Anne. It was a spectacular liaison for the Lygons: once again they rose through marriage with an eminent woman. Anne brought to the marriage her aristocratic associations and the connection to the Beauchamp title which would become relevant to the Lygons four centuries later. It is in this generation that we first find evidence that the family was able to write, and a sense of Anne Lygon as an individual comes across the centuries on a document of 16 June 1532 in which she grants land to a William Clarke. It is signed by her in a round unpractised hand, although she would possibly have been over eighty at the time.

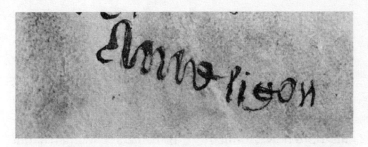

The following year Anne's son, the next Richard Lygon, was knighted at the coronation of Anne Boleyn and in 1548 he served as sheriff of the county. On his death, an inquisition post-mortem was held on 20 March 1556. Like any tax return, it undervalued his possessions, but it leaves us a list of lands owned and income recorded. The Lygons were now a substantial family in the county with manors at Madresfield, Holfast, Acton Beauchamp, Elmley Castle, Farley, Hanley Castle, Mytton, Beauchamp's Court, Braundsford, Powick, Woodfield and Clevelode as well as messuages and tenements dotted throughout Worcestershire. Their income was at least fifty pounds per annum, an income which was handed down to Sir Richard's heir, the next William Lygon (1512–67), who was forty-four when his father died, and his wife Aleanor Denys, daughter of Sir William Denys of Durham, Gloucestershire, whom he married in 1529.

In just two generations and through expedient marriages, the Lygons had risen from minor gentry to become kinsmen of the Earls of Warwick. Their rise had depended upon survival, cautious defence of their lands, trustworthy local service to their king and their community, and above all judicious marriages to women who brought more land and greater status. They had literally and metaphorically dug in and survived. Their advancement in Worcestershire society was not spectacular, and their story contrasts sharply with that of the Pastons, also lower gentry, whose letters are well known to medieval historians. The Lygons did not fly too high. But as the prosperous times of the late medieval period gave way to the turmoil of the later Tudor and early Stuart years, such prosperity as they had gained was threatened.

Chapter Three

THE PORTRAIT

At the heart of the house and overlooking an ancient courtyard, stands the Great Hall. Its wattle-and-daub walls are all that remain of the medieval room and over the years they have been panelled in oak; once in the Tudor period and again in the nineteenth century. The hall, some fifty feet by thirty, serves as a formal dining room. Under its hammerbeam roof and overlooked by a minstrels' gallery stands the multi-leaved mahogany dining table which can seat forty-eight guests. If there is one room which vividly exhibits the medieval tradition of open-handed hospitality on an impressive scale, it is the Great Hall.

In pride of place, at the head of the room, a portrait of Elizabeth I attributed – perhaps optimistically – to Federigo Zuccaro is illuminated from high Perpendicular windows which fall from carved stone trefoil- and quatrefoil-shaped architraves. Her attire is weighted with symbolism. She holds a golden sieve, signifying her virginity, and her robe is embroidered with the politically charged Tudor rose. Four ropes of black pearls, probably cargo from Polynesia or Mexico captured by one of her favoured pirates, hang across her stomacher.

The queen's portrait is surrounded by others, including those of two members of the Cromwell family; William Cecil, the first Lord Burghley; Anne, Countess of Northumberland and – reputedly – Lady Jane Grey. This picture hang is a political statement. It is a line-up of the Protestant manipulators of the Tudor succession. Here, above the oldest and biggest hearth in their home, the Lygons have displayed their political fealty to the Elizabethan succession and their acceptance of the new religion.

During a time when men wore their political loyalties on their sleeve and hung them in the form of portraits about the public reception rooms of their home, it is hardly surprising to see this line-up. A draft proclamation made in 1563 and personally corrected by Elizabeth's Secretary of State William Cecil stated a desire on the part of all her subjects 'both noble and mean' to procure a portrait of their monarch and consequently complex images of Elizabeth freighted with propaganda were produced in great numbers. These images were intended not for popular entertainment but to disseminate a cult of the monarch and to underscore her claims to legitimacy. Looking back on the days of 'Gloriana' it is sometimes hard to remember how precarious her position was.

In Tudor England the highly emotive subjects of religion and succession preoccupied its people and provoked endless conspiracies. Worcestershire, like Yorkshire, was known to be a recusant stronghold. The Lygons were divided between the 'Old' and the Protestant faith, reflecting the religious schism in many English families at the time. William Lygon and Aleanor Denys had seven sons and four daughters. One of the younger sons, Ralph, took part in the Duke of Norfolk's plot of 1572 to remove Protestant Elizabeth from power and received a pension from the grateful Philip II of Spain. Ralph spent the rest of his life in exile in Flanders. Hugh, another brother, who graduated from Oxford and became a barrister, remained a recusant until his death in 1601. But before Elizabeth's accession, the third son, Farnando, played his part in an attempt to remove the Catholic Queen Mary from the throne and replace her with her half-sister.

We do not know why he was christened Farnando, which is a somewhat unusual name for an English family with Norman rather than Spanish or Italian origins; nor is there a portrait of him at Madresfield. All we know of him is that he was not a Protestant zealot; he did not particularly exalt Elizabeth – he was an adventurer. As he was a cadet of the family, his future was not cushioned by inheritance. He would have to make his own way in the world and so, exploiting the political instability of the times, he had trained as a soldier and hired himself out as a mercenary.

His adventurous disposition had long been indulged

by his aunt, Lady Butler of Ferford. On hearing her nephew talk of lands beyond the seas and how tempting profits could be gained from travel and that all he needed was twenty marks per year for two or three years to try his luck abroad, Lady Butler obliged young Farnando. Instead of trying his luck abroad, however, he took her money and entered the service of Nicholas Heath, the Roman Catholic Archbishop of York. His career in the service of Catholicism only lasted until 1555, however, when – with an eye to the main chance – he joined the Protestant 'Dudley Plot' against Queen Mary. He had heard that the French king Henri II was promising a pension to the leading conspirators, and he calculated that Elizabeth, once enthroned, would reward the rebels with positions at court. That was enough to make him change sides.

At the beginning of Mary's reign, a number of influential Protestants had left for the Continent. Typically, these exiles, some one thousand in number, were gentry or minor aristocrats, such as the pirate Sir Peter Carew, Sir Peter Killigrew, the Duchess of Suffolk (Lady Jane Grey's mother) and Sir Henry Dudley, kinsman of the Duke of Northumberland. They settled in Protestant Switzerland and Germany and along the French coast around Calais, which remained in English hands. From there they launched a relentless pamphlet campaign denouncing the queen and her religion, spreading discord and hatching schemes to dethrone her in favour of her half-sister, Elizabeth. Covertly encouraged by Henri II of France, the exiles communicated with like-minded Protestants back in England, such as William Cecil, who, despite holding office at the heart of Mary's administration and feigning loyalty, systematically undermined her by providing encouragement and intelligence to the exiles.

Their first open expression of resistance came in 1554 when the Protestant landowner Sir Thomas Wyatt led a rebellion from Kent. It was this uprising that had aroused Mary's suspicions about Henry Dudley's loyalty. The rebels were defeated at the gates of the City of London and Wyatt and some of his supporters were beheaded.

Two years later, in the early months of 1556, the Calendar of State Papers records that printers in England were issuing a stream of 'false books, ballets, rhymes and other lewd treatises' ridiculing Mary and her husband Philip. The English ambassador to France sent word that another conspiracy of long standing was being hatched. Its aim was to 'deprive Mary of her estate' and to use her 'as she used Queen Jane'. The ambassador warned that many were arrayed against the queen, including those 'such as had never offended the queen before'. In the spring and after much deliberation, for it was an incendiary act, Mary put her signature to the death warrant of the premier Protestant in England, Thomas Cranmer, who had been appointed Archbishop of Canterbury during her father's reign. Mary had reason to hate Cranmer. He had annulled her parents' marriage and then married her father, King Henry, to Anne Boleyn. For several days immediately prior to Cranmer's execution, a long-tailed comet burned over London. To easily suggestible minds, it was a portent. Giovanni Michiel, the Venetian ambassador to England, wrote to the Doge:

> For many consecutive days, a comet has been visible as it still is, and with this opportunity, a gang of rogues, some twelve in number, who have been arrested, went about the city [of London], saying we should soon see the Day of Judgment, when everything would be burnt and consumed. These knaves, with a number of others, availing themselves of this device, agreed to set fire to several parts of the city, to facilitate their project of murder and robbery.

Neither the ambassador nor Mary realized the true significance of these fires. They were decoys ignited to distract attention from a planned robbery of fifty thousand pounds' worth of Spanish bullion from the Exchequer: the audacious first move in a complex, deftly planned and surprisingly well-supported plot to oust her from the throne.

The plot had been ripening since the previous autumn when rumours had begun to circulate that Mary intended to crown her Spanish and Catholic husband, Philip. A number of leading Protestant families were outraged and, encouraged by his fourth cousin, the Duke of Northumberland, Henry Dudley had returned to France in the winter of 1555, to secure, once again, Henri II's support. Though the French king feigned neutrality, it was later revealed that when he heard of the plan to poison Mary, he 'relished the scheme'. The conspirators, aided by the French ambassador, François de Noailles, hoped to underscore Elizabeth's claim by marrying her to Edward Courtenay, Earl of Devon and the great-grandson of Edward IV.

The other leading figure in the plot was the Lygons' neighbour and kinsman John Throckmorton. Unlike Dudley, the twenty-eight-year-old Throckmorton was a man of principle and, it was later revealed, considerable bravery. He had been brought up in the household of Lord Thomas Howard and was an educated and well-travelled man. He felt it was his patriotic duty to wrest the crown from Spanish and Catholic influence. His motives were in contrast to those of Farnando and most of the other supporters of the plot, who by and large were stirred by a desire for profit. Typically they were disaffected and down-at-heel gentry who lived by the sword, but also included thirty MPs, unemployed soldiers, unpaid and discharged royal officers, dozens of public officials and adventurers. One man, John Daniel, a servant of Lord Grey, when asked by Henry Dudley in London if he would support him, explained that he needed time to decide. He was deliberating over whether to marry a rich widow and felt it wise to inspect her first . . . A week later he joined Dudley's ranks.

Dudley and Throckmorton's plans to remove Mary from the throne evolved over a number of meetings which took place at one of three venues: a London inn called Arundel's, Throckmorton's home, Coughton in Warwickshire, or Fyfield, the Berkshire home of the two Ashton brothers. These brothers, ex-soldiers and guns-for-hire like Farnando, were said to be 'skilled in service'. Dudley planned to hire three thousand French troops who, together with the exiles, would make up a band of some four thousand men, who would land on the south coast. The invaders intended to join forces with Sir Anthony Kingston, Comptroller of the Queen's Household. The leaders boasted that Kingston would be 'able to bring a great part of Wales at his tail'. Once amassed on English soil, the band of rebels – some twenty thousand men, they predicted – would march on London.

In order to pay for the French troops, the mercenaries and the boats, the conspirators needed the bullion in the Exchequer which had recently arrived with Philip from Spain. It was to have been removed, rowed across the Thames and hidden amongst the sedges on the Shoreditch bank, from where it would have been transported to France. There a makeshift mint, operated by the alchemist William Hines, would melt it down and forge coins with which to pay Dudley's mercenaries.

While conspirators in London worked on the bullion theft, Dudley and Throckmorton travelled to Carisbrooke Castle, the chief fortress on the Isle of Wight and official residence of its Governor, Richard Uvedale. This was a strategically important site on which they intended to land troops from France. There, under Uvedale's roof, they refined their plans. Dudley assured Uvedale that he was merely en route to France to escape debtors but his host became suspicious when he noticed them poring over maps, writing in cipher and whispering in French. When Dudley's luggage arrived, it contained attire more suited to a courtier than a fleeing bankrupt: a black velvet cloak trimmed with wolverine fur, black velvet hose and a matching hat.

Within days, Dudley had taken a boat to Normandy. On arriving at the French court, Dudley learned that the French king had recently signed a five-year truce with Philip and could not be seen to condone treason against Mary, a Catholic queen and Philip's wife. Nevertheless, behind the scenes, he assured Dudley of his support and recommended that the conspirators lie low until a more opportune moment arose.

Impatience unravelled the plot: the robbery never took place. Thomas White, who was involved in the planning, panicked and confessed to Cardinal Pole, Mary's loyal Archbishop of Canterbury, while others moved impetuously and without authority.

Forewarned by White's intelligence the authorities removed the bullion from the Tower but the plot was allowed to mature in order that a larger number of conspirators would be caught. Within days of the comet's flight forty arrests were made, both in London and the shires: one of the men taken was Farnando Lygon.

Sir Anthony Kingston was summoned from Wales but died on the road to London, while Throckmorton,

Dethick, Daniel, Uvedale, Farnando, who was arrested
in March 1556, and others were taken to the Tower, put
to the rack and questioned under torture.
Throckmorton was placed in a cell immediately above
Dethick. Anxious to instil loyalty in his confrères, after
a bout on the rack, Throckmorton prised back a floor
plank and urged Dethick that, though 'I do assure you
it is a terrible pain', he must remain resolute under
torture. 'For look how many thou doest accuse, so many
doest thou wilfully murder.' He elicited from Dethick a
promise to endure which they sealed with a toast in
thin gruel.

Throckmorton had overestimated his fellow-
conspirators. With the exception of himself – who,
despite prolonged torture, remained loyal to the cause
– the captives all proved unequal to interrogation.
Daniel, cooped up in his dank cell crawling with newts
and spiders, scratched on to the wall: 'Pity me, pity me,
for God's sake', before revealing all he knew to the
Lords of the Council. Farnando was examined on 23
April and was so efficient an informant that he wrote an
aide-memoire listing questions that the Council should
put to various associates in order to incriminate them
further. For fear that he might forget details, he wrote:
'Item – to speak for a table to write on. Item – to declare
my own danger in this case that it is not otherwise used.
Item – I hear that the servants say that the world did
dislike me for that I should accuse Throckmorton, for if
I had held my own he had not gone to the rack.'

Throckmorton and Uvedale were the first to be

executed: hanged, drawn and quartered at Tyburn Abbey on 28 April 1556. Others followed. As a reward for the expansiveness of his information, Farnando was pardoned and in 1557 was granted the post of commander of a company of three hundred soldiers, armed with flintlock guns, on the Scottish border. Meanwhile, Dudley evaded capture; he remained in France incognito, assuming the name de Lisle, one of the Northumberland family names. However, rather than enjoying a handsome pension from Henri II, he was condemned to poverty. His co-conspirators, Carew and Killigrew, whose West Country estates ran down to the sea, both returned to piracy – a family trade. The piratical Killigrews were to play a part in a later Lygon adventure. They made such profits that some of their fellow-plotters approached them for loans, to no avail. It was every man for himself.

In fact a number of gentry families involved in the Protestant plots against Mary took to the high seas as pirates during the Tudor years – the Dudleys had been employed as early as the reign of Henry VIII to police the high seas and had helped themselves liberally to booty. When Elizabeth finally acceded in 1558, she found that piracy had taken hold of the seas around England and had become 'so general as to be scarcely disreputable'. Rather than attempt, without resources, to address the escalation of piracy, the wily Elizabeth exploited these skilled seafarers to defend her shores. In 1564, the Queen commanded Sir Peter Carew to fit out an expedition to clear the seas of any pirates, reasoning that it takes a thief to catch a thief. Similarly, Sir John Killigrew was appointed Vice-Admiral of Cornwall, President of the Commissioners of Piracy and Royal Governor of Pendennis Castle at Falmouth where he was in command of a hundred cannon trained out to sea to police its waters. As the Killigrew family covertly controlled the pirate syndicate along that coast they had no incentive to impose law and order. Killigrew also ran a profitable sideline, selling the gunpowder which had been allocated by the Crown to defend the coast from pirates.

Since the Channel was a vital passage to northern Europe's leading port, Antwerp, merchant ships had to run a narrow gauntlet with the twin hazards of storms and the opportunistic English pirates. The cargoes they lost – Antillean hides, Brazilian sugar, West Indian tobacco, South Sea black pearls, silver from the mines of Zaruma, Zamova and Popaya on the Spanish Main, emeralds from New Granada, Oriental silks, Spanish taffetas, Andalusian wine, Toledo steel – were landed on to remote English shorelines and stored in vacated monasteries and convents. The usual cut for booty was one-fifth to the pirate and four-fifths to the handler. Fortunes were made.

Here, clearly, was a new opportunity for the callow Farnando. He had stayed in Scotland only two years, then, beckoned by adventure and greater rewards, he had taken his flintlock and travelled south. In 1559, he was found in the service of his brother-in-law, Henry Berkeley, but again he grew impatient, and set off for the southern coast of England to try his hand at piracy. It is likely either that he boarded the galleon of his co-conspirator Killigrew or that he joined up with Andrew Barker, an infamous pirate who sailed – coincidentally or not – under a flag bearing the bear and ragged staff (the Beauchamp device or badge). Farnando, like many Tudor gentry, masked his opportunism with patriotism. The English pirates allied themselves to Huguenot French corsairs, renegades and petty nobles, and together they claimed that they were motivated by 'gentlemanly revenge' on behalf of their fellow Protestants who had been killed at the hands of Catholic Spaniards – by the Inquisition in Spain or by Spanish colonial governors throughout the Spanish Main – and by the French Catholic crown. The Spanish consequently dubbed them 'Corsarios Luteranos'. Henri of Navarre encouraged English pirates to attack French Catholic shipping and Sir Francis Drake, an ardent Protestant, travelled with his favourite book, Foxe's *Book of Martyrs*, a text which heightened his Protestant zeal.

Farnando's brothers and sisters left a nobler mark on history than that gentleman of fortune, particularly the history of America. Thomas and his son Richard we shall meet in the next chapter. Margery Lygon married Sir Thomas Russell of Warwickshire and their son, also called Thomas, was an executor of William Shakespeare's will. Her second marriage to Sir Henry Berkeley links the Lygons to the Berkeleys once again and their grandson became the Royal Governor of

Virginia. Margery's younger sister Cicely married Edward Gorges and their son, Sir Ferdinando Gorges, became known as 'the Father of Colonization in America'. In 1639, King Charles I granted him 'a parte & portion of the countrie of America called by the name of New England' and Fort Gorges in Maine still bears his name. Elizabeth Lygon married William Norwood and their grandson wrote *A Voyage to Virginia* in 1649.

The indomitable mother of this generation of Lygons, Aleanor, became a widow in 1567. As her eldest son, William, inherited Madresfield on her husband's death, she returned to Arle, her dower, a manor brought into the Lygon family upon her father-in-law's marriage to Margery Greville in 1511. Two years later she was joined there by her wayward son Farnando, who received an annuity of eight pounds from the manor of Madresfield. Records reveal that his mother was still alive in 1579, but nothing further is recorded about Farnando. He never married. Was his passing as dramatic as his life? We don't know: as he was a renegade, we have no account of his death.

We catch sight of Farnando's great-nephew William (1568–1608) in a portrait, painted in 1599, which hangs alongside that of the Virgin Queen in the Great Hall. This painting shows a gimlet-eyed man in his thirties dressed in black doublet, belted in cloth of silver, and ruffed and cuffed in iridescent white lawn, leaning outwards with an urgency suggesting that the viewer has something he wants. His dandified dress – with its nod to Spanish court fashion and to unnecessary expense – announces an Elizabethan opportunist.

William inherited the estate in 1584. He was born into an era in which the landed classes were keen to display their wealth and position and reflect the new prosperity of the Elizabethan era with its reach across the globe. It was not sufficient simply to receive a handsome income, it must be conspicuously spent because, as a contemporary diarist, Sir Thomas Smith, recommended, 'a gentleman (if he will be so accounted), must go like a gentleman'. In an effort to maintain or improve their status many Elizabethans over-reached themselves and the Lygons, like so many other English families, might have lost all their lands as a result of William's profligacy. Nicknamed 'William the Wastrel' by the family, he brought them to the brink of bankruptcy.

An inventory dated 1584, the year in which the Wastrel inherited the estate, shows that his lands stretched over three counties – Worcestershire, Warwickshire and Gloucestershire – and his home, Madresfield Court, included a 'chamber over the gate', a 'little chamber over the gate', a south chamber, a 'le mer' chamber (perhaps referring to a sea image in the form of a tapestry, mural or carving in it), a nursery, a maid's chamber, the Liggons' chamber, William Liggon's chamber, a gallery, a cheese chamber, a parlour, a chamber from the parlour, a 'chappell' chamber, four more small chambers, a long house, a buttery, another room, another little chamber, a

Sir William Lygon, 'William the Wastrel', brought the family to the brink of ruin by lavishly extending Madresfield. He and his wife, Elizabeth Harewell, were both painted in 1599.

The River Severn meanders close to Madresfield's boundary, and is depicted in a map from Michael Drayton's 'The Poly-Olbion', 1613.

chamber next to the privie and a 'great chamber'. The list of furniture in one of the main bedrooms, 'a truckle bed, white rug, jointed chair', gives us a sense that even an affluent knight's home was still frugal at that time. Even wealthy noblemen until the mid-sixteenth century continued to live in a style that differed little from their medieval antecedents in fortified, draughty buildings with little privacy from their household.

Following the Dissolution of the Monasteries and the social fluidity arising from the political actions of the Tudor regimes, numerous country houses were rebuilt from the monastic ruins; some quite literally from the stones left abandoned on these religious sites. Although the Lygons did not personally benefit from the Dissolution, the Wastrel did avail himself of the rapidly growing output of the brick-maker and, on inheriting the manor house, rebuilt and extended it, providing his family with superior standards of comfort and privacy. As property was now held more securely, the old house no longer needed to turn its back defensively on the world around an internal courtyard. Now Madresfield turned its face more confidently out to face it. The Wastrel did not employ an architect but worked from his own plans, oversaw his workmen, kept accounts and masterminded the whole successful project. He retained the twelfth-century Great Hall at its heart and encased its timber frame and walls with bricks made from the clay which he had excavated from the considerably enlarged moat. The interior of the Hall was panelled with oak from the park.

Ignoring classical or foreign influences he created a picturesque pink-bricked Elizabethan building with crow-stepped gables, tall chimneys and mullioned windows. Now it was considerably larger than the previous house and included a number of new chambers, with the important addition of a sixty-foot Long Gallery overlooking the park. A solar wing, a section of the house into which the noon-day sun shone brightest, was also added where the women of the house could pursue embroidery and needlework in the light which shone through the modern glass windows which had replaced the ones made of horn. Various domestic offices were added to the back of the house to complete the facilities required of a substantial Tudor manor house. To commemorate the completion of the rebuild, a piece of stone inscribed with the date 1593 was set into the brickwork of the building. Glorious though the Wastrel's project certainly was, it plunged the family into generations of debt.

William Lygon was appointed a justice of the peace before 1591 and sheriff of the county between 1592 and 1593. He represented the county in Parliament between 1589 and 1608. In 1603 the Wastrel received a knighthood, probably due to the support of his uncle, Sir Thomas Russell.

William was knighted by James I who was wont to scatter honours like confetti, frequently for cash rather than merit in order to fund his expensive tastes. The resultant swelling of the upper ranks bred social insecurity which in turn fostered yet more conspicuous consumption as the nouveaux riches scrambled to flaunt their new-found wealth and rank while the established families tried to out-spend these upstarts and turned to genealogy to distinguish themselves from them. Since the time that Anne Lygon had signed the 1532 grant of land in her childlike hand, the landed classes of England had become a literate and record-conscious society. The Wastrel's kinsman and neighbour Henry Berkeley, for example, kept such extensive family records at his seat, Berkeley Castle, that a decade after the Wastrel's death, John Smyth could publish *The Lives of the Berkeleys*. Although they did not inspire a book at the time, the Lygon Muniments leave us details of the Wastrel's profligacy and his struggle to raise loans.

The late sixteenth century was the first period in which the landed classes of England became heavily dependent on credit, but the use of a mortgage to finance expenditure was a dangerous device since loans spanned only six months and non-payment threatened the loss of the land or the manor. It was a high-risk gamble. The Wastrel began seeking credit in 1591 when, jointly with his brother-in-law, Edmond Harewell – another spendthrift who completely dissipated his estate – he borrowed 100 *librae* (pounds) from a Roland Barkely of Worcester, to whom he sold the manor of Warmendon in 1594. In 1602 he was forced to sell the manor of Acton Beauchamp. He then borrowed significant sums from a pair of merchant traders from London and was forced to sell more manors and rent others out. The Wastrel was not above skulduggery. Three bonds were conditioned whereby payments were to be made within a month of his return from Venice. This journey was probably a fiction devised to cover transactions between himself and his friends. Generous hospitality continued to be the mark of a man of rank and the Wastrel spared no expense to provide a rich table under the Great Hall's roof. Indeed, many decades later his great-grandson wrote that Sir William Lygon's extravagance in great housekeeping brought the estate to a low ebb.

Sir William and his profligate friends persisted in juggling creditors until, on 7 December 1608, it was stated in a writ of the Court of Chancery that Sir William Lygon was too ill to travel. In fact he died the following day at Madresfield and was buried on 10 December at Malvern. His eldest son, another William Lygon, inherited the estate and as he was under age he became the king's ward. The lands were consequently taken into the custody of the Court of Wards.

At nineteen young William was knighted and in July 1611 he married Elizabeth, daughter of John Playdell, late of Aldington in the neighbouring county of Gloucestershire. But their time at Madresfield was relatively brief. William died aged only twenty-nine and once again the mortgaged estate was inherited by a minor, yet another William, who became, like his father before him, the king's ward. This dependent state was to cause the boy, in due course known as William the Colonel, much rancour and would affect his loyalty to the Crown.

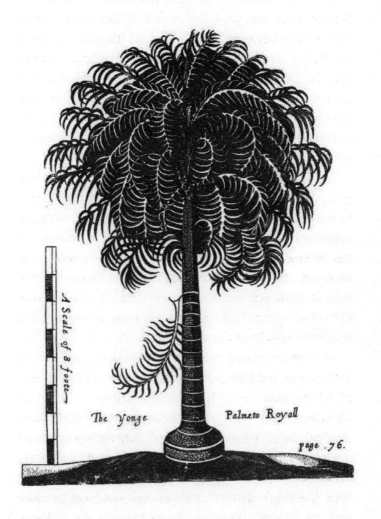

A Scale of 8 foots

The Yonge   Palmeto Royall

page .76.

The Royal Palm, from Richard Ligon's History of Barbadoes.

Chapter Four

THE HERBS

It's dawn at Madresfield. Dogs are barking in the Moat Garden. The din of heavy iron bars shifting to unfasten the colossal oak doors can be heard at the front of the house and, out at the back, the poultry protest as a gardener marches through their yard, carrying sprigs of fresh herbs. In summer his posy includes basil, lovage and marjoram, in winter he brings bay, rosemary and thyme. He crosses the Bridge of Sighs, passes along the flagstone corridors by the Old Kitchen, the pantries, the dairy and the cold stores and enters the New Kitchen. He places the herbs in a jar on the window sill for the cook to use throughout the day. The herb garden is not an ornately laid out knot garden or a fastidious parterre; it is a simple affair stocked with most of the English herbs known to us. At its best, English country house cooking has always depended on the subtle application of fresh herbs.

It was seeds from Madresfield's herb garden that

Richard Ligon [*sic*] (1590–1662), son of Thomas and grandson of William and Aleanor, took with him when he set sail for the West Indies nearly four centuries ago. Along with his culinary knowledge he brought a bag of English herb seeds – rosemary, thyme, winter savory, sweet marjoram, pot marjoram, parsley, pennyroyal, chamomile, sage, tansy, lavender, lavender-cotton, garlic, tarragon and southernwood – a taste of home. These yielded the first European herbs planted on the island of Barbados. His other legacy to the island was an architectural template for a planter's house, known as the 'double house'. In time, it was duplicated throughout the West Indies and the southern states of America. We know this because Richard, the first author in the Lygon family, wrote *A True & Exact History of the Island of Barbadoes* [*sic*] which was published in 1657, and in which he passed down to us an extraordinary tale.

Richard was born during the reign of Elizabeth I. His father Thomas had been brought up at Madresfield, but as he was a younger son, he did not inherit Madresfield and lived fifty miles away, with his wife, five sons and three daughters, on a farm at Elston on the Salisbury Plain, near Stonehenge. There, Richard enjoyed a country childhood. He bred a falcon and developed a keen interest in botany and animal husbandry. He visited his cousins at Madresfield which, like most country houses at the time, was self-sufficient. The Lygons baked their own bread, made preserves and jellies, concocted violet petal and honey syrups, kept cultures in the Still Room to make fruit-flavoured vinegars, matured milk products in the dairy, cured and preserved meats in the spicery for winter and hung game in the cold store. Sugar, an extremely expensive commodity, was known only to the élite at court and so beehives were kept to yield honey to sweeten the cooking. Water, homemade ale and wine were the most common drinks. Drinking chocolate, coffee and tea would not be available for another half-century on even the most affluent London table. The family continued to stock the stewes on the far side of the moat with freshwater fish for Fridays and Lent just as Joan de Braci had done two centuries earlier; fowl ran in the poultry yard and deer in the park provided venison. Extensive orchards lay behind the house. Berries, vegetables and salad greens grew in the kitchen garden and the produce of Home Farm rounded off their provisions with suckling pig, beef and mutton, lamb being considered too insipid a meat for the seventeenth-century palate. As a boy, Richard would have been familiar with the smithy, sawmill and the carpenter's workshop and might even have witnessed a local stonemason at work on his cousin's updated manor house. All these crafts were regularly practised both at his own home and – more extensively – at Madresfield where the fabric of the family home and its stock of household goods, such as chairs and chests, were being upgraded.

Details of Richard's early life are sketchy. His father died in 1619, and three of his four brothers probably died young. We can assume this because his mother's will, written in 1622 and executed in 1624, named only Thomas, her eldest, and Richard, her fourth son, as beneficiaries. In 1625, the two brothers sold the farm. Thomas accompanied his kinsman Sir William Berkeley to Virginia, where Berkeley had been appointed Governor in 1641, and remained in America where he died aged ninety. It is from Thomas that the American line of Ligons is descended.

Richard had been for some years dividing his time between Elston and London, where he attended the court of James I, the profligate king who had knighted the Wastrel. Richard was probably page to the equally extravagant queen, Anne of Denmark. As a witness to the royal dining table, Richard honed and widened his knowledge of fine food and probably tasted for the first time such exotic meats as peacock, swan, crane, heron and whale. The new Stuart dynasty was notoriously ceremonious and its dining scaled the heights of conspicuous consumption when a courtier introduced the 'ante-supper': a spread of the most sumptuous food that the chefs could prepare which, once the guests' appetites had been whetted, was thrown away and replaced by exactly the same fare sent fresh from the kitchens. The king and queen held lavish banquets. In 1621, for example, 100 cooks took 8 days to prepare 180 dishes, including 240 pheasants, at a cost of £3,000.

At court the young Richard also profited from a rarefied education in literature, classical and contemporary languages, painting and music. He had a particular interest in architecture. He hunted stag with the royal buckhounds in Windsor Forest and became an accomplished falconer, a sport confined to privileged circles. The court musician John Cooper, known as Coprario, became a friend and together they travelled to Italy where they inspected new musical instruments. Here Coprario completed his training before returning to the court as composer to James's son, Charles I, when the latter ascended the throne in 1625. Richard also befriended the royal gardener, John Tradescant, who deepened his botanical knowledge.

Richard was a landless bachelor in need of an establishment and to this end he became involved in a significant royal project, the draining of the Fens, in the hope that the speculative venture would secure him an estate. The Fens, an inhospitable, swampy area of land stretching over 1,400 square miles, lie to the south and west of the Wash. At the beginning of the seventeenth century this marsh could not support farming but Caroline entrepreneurs determined to reclaim it. The area was divided into four sections, called 'Levels', and the entrepreneurs were known as 'Undertakers'. Through court circles, Richard was invited to become an Undertaker, joining a partnership which included the Earl of Lindsey and Sir William Killigrew.

'The Lindsey Level' in Lincolnshire was drained but it was a controversial task, seen as a threat by the fen men who eked a subsistence from this bleak, sodden terrain by wildfowling, eeling and digging turf to fuel the salt-works. Violent riots broke out, incurring significant losses for the Undertakers. In November 1641, Killigrew and his associates submitted a petition to the House of Lords itemizing damages of £180 arising from the rioters' actions. Richard was a signatory. The following May, a second petition was brought before the Upper House signed, 'Sir William Killigrew, Edward Heron, Esq., Richard Ligon and other participants with the Earl of Lindsey'. These men claimed that they had been 'thrown out of their lawful possessions, their works and drains that have cost near £60,000' thanks to the actions of hundreds of rioters.

Despite elevated connections and persistent remonstration with Parliament, the Undertakers – Royalist to a man – were ignored. More urgent matters were now claiming parliamentary attention. On 22 August 1642, King Charles I raised his standard at Nottingham to defend the monarchy against the Parliamentarians. The English Civil War had begun. Large tracts of England, including the Fens, fell to the Parliamentarians.

Given his royal association and this significant speculative loss, it is hardly surprising that Richard's loyalties lay with the Crown. He remained in London which, though controlled by the Parliamentarians, provided ideal sanctuary for the opposition. The port of London offered a line of communication with the Royalist sympathizers on the Continent. Despite blockades and border controls between Royalist and Parliamentarian territory in England, Richard managed to attend the king on at least one occasion at Oxford, the Royalist capital. There Richard also saw his friend

Brian Duppa who had tutored Charles as a boy and had become chaplain to the royal household and bishop of Chichester and Salisbury. Duppa was to be instrumental in Richard's life after the war.

Richard's role during the Civil War is unclear. He was not in military service but may have been a spy and in his recollections, written in the early 1650s, he is understandably reticent about this period of his life. The English Crown was contested three times within a twenty-mile radius of Madresfield, at the battles of Evesham, Tewkesbury and Worcester. The first skirmish of the war took place between Prince Rupert and Nathaniel Fiennes' troops close to Madresfield. As the house was situated near the routes to and from Upton-on-Severn, Ledbury and Hereford, it was besieged three times during the Civil War and was occupied in turn by both sides. Throughout the war, the city of Worcester remained loyal to Charles II and, as a consequence, still enjoys the title the 'Faithful City' – faithful to the Crown.

Colonel William Lygon (1613–81), Richard's cousin, had inherited Madresfield while still a child from his father, William, who had died young. He married Mary, the daughter of Sir Francis Egiocke, and together they had ten children. In contrast to his cousin, the Colonel served in the Parliamentarian Army, though he was a half-hearted Roundhead. It has been suggested that he had turned against the Crown because of a protracted struggle, on coming of age, to free his lands from the Court of Wards. When the Colonel's troops were routed by the Royalists stationed at Worcester in 1646, Madresfield was garrisoned for the king by Captain Aston who, during the siege of Worcester, was charged to hold it for a month. At one point during hostilities, the Colonel was commanded as a punishment to raze Madresfield to the ground, an order he (understandably) failed to carry out. And throughout the negotiations of June and July 1646 for the surrender of Worcester city to Cromwell's forces, he was a conciliatory rather than bellicose member of the Parliamentary delegates. Yet fortunately, at the end of the war, on payment of a fine, the house was returned to him, though the estate was mortgaged to the hilt owing to his grandfather's high spending. It would take another two generations to restore the Lygon finances. To celebrate the recovery of his family home, the Colonel planted the elm and oak drives which approached the house from the west: these oaks still stand.

By this time – in May 1646 – the king had surrendered in Nottinghamshire; Exeter had already fallen on 13 April of that year. Richard was among the Royalists captured there along with two friends who would change his life: Thomas Modyford, a barrister and a Royal Commissioner for Devon, and Modyford's brother-in-law, Thomas Kendall, son of the Collector of Customs of Exeter. As a London-based merchant, Kendall had considerable overseas trading interests. It was said that it was through Modyford, an opportunist rather than a dependable Royalist, that the city had fallen to the Parliamentarians. Nevertheless, all three were placed under arrest.

Commissions were established by Parliament to deal with those who had actively supported the king and the Committee of Compounding, which sat in London, determined whether those found guilty should be fined or should have their property sequestered. However, Richard – an unrepentant Royalist – did not wait for the Committee's verdict. Reduced to being a gentleman without land or vote, a courtier without a court, an entrepreneur without a venture, a man without family and 'a stranger in my own country', he heeded the old proverb 'Needs make the old wife trot' and at fifty-seven, and having 'lost (by a barbarous riot) all that I had gotten by the painful travails and cares of my youth', he took flight, accompanying Modyford to the West Indies where they planned to buy land on Antigua.

His story has been left to us thanks to Bishop Duppa who, upon Richard's return in 1650, encouraged him to write an account of his three-year exile. *A True & Exact History of the Island of Barbadoes* is the first history of the island. Richard's story begins with the departure of a sister ship laden with men, provisions and equipment, which was sent ahead, via the Ivory Coast, to Barbados, where Richard and Modyford would join it, take on more equipment and slaves and move on to Antigua. Richard and Modyford (later to become the Governor of Barbados and then of Jamaica) followed, setting sail on 15 June 1647 aboard the *Achilles*, a 350-ton ship with a cargo of cloth, linen and broad-brimmed hats 'such as Spaniards use to wear' for the purpose of trade. On board was also a consignment of prostitutes from Bridewell prison and Turnbull Street in London. Adopting a south-westerly course to avoid 'pirates and pickaroones', they headed for the coasts of Barbary and Spain.

According to Richard there was 'no place so void and empty' as Madeira, whereas the island of St Jago in the Cape Verde archipelago was a garden paradise. After a heavy rainfall the valleys 'put on new liveries: so fresh, so full of various greens, intermixed with flowers of various kinds', such as that which he christened the 'St Jago' and from which he took cuttings. The passengers and crew rested there for nineteen days. Water and provisions were taken on board and hats and linen exchanged for cattle and horses. Richard was appalled by the hovels inhabited by the Europeans. Meaner than the 'meanest inns upon London-way', they consisted of four poky rooms with filthy earth floors, miserable cobwebs for hangings and frying pans and grid-irons for pictures. Far more pleasing to his eyes was his host's shapely black mistress who was surely 'of the greatest beauty and majesty together, that ever I saw in one woman'. She moved 'with far greater majesty and gracefulness than I have seen Queen Anne descend from the Chair of State to dance the measures with a baron of England' and was dressed in a green and white striped taffeta turban, a beguiling veil which she removed and replaced to alluring effect, a tawny orange and sky-blue striped petticoat and a purple mantle tied with a large black ribbon and fastened to one shoulder with a large jewel, from where it hung 'carelessly' to her ankles. Her legs were encased in silver-laced and fringed buckskins and her shoes were of the finest white leather laced in sky-blue to match her petticoat. Large pendants swung from her ears and pearls decorated her throat and arms, though 'her eyes were the richest jewels, the most oriental that I have ever seen'. Richard was transfixed and offered her some trinkets but ultimately backed away from her uncorsetted temptations when he realized that the islanders were 'as jealous of their mistresses as the Italians of their wives'. The recalcitrant bachelor confessed 'had not my heart been fixed fast in my breast, and dwelt there some sixty years, and therefore loathe to leave its long kept habitation, I had undoubtedly left it.'

At sea once again, Richard was reminded of hounds chasing stag in Windsor Park as shoals of porpoises crossed the prow in pursuit of prey. He admired the sea hawk's 'swiftness of wing' as it stooped from great heights, freer and faster than the best haggard falcon he had trained, and, using the dolphins as 'spaniels', located its prey, the flying fish. The raptor, being five hundred leagues from dry land, would then find rest on the back of a green turtle. Richard savoured turtle meat and judged it beyond compare in 'wholesomeness and rareness of taste'. Feasting on fish – mackerel, bonito and albacore – the crew used flying fish or shark as bait for dolphin, which was prepared, Richard approvingly recounts, with wines, spices and sweet herbs probably improved under his culinary instruction.

At last, after ten weeks, Barbados hove into view. It lies at the eastern end of the Lesser Antilles and the first Englishman to step on to the uninhabited island was probably Captain Simon Gordon in 1620. Five years later, en route from Brazil to England, John Powell landed, calculated the potential of these 166 square miles of virgin rainforest and returned two years later with ten slaves captured from a Portuguese ship and the first eighty English settlers. In late August 1647 Richard sailed along its western shore towards Carlisle Bay and observed that the highest terrain lay in the middle of the island and then sloped gently down to the sea where the sands were fringed with 'the most magnificent tree growing on the earth', the royal palm – its slender trajectory ending in a neat explosion, like a green firework. Behind the beach, 'one above the other, like several stories [*sic*] in stately buildings', lay the plantations, giving inhabitants all over the island an uninterrupted view of the ocean and the benefit of its cooling breezes. Twenty-two ships stood in the bay when they dropped anchor. Altogether, it was a pleasing sight.

On land, however, Richard's spirits fell. A plague was raging so virulently that 'the living were hardly able to bury the dead'. Six thousand would die during the 1647 outbreak of yellow fever and as the bodies were thoughtlessly thrown into the swamps around Bridgetown, they contaminated the drinking water and

perpetuated the cycle of death. Barbados has no freshwater lakes and few rivers and so drinking water was
taken from stagnant pools. Alternatively, rainwater
was collected in ponds in which, to Richard's astonish-
ment, slaves were allowed to wash. Having landed,
Modyford and Richard learned that their sister ship was
lost at sea and, unable to proceed to Antigua, they
explored opportunities on Barbados. It was far better,
they were advised by planters, to buy a 'ready furnished'
plantation stocked with servants, slaves, livestock and a
sugar-works than to endure the hardship of clearing
virgin forest, a task that Richard's medieval ancestor
Robert de Braci had painstakingly completed at
Madresfield. On Antigua the job could take twenty
years since the trees, particularly fustic and ironwood,
were so hard that they broke all tools. The Governor
introduced them to William Hilliard, a successful
planter and island councillor who, having been on
Barbados for many years, was yearning for 'the sweet air
of England' and looking for a partner to buy half, and
manage all, of his 500-acre plantation. Paying seven
thousand pounds for the half share, Modyford bought
himself a place in the island's fledgling sugar
'Plantocracy'.

Sugar was a relatively new cash crop on Barbados.
The first English settlers had grown tobacco, ginger and
cotton on twenty- or thirty-acre plots. However, in the
early 1640s entrepreneurs such as James Drax and
James Holdip learned from Dutch and Jewish traders
operating in the Spanish Main that sugar was three

times as profitable as tobacco and they switched to sugar cane. Fortunately, the Bajan climate and the rich black volcanic and red clay soils proved to be perfect, but it was only after a decade of trial and error that they perfected its manufacture. When Richard arrived, the planters were harvesting their crop prematurely and struggling to master the chemistry of sugar-making. Their inferior muscovado sugar was too moist and full of molasses to command a high price but by 1650 they had managed to produce pure white sugar and found a voracious market in Europe.

As sugar production advanced, land values rose by 200 per cent in just a decade, and enterprising planters bought out the smallholders. Many recent entrepreneurs were Royalist émigrés from the Civil War and considerably more affluent, or better placed to access credit, than the modest early settlers. Though Richard himself did not enter the sugar trade, he witnessed first hand this dramatic change in the island's fortunes. Within a decade the island's topography had been transformed. Square miles of hardwoods were felled and in their place a matrix of sugar cane was planted, calling to mind the precision of a Bordeaux vineyard rather than the verdant disorder of the tropical rainforest.

The planters nicknamed Barbados 'Little England' and were determined to make their fortune from what Richard called 'efficacious sugar', which was said to preserve both health and fortune. Doctor Butler, one of the most learned and famous physicians that this nation, or the world, ever bred, was wont to say that:

> *'If sugar can preserve both pears and plumbs,*
> *Why can it not preserve as well our lungs?'*

The doctor counselled the addition of sugar to claret and prescribed it to patients suffering from colds, coughs and catarrh in cold damp climates.

Planter society was opportunistic, competitive and highly materialistic. James Drax, the planter-king, was an Anglo-Dutchman who had landed with only three hundred pounds but he had the advantage of being a pioneer. He vowed that he would not leave until he could afford ten thousand acres in England plus the wherewithal to run a handsome estate there and he was well on the way to achieving his goal. Richard and Modyford arrived a decade after him and Modyford set himself the target of amassing a hundred thousand pounds 'all by the sweet negotiation of sugar'. Richard describes in detail this business, the most pre-eminently profitable of the late seventeenth and eighteenth centuries. He reasoned that only a man with some considerable investment, approximately fourteen thousand pounds, could by 1647 afford to set himself up as a planter. Adventurers, aristocrats and entre-preneurs found the prospect irresistible and Richard's frank and practical account encouraged them. Over the next 150 years, while many failed, others made the for-tunes that financed some of the great houses in England: Harewood built for the Lascelles family,

Alderman Beckford's Palladian – and later his son William's Gothic – Fonthill and Christopher Codrington's magnificent library at All Souls, Oxford.

Within a couple of decades, sugar was no longer an exotic rarity but an everyday staple on European tables, stirred into drinking chocolate, coffee and tea, which was made widely available in London coffee houses in the third quarter of the seventeenth century. The English sweet tooth was born.

Richard was a realist. His book deters those with 'sluggish humour' or 'too volatile to fixe on businesse' from considering a trade that could be financially and physically ruinous. Planters had to be patient and skilled managers of men and materials. Only reliable contacts would ensure the necessary slaves and supplies. They must endure great discomfort, and be prepared for poor harvests, fire, slave insurrections and mortal illness. While the tropical island provided the perfect growing conditions for sugar – sixty inches of rain a year, heat and breezes – for eight months of the year the air was so humid that all knives, swords, locks, clocks and ammunition rusted. Even if a blade was rubbed clean of rust on a grindstone and replaced in its sheath, 'in a very little time, draw it out, and you shall find it beginning to rust all over'.

So preoccupied was the 'Plantocracy' with sugar profits that its housing was extremely crude. The planters lived in log cabins and their slaves bedded down on wooden planks under the sky. Their meagre timber houses were so 'insufferably hot' that Richard

wondered why they had not applied the sound architectural principles of thick walls, high ceilings and deep
cellars. Tiny windows kept out the driving rains and the
roofs were so low that a gentleman could not stand
upright in his hat. Had they not heard of shutters? he
wondered. And, contrary to logic, they closed their
houses to the refreshing easterly winds so that in the
heat of the afternoon the houses became 'stoves'.
Having seen the results of the recent work at
Madresfield and counting architecture among his
passions, he was able to show the planters how to
employ the carpenters and masons who had recently
arrived on the island. He drew up nearly twenty plans for
planters' houses, though only two were built to his
prescription.

A third of the house, he proposed, should be built on
an east/west axis and two-thirds across the west end of
this block on a north/south axis. To provide shade in
the afternoon for the rest of the building the
north/south section should be two storeys high. Ideally,
the whole edifice should be raised at least three feet
off the ground, leaving viaducts underneath for venti-
lation. A large porch and front door should open to a
hall stretching from the front to the back of the house
to allow cooling winds to blow through. He was keen
to add decorative detail: monograms carved into the
stonework like those above the entrance at Madresfield
would lend a similar refinement. Despite their talk, few
planters carried out his plans, calculating that the
labour required in building a decent house cost

'the want of those hands in their sugar work'. However, Richard's 'double house', an expression which is still used today, was widely copied in the southern states of America where the Ligon-style plantation house can still be seen.

Before Richard's arrival, planters tended to boil or roast their meat plainly but having given them 'some tastes of my cookery in hashing and fricasseeing this flesh', he began to impart some of the culinary knowledge that he had learned at court, including the principles of curing, seasoning and dressing meat with English herbs. 'I know of no herbs growing naturally on the island, except purcelane,' Richard reported, but having fortunately 'carried with me in seeds' fifteen types of English herb, he sowed them and watched them thrive – unlike English flowers, such as roses, which could not tolerate the climate. He then applied them to his cooking. He would have known, for example, that the bitterness of tansy, if applied to meat, could repel flies. He also propagated the St Jago flower from the cutting he had taken en route to the island. It has since been renamed the Barbados Pride and is one of the most popular plants on the island.

Richard marvelled at the wildlife and the variety of indigenous fruits on Barbados. The noble shape, sprouting coronet of leaves and symmetrical checked patterning of the pineapple particularly pleased this classically educated aesthete. It obeyed in every detail the rules of Divine Proportion. He observed:

When you bite a piece of the fruit, it is so violently sharp, as you would think it would fetch all the skin off your mouth; but, before your tongue have made a second trial upon your palate, you shall perceive such a sweetness to follow, as perfectly to sure that vigorous sharpness, and between these two extremes, of sharp and sweet, lies the relish and flavour of all fruits that are excellent.

Pineapple juice, he reported, was surely 'the Nectar which the Gods drunk [*sic*]'. Not only did Richard describe these plants but he also drew them and urged experts to come and catalogue the island's flora. Thirty years later, in 1686, the botanist Sir Hans Sloane made a study entitled *Voyage to the Islands of Madeira, Barbados, Nevis, St. Christopher and Jamaica* and on his return founded the Chelsea Physic Garden which, to this day, specializes in herbs.

Richard did not back away from describing the horror of the sugar trade. In the Barbados Museum in Bridgetown there is an exquisite and finely wrought silver object lying in a glass case. With the artful precision of a calligrapher, a silversmith has twisted this precious, polished metal into arabesques which spell out three initials 'G.H.C.' They stood for George Hyde Clarke. Peering down at it in the dimly lit gallery, one might mistake the monogram for a name plate from a fine writing box until its true purpose becomes clear: 'slave-branding iron'. That such an ostentatiously fine and beautifully wrought tool had been commissioned for such work communicates, at a glance, the brutality of the plantation owner towards the *sine qua non* of his trade: slaves. Just like a trunk, a book or a walking cane, the slave was part of his inventory.

The profitable edifice of the sugar trade was built on the back of the enslaved African, whose plight makes grim reading. By the end of the 1640s, in just twenty-five years, the planters on Barbados had enslaved – 'panyared' – thirty thousand. They were brought over by the Middle Passage of the Triangular Trade, from coastal towns such as Axim, Takoradi, Shama, Lagos, Bonny and Old Calabar in West Africa to the West Indies. This was a two- to three-week voyage during which, on average, a fifth died. Shackled in pairs and stacked like logs in a woodshed, they were deprived of sufficient water and food, frequently losing twenty per cent of their body fluid due to dehydration and the 'flux'. Fever and disease quickly spread through the ship and though boards were sluiced with vinegar in an attempt to overpower the stench of human excrement, so fetid was the smell carried by the salt breeze that other shipping sailed a couple of miles upwind to avoid the foul reminder of a foul trade. Rather than endure the voyage and a life of enslavement, many Africans attempted hunger strikes or threw themselves over-board to be eaten by sharks, which opportunistically patrolled the shipping lanes.

Sugar is an exacting, implacable crop. The Africans laboured for between ten and twelve hours a day in the humidity and heat. The heavy cane was cut, transported on carts to a mill and swiftly ground between stones. The juice was then transferred to boilers, moved on to a curing house and finally to a distillery before the crystallized grain was packaged and sent down to the docks to be exported. Working at speed and encouraged by a cat-o'-nine-tails, it was not unusual for a slave to lose a limb in the grinders or to die falling into a boiler from fever or exhaustion. Richard observed their lives – toil, rituals and relationships – at close quarters. He dispassionately describes the physiognomy of the Negro with the accuracy of a man trained to consider aesthetics.

> I have been very strict in observing the shapes of these people; and for the men, they are very well-timbered, that is, broad between the shoulders, full breasted, well filleted, and clean legged and may hold good with Albrecht Dürer's rules, who allows twice the length of the head to the breadth of the shoulders, and twice the length of the face to the breadth of the hips, and according to this rule these men are shaped. But the women not; for the same Great Master of Proportions allows to each woman twice the length of the face to the breadth of the shoulders, and twice the length of her own head to the breadth of her hips. And in that, these women are faulty, for I have seen very few of them whose hips have been broader than their shoulders, unless they have been very fat.

Disdaining the popular European view that they were

just 'beasts of burden' or chattels which could be traded and worked to death in the interest of profit, Richard was – though by no means an abolitionist, the abolitionist movement being founded over a century later – unusual for his time in his humane obser-vations. During his short stay on Barbados, he built up relationships with a few of the slaves and in doing so came to hold them in respect. He describes the cruelty of the slave market, the conditions under which the slaves worked and their barbaric living quarters. At the Bridgetown slave market, those Africans who had survived the Middle Passage were herded naked – save for the ship's name branded into their flesh – before the planters so that nothing could be hidden from a prospective buyer. A humiliating stampede then took place as planters or their agents scrambled to place a hand on a desired slave to claim ownership. While a strong young male slave could command thirty pounds for his trader, the old or infirm were virtually worthless. Consequently, traders were not above de-ception. The old men or women had their grey hair dyed black and those with acute diarrhoea or the 'flux' were plugged with cotton wool as a temporary measure.

Observing the systematic cruelty meted out to the Africans, Richard was amazed that, despite being double in number to the white population, and despite their many grievances, the slaves did not rise up and 'commit some horrid massacre upon the Christians, thereby to enfranchise themselves and become masters of the island'. But the Europeans were adroit. Slaves were forbidden to handle weapons and were consequently gun-shy. Their spirits were 'subjugated to a low condition' so that listlessness rather than defiance was instilled, and the various African tribes, from Guinea, Angola and the Gambia, were segregated by language to prevent plotting and rebellion. A riot did break out in 1649 but it was efficiently crushed. Nor did Richard share the slave-owners' self-serving view that the African was without a soul. He observed:

> Religion they know none; yet most of them acknowledge a God, as appears by their motions and gestures, for if one of them do another wrong, and he cannot revenge himself, he looks up to heaven for vengeance, and holds up both his hands, as if the power must come from thence, that must do him right. Chaste they are as any people under the sun.

In an attempt to humanize the African in the eyes of his European readers, Richard describes two encounters on the Modyford plantation, one with a slave called Macow and another with one named Sambo. Macow, a man of great dignity, kindness and wisdom, arrived at the planter's house one day when Richard was playing a theorbo, a long-necked lute. He handed the instrument to the curious slave who began to pluck at the strings and examine it. A day or so later, Richard was walking through the grove where he found Macow sitting on the ground working on a piece of timber with a chisel and saw. He was fashioning his own theorbo.

Richard tested the instrument and it 'put me in wonder how he of himself, should without teaching do so much'. He shared with Macow some rudiments of music, including the use of sharps and flats, and then 'left him to his own enquiries. I say thus much to let you see some of these people are capable of learning Arts.'

Sambo, another of Modyford's slaves, was so dependable that he had informed his owner of a slave conspiracy to rebel. When he was offered a holiday in recognition of his loyalty he declined on behalf of both himself and his slave crew, arguing that he was simply carrying out his duty. While cutting through the vegetation to clear a path to church with Sambo and three other slaves, Richard was asked by him to explain how a compass worked. The two men fell into conversation, whereupon the African, thinking it would provide him with 'all the knowledges he wanted', asked whether he could become a Christian. Richard promised to help but on discussing it with Modyford was informed that under English law no Christian could be made a slave. But, Richard argued, that was not what he was requesting – quite the opposite – Sambo the slave wanted to be made a Christian. Impossible, Modyford retorted. It would set an unacceptable precedent as 'all the planters in the island would curse him'. The planters feared that through Christianity the slave might learn that all men are equal in the eyes of God and then challenge the status quo. Also, to study the bible the slaves would need to read, which, it was feared, would lead to revolt.

'So I was struck mute,' Richard reports, 'and poor Sambo kept out of the Church; as ingenious, as honest, and as good natured a poor soul, as ever wore black or ate green.'

In his third year on Barbados, Richard was struck down with fever and was close to death for three months. Modyford sheltered him and Walrond, another planter, showed great kindness too. When he was strong enough to travel he went down to Bridgetown and negotiated his passage home on an English ship which sailed on 15 April 1650 – at midnight, in order to dodge a well-known Irish pirate, named Plunquet, whose ship lay in wait for passing trade just outside the harbour. Modyford, ever the opportunist, in his later career as Governor received back-handers from a number of these Caribbean pirates, including the infamous Henry Morgan who was later knighted by Charles II.

On the homeward journey, the captain, despite re-assuring the sickly Richard that he was well stocked with provisions such as beef, pork, peas, fish, oil, beer and wine, had little to offer his passengers. Even the fresh water was fifteen months old. He had not taken fresh water on board at Barbados. Calamity struck when the sails were torn down by high winds and there was not even thread aboard to repair them. Supplies were so low that the crew, who represented the majority, planned that the passengers should be 'dressed and eaten' – the fattest and healthiest first. Since he was still nothing but skin and bone, Richard reckoned that if they tried to eat him he would 'dissolve and come to nothing in the cooking', and so he might be last on their menu. When all seemed lost, 'a little virgin' stood up and said that if the ship's carpenter would carve her a spindle, she would make thread and repair the sails. She saved the day and they returned safely to England.

Richard was promptly imprisoned for debts and it was while in gaol that he wrote his story. Bishop Duppa was the midwife; he urged Richard to write his tale. He concludes his book philosophically, predicting that since God had restored him from sickness, ship-wreck and pirates, he would also 'deliver me from this uncircumcised Philistine, the Upper Bench' – the King's prison for debt at Fleet Prison. It is probable that his friends paid his outstanding fine and he was released. Richard died in 1662 at Pill, on the outskirts of Bristol, a city whose wealth was founded on the Triangular Trade. Optimistic to the end, the childless bachelor left 'Lord of the Manor of Pylle' and the (theoretical) rights to his land in the Fens to his cousin, Edward Berkeley. The fen property never materialized.

By the time of Richard's death, sugar and various spices were being imported in bulk from the West Indies and distributed by grocers on to provincial tables up and down the land. Despite the debts left by the Wastrel, Richard's cousins had managed to hang on to the Madresfield estate. They did so by entering trade – the grocery trade – importing sugar, spices and exotic herbs. Whether this was inspired by the travels of their kinsman is not known.

Chapter Five

THE HAMPER

The kitchen corridor runs for sixty paces along the dark, northern side of the house, from the back entrance, by the Bridge of Sighs, through to the front of the building. As a busy thoroughfare down which casks, barrels, sacks and hampers were carried the corridor is necessarily wide, flagstoned and painted a utilitarian cream. At the bridge end, fifty-two black wrought-iron bells hang high on the wall, each identified with a handwritten, yellowing paper label indicating which room requires service: the Lygon, Stanhope, Pyndar or Somerset Room, Her Ladyship's Sitting Room, the Day or Night Nursery, the Solar Room or the Flower Room . . . On an adjacent wall hang two large black-boards: one is marked out with a weekly calendar, the other with the principal bedrooms waiting to be chalked with the names of guests and their requirements. At the other end of the corridor, by the New Kitchen, leather fire buckets, ladders and shopping baskets hang from wooden pegs above dog- and log-baskets on the flagstones below. Alongside the baskets stand rows of grocery hampers.

After the Civil War, several cadet members of the Lygon family turned to the grocery trade as they had no collateral in the estate. The example was set by William the Colonel's second son, another William (1642–1721), nicknamed 'William the Correspondent' because he left a collection of over eight hundred letters dating from the Glorious Revolution in 1688 until 1721. The majority of these were addressed to him by his business partner, Thomas Tuckfield, his sister, Ann Bull, and his two elder sons. Since he drafted replies to them on the back of each sheet, they provide a significant insight into his business matters and familial preoccupations.

Keenly aware of his ancestor's profligacy, the Correspondent wrote: 'my dear father's paternall estate was reduced to a low ebb by his Grandfather's extravagances (tho' that was only in great housekeeping)'. In the Wastrel's wake, debts had mounted and by 1650 three-quarters of the estate was mortgaged. Throughout the Civil War and for some time after, many English estates changed hands as a result of altered circumstances but thanks to the Correspondent's sound management, the Lygons managed to wrest Madresfield from debt.

While Richard, the Colonel's heir, and his three youngest brothers pursued gentlemanly careers at the bar, the two middle brothers, William and Thomas, were apprenticed to grocers in London. It was not unusual for members of the gentry or the aristocracy to turn to a trade in order to restore their finances and to claw back mortgaged lands. The Lygons chose this route to financial recovery.

Being a younger son, the Correspondent received a more modest education than his elder brother and, showing an aptitude for mathematics, in a shrewd move he was apprenticed to Richard Izard, a member of the powerful Worshipful Company of Grocers, in the City of London. This merchants' association had evolved from the amalgamation in 1345 of two smaller guilds: the Pepperers of Soper's Lane, the first recorded mercantile association in the world, and the Spicers of Cheap. The guild took its name from a gross, the measure by which goods were traded, hence the title 'grosser' which evolved into 'grocer'. Its principal concerns were the protection of trade, the companionship of its members and the training of apprentices. In the Middle Ages, its members had pioneered trade with the Mediterranean and Byzantium and, from this adventurous fraternity, the Levant Trading Company (founded in 1581 for trade with the Near East) and the East India Company (granted a royal patent in 1600) had emerged to establish a global network of trading alliances. In pursuit of lucrative trade, members undertook voyages of exploration, discovering routes to India and the East from whence they brought back exotic spices, peppers, figs, currants, raisins and dates from Japan, Java, Sumatra, Borneo, Barda, Malacca, Celebes,

Siam, Coromandel, Malabar and the sub-continent of India. The discovery of new sources of exotica along with the identification of new markets coincided with the successful development of England's long-distance shipping and by 1700 England had superseded Holland as Europe's main entrepôt. Among the City guilds, which included the Mercers, the Glove-Makers and the Goldsmiths, the Grocers soon became the wealthiest and most important in the City.

The Correspondent was indentured as an apprentice in his early teens. It was a most sought-after position which would have cost his father a handsome fee, perhaps as much as one hundred pounds, payable to Richard Izard, his 'master'. In return, Izard guaranteed a thorough grounding in the profitable trade. Owing to the un-precedented social mobility of the time, the governing class of the previous century had introduced elaborate etiquettes of courtesy and sumptuary restrictions in an attempt to keep aspirants in their place. James I had further complicated Elizabeth I's sumptuary laws by stipulating rules concerning apprentices' and maid-servants' dress. For fear that they might presume to rise above their station by adopting rich dress, in 1611, by order of the Lord Mayor to the Wardens of the Worshipful Company of Grocers, the king inaugurated a precise dress code for apprentices.

Starting from the top, young Lygon's hat should not cost more than five shillings and must not be lined in fur, silk or taffeta. Its band should be either modest 'holland' or another kind of linen but it certainly could not boast a lawn or cambric trimming. Under the hat, his hair should be 'cut short in a decent and comely manner' without fancy tufts or locks. Lace was banned and his hems had to be plain and stitched. Any neck ruff was limited to a modest two inches in depth. As silk or silk-mix was deemed extravagant, only fustian (corduroy), canvas, sackcloth, khaki, English leather or 'English stuff' were permissible for his doublet and breeches. No broadcloth for a cloak, coat, jerkin or doublet should exceed ten shillings a yard and it should be worn plain and unembellished, save for silk buttons. Gloves must not cost more than twelve shillings – fringing or gold or silver lace trims were beyond budget – garters and hose had to be knitted from wool rather than woven from silk, and rosettes at the side of his knees or on his shoes were forbidden. Finally, shoes had to be cobbled from modest English leather. 'Spanish' shoes or those flaunting a 'Polonia' heel were unacceptable. If an apprentice dared to breach these regulations, he would be thrown into 'Little Ease', a prison in the Guildhall, for eighteen days. The prison derived its name from the rumour that the culprit could not sit, stand or lie down with any comfort and so, it was supposed, would not forget his lesson. The poor lad could also be imprisoned for other gentlemanly presumptions, such as taking dancing or fencing lessons, frequenting a tennis court, bowling green, cockfighting ring or brothel and for keeping a trunk full of apparel or a horse or pet without his master's permission. Despite these rulings, an apprentice did have recourse to the wardens of the guild if he considered that his master was not training, feeding or dressing him appropriately, or if he was being abused. If the wardens found the master wanting, he would be heavily fined.

The Correspondent entered this rule-bound world in 1655, followed, two years later, by his younger brother Thomas. Thomas served under Francis Lucy, another London-based grocer, and upon completing his apprenticeship formed a partnership with Edward Asgill, a 'painter-stainer' by background. The two traded as druggists. As both young men were bachelors, they shared a home at the Rose and Talbot inn on the south side of Poultry. Meanwhile, once his apprenticeship was finished, the Correspondent used his share of the family money, six hundred pounds – £83,000 at today's value – to buy a warehouse and began importing produce, including sugar, within two decades of his kinsman Richard's return from Barbados. Perhaps Richard had advised his cousin of the profitability of sugar and suggested contacts.

Seventeenth-century London was a thriving city for traders. Greater quantities of sugar, tea, coffee, chocolate, fruits and spices passed through its docks than ever before. Once established, the Correspondent prospered and was granted the Freedom of the City of London in 1665, the year in which the catastrophe of the Great Plague struck the capital, followed in 1666 by the Great Fire. The Plague was described by the statesman and historian the Earl of Clarendon as 'another enemy, much more formidable than the

Dutch' and it was to kill ninety thousand people. The Correspondent escaped the plague, probably retreating to Madresfield like many with country connections – speedily followed by their fashionable physicians, who excused themselves 'on the grounds that it was their duty to follow their patients'. Within a year his business, established within the City's walls, was burned to the ground in the fire which broke out in the early hours of Sunday 2 September, 1666 in a bakery in Pudding Lane. Over three days it devoured most of the wooden City, including many grocers' establishments, warehouses and docks, and the Grocers' Hall and all the guild's houses and properties, with the exception of a few tenements in Grub Street. 'The effect was very terrible, for above two parts of three of the great city were burned to ashes, and those the most rich and wealthy parts of the city, where the greatest warehouses and the best shops stood,' Clarendon reported.

Fortunately, the grocers' records, which had recently been moved to a turret in the garden, survived and include a later account by Mr Somers Smith, Clerk to the Company: 'The destruction of the Hall and property was not the full measure of the calamity. The Company were [*sic*] heavily in debt . . . For almost a century from the date of the fire the history of the Company is that of a continuous struggle to maintain its existence.' Not until the mid-eighteenth century did the livery company recover from its losses, though some immediate relief was found for its members by melting down and selling off the guild's plate, which amounted to over two hundred pounds in weight of solid silver.

The Correspondent was forced to rebuild his business. In 1671 he formed a partnership with a distant cousin, Thomas Tuckfield, a grocer in Broad Street. They became lifelong friends. It was a profitable liaison and the pair were well placed to exploit the expanding market in grocery produce, specializing in trading spices, teas and dried fruits. Successful traders could, in one generation, accrue wealth to rival that of many a peer of the realm, provoking the social satirist Daniel Defoe's observation that 'an estate's a pond, but a trade's a spring'. Keen to elevate their standing, the merchants could spend these fortunes on buying a title from the Exchequer or enticing members of the aristocracy to marry into the family.

As individuals, successful tradesmen could wield some social clout but once attached to one of the livery companies they could enjoy the advantages of being aligned to an institution of considerable political and economic power. The Correspondent had been admitted to membership of the Grocers' livery company in 1667. A guild played its role in the grand, municipal machinery and, regardless of cost, livery companies organized City pageants to trumpet their power. Frequently a grocer was elected Lord Mayor of London and his livery company would stage a spectacle in which no expense was spared. As a member of the Grocers' Guild, the Correspondent participated in this pageantry. The masters, wardens, freemen, assistants, bachelors, gentleman ushers and pensioners of the company would process through the City behind extravagantly themed chariots, manned by a young Negro, finely costumed in multi-coloured Indian attire, sitting high up on a stage camel between two silver panniers piled high with raisins, almonds, figs, sultanas and spices. To the left and to the right the 'blackamoor' scattered his bounty of costly sweetmeats to the crowd which scrabbled in the dirt to taste the exotica. In a crude public relations exercise, the grocers displayed their wealth and encouraged consumerism.

For nearly two decades, the Correspondent thrived within this powerful cartel. He had married Elizabeth Bridges, but she died young – perhaps of the plague – and childless. The widower took a lively interest in politics and frequented the new coffee houses with his friends, the MPs Richard Dowdeswell, Thomas Wylde and Samuel Pytts. This bustling, happy existence came to an end in 1687 when his older brother Richard died without an heir. Reluctantly, the Correspondent sold up and abandoned London to take on Madresfield.

He succeeded to an impoverished estate whose fragile finances had been further compromised by a generous settlement made on his mother who, as a widow, enjoyed a liberal jointure which entitled her to a large stake in all the estate's manors. Considerable annuities were also paid to his sisters. As the new squire of Madresfield, the forty-five-year-old widower now had to find a second wife and sire an heir. He chose Margaret, the only surviving child and heiress of Thomas Corbyn of Hall End in Polesworth,

Warwickshire, whose family was known to him because of its trading interests in the West Indies. The couple produced four children, William, Corbyn, Thomas (who died of smallpox aged sixteen) and Margaret. In their turn, two of the three surviving children succeeded to Madresfield.

Though the estate was still heavily mortgaged, throughout the seventeenth century land values rose rapidly and business-minded landowners like the Correspondent were swift to enclose common land, consolidate holdings, evict unprofitable tenants and rationalize their agricultural production when the price of foodstuffs rapidly inflated over the second half of the century. Aside from land, William was also rich in cultural assets, inheriting 530 books, 11 maps and 43 pictures, which certainly amounted to the chattels of a gentleman of culture. Now, with the same tenacity and business acumen that he had applied to the grocery trade, he set about painstakingly rebuilding the Madresfield finances, regularly consulting Tuckfield for advice. Letters between them illustrate the day-to-day business matters and problems faced by men in trade, along with the contemporary political scene, for William liked to keep abreast of the grocery business, the stock market, proceedings in the House of Commons and city gossip. Calling on the market intelligence of his old London friends, the Correspondent wisely pieced together a sound port-folio of investments and, though he did buy a few shares in the South Sea Company, he resisted the frenzy of speculation that resulted in the bursting of the South Sea Bubble in 1720 and bankruptcy for many.

By the beginning of the new century, he had underpinned the finances of Madresfield. It was time to think about the future of his children. His first-born, yet another William Lygon, was educated at Balliol, Oxford, before entering the law. But the future for their second son, Corbyn, looked less promising. He had a club foot and an acute speech impediment. Placing this high-shouldered, nervous young man into a trade was going to prove difficult. The first step was to find a cure. The eighteenth century has been called 'the golden age of quackery' and Corbyn certainly met his share of quacks as his father approached various conmen offering cures, such as Mr Mountjoy, a 'sopeboyler in Bristoll'. The Correspondent drafted a reply to this charlatan on the back of a letter from him on All Saints' Day, 1 November, 1701. It reads: 'Good Sir, My cosin Whittingham tells me that you would . . . come hither to perfect the cure of my son, whereby to bring his leggs straight, which he gives me hope you can effect.' In the meantime he guarantees to continue to apply the ointment, which evidently did not work.

What was to become of Corbyn? Tuckfield made a suggestion in a letter dated 7 June 1709:

> I was glad to hear by your son, Mr. Corbin, that you were well returned out of Warwickshire . . . I did enquire of him if hee had thought of what imployment hee should like best . . . hee told mee that he should

choose to bee a grocer, the same trade that you were. I told him that would be a dirty and laborine trade, and required some strength. Hee told mee that hee was informed the aprentaces now were not put to do so much of the labouring work as wee were when wee were aprentaces (neither indeed are they) ... his infirmity in his speech will bee a great hinderance in setting of him in any buisnes ... I did hear that there was a man about Kingsington [*sic*] that made it his buisnes to instruct those that had that infirmity, and had much mended them speaking. If anything could be done, it would be a great advantage to him.

Dr fford, the man from Kensington, was interviewed by Tuckfield on Corbyn's behalf. Tuckfield informed the Correspondent on 5 July 1709 that fford claimed that he could 'teach him in little time to speake as well as aney of us' but that he would charge fifty pounds, claiming that the fee was high because of his reputation for curing bad stammers. Tuckfield bargained, finally agreeing, on Corbyn's behalf, to pay twenty guineas (less than half); ten in hand and ten if he was cured. By late July, Tuckfield could report that after a fifteen-minute session with fford, Corbyn 'came to us, spoke verry well to admiration ... all the time without stammering'. Corbyn had been instructed by fford 'as a gentleman' not to reveal his methods. Despite entreaties, the worldly Tuckfield withheld the outstanding ten guineas until success was assured. Over time Corbyn seemed to improve and the ten guineas were paid. While Tuckfield was struggling to oversee Corbyn's cure and place him as an apprentice, the two Lygon sons spent money recklessly, William incurring excessive battel bills in college while Corbyn, who fancied himself a dandy, ordered numerous 'dragget coats', waistcoats and leather breeches. Perhaps he hoped that handsome clothes would lend him a confident air and distract from his disability.

Eventually, in September 1709, Tuckfield found a Mr Waldo of Watling Street who was prepared to indenture Corbyn as his apprentice, following a month's trial, for a sum of 150 guineas. As Waldo had 'a man to do all the ordinary work' and Corbyn would be his only apprentice, Tuckfield was satisfied that Corbyn would have a good grounding in the grocery trade from this 'sober discreete young man'. But his excessive extravagance on clothes continued, and he was sharply reprimanded by his father. On 15 September 1710, Corbyn wrote to make amends, suggesting to his father that he might 'be pleased to sell' his 'Plate' perhaps to repay his father. He added that he wished to 'return my most humble thankes for your fatherly Correction to me which I will never [*sic*] take care never to deserve again'. However, the letter concluded with an account of recent purchases: nine shillings and sixpence on stockings, twelve pounds on three pairs of shoes, a pound on 'pocket expenses', two pounds and ten shillings on his mercer's bill, a pound on 'ishue plasters', two hats at eleven shillings each and one and six on shoe repairs. Clearly, Corbyn was defying the sumptuary laws.

Six days later, a letter from Mr Waldo brought further disappointment. In Waldo's opinion, Corbyn was 'under such a misfortune by the impediment in his speech, that he's no way (nor like ever to be) fit for a Grocer; the Poor Lad indeed does what he can, and he's sober, and very honest'. Obviously fford's cure had only been temporary. He offered to reimburse Lygon a proportion of the apprentice fee. Another situation had to be found for Corbyn.

The next pressing issue to concern the Correspondent was to arrange good marriages for his children. Just as he had mastered the grocery trade and then estate management, so he now turned his negotiating skills to another market: the marriage market. It was vital for the future of Madresfield. His correspondence throws light on the candid horse-trading that took place between fathers or their agents, matchmakers, lawyers or brokers, while layers of subterfuge were deployed to protect the subject from such worldly transactions. William the Correspondent was quite unusual in requiring some genuine affection to exist between the parties before negotiations were concluded. It was clearly his ambition to marry his boys into the aristocracy. It would prove to be a challenge as both were plain, to say the least, and Corbyn, of course, was handicapped.

In Stuart times a clear distinction was made between 'wooing', merely flirtation without commitment, and 'wiving', a serious attempt to court a woman with a view to marriage. Contemporary letters and diaries are peppered with the vocabulary of battle, a chess game, a hunt or even downright war. William Lawrence, writing to his brother in 1667, reported that 'after the discharge of some sighs, after I had made many assaults upon her white hand, and stormed the blushing bulwarks of her lips, the fortress upon the 24th of September was surrendered, and at night I triumphantly entered into my new possession'. For a man in search of a bride, the challenge was proportionate to his target's social status; the higher the prize, the more protracted the negotiations became, since considerable property was often at stake in the higher echelons of the gentry and aristocracy. Negotiations traditionally hinged on three factors: dowries (the money or property a wife brought to her husband), portions (the share of an inheritable estate given on marriage) and jointures (the estate reserved for the wife in the event of her widowhood).

To protect an estate from being broken up into virtually worthless fragments to be shared between the competing members of a family, in the mid-seventeenth century conveyancers had introduced 'strict property settlement'. The heir was a life-long 'tenant' of the estate which he inherited but ownership of the estate was entailed for the next generation – the unborn first son of his marriage. The inheritance mechanisms of primogeniture and entail ensured that estates were shielded from a profligate 'tenant' (the eldest son) so that a stable ruling class could consolidate and build upon its wealth. If the Wastrel had been confined to strict settlement he would not have been able to plunge the family into debt. Over the next century, the wide adoption of strict settlement by landed families combined with an active land market following the Restoration gave rise to great magnates in possession of great estates at the expense of the lesser gentry whose lands were swallowed up and who moved to the towns and entered a trade or profession. The Lygons were precariously poised between these two strata: merchants and gentry.

Marriage settlements were an essential element in the expansion of estates because, whatever a bride's circumstances, she was expected to contribute her 'portion' towards the enlargement of her prospective husband's estate with land or cash. Inevitably, brides with the largest dowries were the most eagerly sought and there was a surfeit of them since, within the peerage between 1650 and 1725, males were not replacing themselves. Through hard work and judicious land management, the Correspondent had now unburdened his estates of mortgage and in 1713 he entered the marriage market on behalf of his eldest son and heir. William junior had graduated from Balliol College, Oxford in the spring of 1708 and his father sought a match with the eldest daughter of the fifth Lord Digby. While hard bargaining underlay this correspondence, the negotiating patriarchs dressed up their horse-trading with laboured courtesies.

A Mr George Glyn acted for the Lygons and a Reverend M. Cotterell for the Digbys. On 26 August 1713, Glyn received a letter from Digby which read: 'I

am now so farr satisfied as to permit the young
Gentleman to see my Daughter at Holm Lacey: but
matters of this nature must be managed with great
caution and secrecy.' Digby proposed that the young
people should encounter one another by apparent
accident:

> He [William junior] should go to Mr. Pyndars
> [William's sister was married to Reginald Pyndar] and
> whilst he is there get Mr. Westfaling to convey him to
> dinner to my Lord Scudamore's under pretence of see-
> ing the house, or out of a desire of being acquainted
> with my Lord . . . it is absolutely necessary to be careful
> of the secret in the first stepps that are taken in an affayr
> of this nature . . . Take care of this letter.

On 2 September 1713, the Correspondent wrote
directly to Digby: '. . . The Honour your Lordship does
me in accepting of a treaty for my alliance with your
family I receive with all imaginable deference.' Lygon
assured Digby that this was the first marriage attempt
made on behalf of his son and, assuming that Digby
was 'already acquainted with what fortune I think my
Son's circumstances doe very wel deserve,' begs 'the
favour to know what settlements your Lordship does
expect for it'. In plain English, how much would Digby's
daughter bring to the Lygon coffers? Digby reminded
the Correspondent that he had six daughters to marry
off and therefore could not 'give one of them more
than four thousand pounds; for which I shall expect no

more than is generally thought reasonable for a joynture, which is five hundred pounds per ann. That has been the proportion in the Settlements I have been acquainted with and particularly in my own.' Disappointed, the Correspondent responded that six thousand pounds was expected, pointing out 'the now usual settlements of 100 [pounds] per ann. for 1000 fortune'. Digby came back with a closing offer of five thousand pounds which was accepted and arrangements were made for the couple to meet. Unfortunately, young Lygon was spurned in his first attempt: Digby's daughter did not like what she saw and, via Cotterell, sent the excuse that she must call off any thoughts of marriage 'till shee could enjoy a better state of health'.

Undeterred, the Correspondent turned his sights on Digby's second daughter, expecting similar terms. 'I would only beg, if it might be, that the two sisters be not together til he is come acquainted with the 2d, if my Lord please to give his permit to an interview.' As Cotterell was away in Bath, a reply was not given until 10 May 1714 informing the Correspondent that the Digbys had gone away to Dorsetshire for ten weeks and Cotterell suggested that he could 'make haste to his Lordship' with the proposal. The Correspondent chose to write to Digby directly: 'My Lord. Your eldest Daughter's sickness continuing and therewith her averseness to marriage, I desire your Lordship's consent my Son may wait upon your second Daughter, both of us being ambetious to match into your honorable family. I presume your Lordship does not design to lessen the proposed fortune with your other daughter and your Lordship shall not fayle of the same settlement I intended for my son.' Digby replied on 25 July agreeing to the same settlement on his second daughter, adding that 'when you are pleas'd to acquaint me with the circumstances of your estate, and with the settlement you propose to make as well in present as after your death, you shall receive a further answer.' After more parrying, a deal was reached, each side drawing on precedents found among their own family and acquaintances. The Correspondent agreed to 'settle for present maintenance and joynture: [the estate of] Hallow for life only and then leave it to my Son's disposal at pleasure, unless in case of Daughters only, and then to stand security for part of their fortunes. I propose to entayle the Warwickshire Estate on the heires mayle reserving a power for my Son (tho' there be heirs male by this match) to settle the same in joynture to any other wife, but for life only.' Various caveats were made for a marriage without issue or only female issue. In October, the Correspondent assured Digby that 'my integrity is all I can mostly call my own which I have (praysed be God for his goodness) hitherto kept unspotted' but that should His Lordship desire to see 'any wrightings or any other accompts to be layd before you' to confirm the value and repairs of his estates, he would be happy to oblige.

Sadly, no amount of negotiation could prepare for the young lady's immediate refusal. Like her sister, she did not like what she saw and on 19 November 1714 Digby finally closed negotiations stressing that 'I cannot upon any account pray her to marry against her inclinations.' The crestfallen Correspondent requested that all relevant letters be returned to him for fear of compromising his family's marriage prospects. He later learned another reason why the younger Miss Digby had spurned his son. She had been misinformed by a young gentleman that old Lygon was a Whig, 'or at least a very low Churchman', and, the Digbys 'being generally very high', the match was unacceptable to her. Smarting from such an insult, the Correspondent wrote to M. Cotterell, 'I have during my whole life constantly frequented prayers of the Church, Dayly whilst in London and the Sacrament monthly in my own parish Church there.'

Despite a thriving estate and a good character, it took six attempts to find a bride for the Lygon heir. In the spring of 1716 a Miss Jennens of Gopsal was suggested by a go-between who intimated that she could bring ten thousand pounds to the alliance, but negotiations foundered. Forced to lower his sights, William junior eventually, on 2 August 1716, aged twenty-five, married Margaret, daughter of Charles Cocks, scion of long-established lawyers from Worcester. Miss Cocks brought a dowry of five thousand pounds. Even then the nuptials required the Correspondent's accountancy skills. A few months before the marriage he had written to his son advising him to present his new bride with:

A Coach etc,	[pounds]	100: 00: 0
and four horses for it		100: 00: 0
a present in Gold the wedding		100: 00: 0
for what they please		300: 00: 0

Alas, William junior died one month after his marriage.

Similarly protracted negotiations as had attended William's marriage were endured to marry off the stammering and club-footed Corbyn. Edmund Bray's daughter of Barrington Park in Gloucester was proposed but she took one look at Corbyn and ran. Eventually the dependable Mr Waldo, Corbyn's master in the grocery trade, introduced him to Jane, daughter of Isaac Tullie, a silk mercer and the brother-in-law of Edmund Bray. Though she was 'very much marked by the Small Pox' Corbyn found her to be a suitable match and the couple married on 4 June 1717, Mr Waldo promising that Jane would bring 'five hundred pounds of lawful money of Great Britain for her marriage portion'.

The Correspondent died on 16 March 1721. An inventory of his goods and chattels made on 15 February 1716 included the 'furniture of a drawing room with a watch, a clock and two pictures, in his closet two small cabinets, a pair of globes, the books there and in other places'. There was cash in the house, money in his purse, 'grain of all sorts', a coach, four horses, four saddle horses, saddlery, harness, silver plate, shillings, cutlery and 'old lumber and things forgotten or omitted'. He had been a man of substance.

Corbyn now became the master of Madresfield, a property saved from mortgage and bolstered by the riches of the grocery trade. He inherited a handsome estate at the heart of England's mistletoe lands which stretch across Worcestershire and into the Welsh borders. Tangles of mistletoe rest in the bare branches of the oaks in the park: it is easy to imagine Corbyn and Jane admiring their sweet prospect through mullioned windows during their first winter together at Madresfield. Since earliest times mistletoe has been venerated for its healing powers and aphrodisiac charms. According to folklore, each hoar-frosted berry permitted the couple another kiss. Their gardeners would have harvested the mistletoe and piled it into wicker baskets to bring into the house. The boughs would be suspended above fireplaces and doors, in the hope that they would not only bring fertility but also protect the home from fire. It boded well and together they had three children. Their happiness seemed assured.

Chapter Six

THE RED HEELS

In pride of place above the fireplace in the Saloon, a small, richly appointed sitting room which leads into the Drawing Room, hangs a portrait of a fey youth depicted in oils circa 1710 by Charles Jervais. He is dressed in a lavishly embroidered waistcoat, a scarlet silk jacquard coat buttoned and braided in silver gilt, dove-grey satin breeches and a pair of black silk shoes balanced on high red heels. He poses as the epitome of the 'well-heeled'; cane in hand, parkland behind him, groom and thoroughbred in attendance. It is a fanciful portrait. Just as the grocery apprentices had flouted the sumptuary laws by wearing shoes that boasted 'Polonia' heels, so this youth's red heels are freighted with presumption. Louis XIV had introduced red heels to the French court to signify that their wearer held the correct genealogical credentials to be presented at court. Impractical red heels flaunted a life of conspicuous leisure. The fashion spread from Versailles throughout

Europe. Not only did the Hanoverian monarchs George II, George III and George IV all wear red heels at their coronations but to this day at the annual Garter ceremony the Queen's pages wear red-heeled shoes. The fashion came to imply that the wearer was high-born – *vrai talon rouge* – and consequently became symbolic in portraiture.

The man in this portrait is William Jennens, nick-named by the Lygons 'William the Miser'. It was from this distant relation that, in the early nineteenth century, the Lygons acquired a fortune which would ensure their continued security and enable them to keep Madresfield to this day.

Young Jennens was painted in his finery approximately two decades before Corbyn and Jane and their three children were struck down, perhaps by smallpox. Their happiness had been relatively short-lived. The estate passed in 1728 to Corbyn's sole surviving sibling, Margaret Lygon, who had married Reginald Pyndar. Margaret and Reginald were succeeded by their eldest son, the young Reginald, who added his mother's maiden name to his own, becoming Reginald Pyndar Lygon. This device, known as fictive kin, was used when a man married into great property. He or his children changed their name to that of the heiress to give the impression of continuity through the male line. This ploy, along with the double-barrelled surname, was designed to deal with the demographic crisis of the early eighteenth century in which there were far fewer males than females born into the land-owning classes.

Thus it was the house, Madresfield, which became the continuity and the Pyndars simply adjusted their name to substantiate this. It was through this Pyndar line that Jennens's unimaginable riches fell into the Lygons' laps.

Reginald Pyndar Lygon's son and heir William (1747–1816) went further than his father and dropped the name Pyndar altogether. As plain Mr William Lygon he was elected, uncontested, MP for the county in 1775. Sir William Beechey's portrait of him in the Drawing Room shows a mild-looking, slack-jawed squire. The fat of the land fills him out, making him appear gouty and stolid. Surprisingly, he took as his wife what – in Worcestershire parlance – would have been called a 'vaunty dame'. The sprightly Catherine Denne (1760–1844) was nearly fifteen years his junior. She is the third important woman in our Lygon tale and she played as crucial a role in the family's advancement as did Joan de Braci who brought the estate and Anne Beauchamp who brought the noble connection in the medieval period. Thanks to the clever and pushy Catherine, the family swiftly rose through the social ranks.

And yet William Lygon had married Catherine in 1780 under a cloud of controversy. His bride was not high-born, having been brought up on the margins of what Georgians called 'the quality' or 'the *ton*'. The Muniments yield no evidence of extended negotiations attendant upon the betrothal of the heir to Madresfield. Perhaps they married against the Lygon family's wishes? Little is known about her, save that her mother

*Sir William Lygon, the first Earl of Beauchamp,
by his kinswoman Frances, Lady Crewe, c. 1800.*

A still substantially Tudor Madresfield in 1776.

was the daughter of a Somerset gentleman and her father, James Denne, was a banker in London and had the arms of the Dennes of Grenane in Co. Kilkenny, Ireland, as his seal. The Dennes had been long-established landowners in Kilkenny but would not abandon their Catholic faith once the English seized control of Ireland. They sheltered priests and refused to attend Protestant church services as the English law required and consequently their lands were sequestered. James Denne's grandfather fled with his twelve children to begin a new life in Bristol.

A letter in the Madresfield archives from Lord Raglan, dated 29 April 1917, observed that Catherine had 'dark hair and blue eyes' and 'her descendants look Irish'. The number of times she was painted might suggest she was vain; she was certainly beautiful. Two portraits of her by Royal Academicians hang either side of the fireplace in the Drawing Room; one is by John Hoppner and the other by Sir Joshua Reynolds. Hoppner's Catherine is a girlish beauty whose sole ornament is a ribbon tied nonchalantly in her tresses. She is dressed in a *chemise à la Reine*, a style popularized by Marie Antoinette during pregnancy and which was taken up by fashion-able – and not necessarily pregnant – ladies in the 1780s. It was usually of a white and light, almost diaphanous, material, such as Tana lawn or muslin, with a draw-pull waist and neckline which lent the wearer an air of pastoral beauty or, in Hogarth's phrase, 'the beauty of intimacy'. Her gaze is direct, her carriage lively: she looks approachable. Reynolds' Catherine on the other hand is a *mondaine*, fashionably dressed *à la turque* in a coat, sash and bandana, worn over a sprigged muslin dress. Eye-catchingly large pearls hang from her ears. Catherine's unloosed chignon of hair hangs asymmetrically down one shoulder, her knowing gaze is turned from us and there is the hint of a smirk in her expression. European ladies had been dabbling with Ottoman costume throughout the eighteenth century, a style pioneered by Lady Mary Wortley Montagu. Catherine was no dowdy provincial when it came to fashion.

Catherine and William had four sons and six daughters, eight of whom survived to adulthood. The vivacious and resourceful châtelaine ran Madresfield on a tight rein. Her notebooks and recipe books in the Muniments show her meticulous accounts and economical recipes for 'scarcity of eggs', medicinal concoctions for 'curing a Cancer [ulcer] or sore mouth' and frugal tinctures for 'Cheap Paint' which involved stirring four pounds of 'Roman Vitriol', potash and pulverized yellow arsenic into boiling water. Although on the relatively modest budget of a landed squire, the Lygons nevertheless frequented Society and the studious William could count the Prime Minister, William Pitt the Younger, whom he had met at Oxford, as a friend. The Lygons divided their time between Madresfield and their house in Great George Street, Westminster, which stood within hearing of Parliament's Division Bell. He was one of only five county MPs who voted for Pitt's unpopular inheritance tax.

William had originally been a Whig but as he grew older his conservative instincts got the better of him and, perhaps under Catherine's influence, he crossed the House in 1783 to become a 'wavering Tory'. Within the next decade, for William as for many liberal-minded contemporaries, the brutality of the French Revolution reinforced this conservatism. He was hardly an active member and there is no record of his having spoken in the House before 1790, when, in recognition of his political loyalty, he was appointed to the Board (later the Ministry) of Agriculture in William Pitt the Younger's government. Within eight years of William's maiden speech he unexpectedly inherited vast wealth from a distant kinsman, William Jennens the Miser. Life for the Lygons of Madresfield would be utterly changed.

In 1798, William Jennens, squire of Acton Place near Long Melford, Suffolk, died intestate at the great age of ninety-seven. A will was found in his coat pocket, sealed but not signed and therefore useless. The passing of this childless bachelor would have gone unnoticed had he not been the richest commoner in England. He had out-lived all known relatives. Who would inherit his substantial estates, spanning eleven counties, and a personal fortune of over two million pounds, yielding an annual income of forty thousand pounds? The Crown Authorities had taken possession and advertised for next-of-kin. Within days, three claimants stepped for-ward, taking out letters of administration: William Lygon of Madresfield Court; Mary, Viscountess Andover of Elford, Staffordshire; and the trustees for the ten-year-old

George Augustus William Curzon of Penn, Buckinghamshire. Each was distantly related to the Miser through the female line.

The Miser's wealth had been amassed over three generations by his ancestors, Birmingham ironmasters. His father, Robert, a younger son of Humfrey Jennens, had insinuated himself into the court of William III, served as his aide-de-camp in Flanders and, in recognition of his services, was granted the sinecure 'Groom to the Bedchamber Extraordinary'. He also won the heart of Ann Guidott, the heiress descendant of a Florentine noble family and an extremely parsimonious woman. William Jennens was their only child and King William III conferred on him the honour of being the king's godson. As a boy, Jennens served as page of honour to Queen Anne. Yet it soon became clear that he had inherited his mother's parsimony.

By 1708, Robert had risen sufficiently as a lawyer and courtier to afford a country estate, financed partly with a loan from the Duke of Marlborough, whose wife Sarah was his cousin, and for whom he acted as spymaster during military campaigns. He bought the estate at Acton and commissioned the architect James Gibbs to build a mansion. Though habitable, it was never finally completed. In his turn, William the Miser inherited not only this estate but also, shared with his cousin Charles, those of three uncles who had died without male issue. Not content to live on his inherited wealth, William started investing – buying lands, mortgages and government bonds – and also established himself as a moneylender, at usurious rates, to the aristocracy's high-stakes gamblers. Most evenings, he settled himself down at a table in the corner of the dining room at White's, the gentleman's club on St James's, and in a large ledger, populated with names from both the *Almanach de Gotha* and *Debrett's*, he recorded the sums he lent and to whom. It was said that for every thousand pounds a player borrowed from him, the following morning he would owe one thousand guineas. William quickly earned the nickname 'The King and Pattern of Usurers'.

Rumours circulated that this strange, pock-marked bachelor was a miser. It was said he lived in three poky rooms in the basement of his unfinished mansion, abandoning the Palladian state rooms above to the spiders, who added their filigree to the silver chandeliers, and to the birds that had flown through the broken windows and nested in the shredded velvet curtains and mildewed silk upholstery. His meagre bedroom was lined with the cast-off shirts of his godfather, William III. People said that he fed to his dogs, rather than to his servants, the scraps from his table and that he opened the house to the paying public to offset the housekeeper's wage. Could it be true that he would light a stinking tallow candle, rather than a more expensive wax one, only if a guest needed to read a document or ledger, otherwise they were expected to sit in the dark? Did his neighbours really see, night after night, eight ghostly black horses gallop down Acton's mile-and-a-half-long drive, drawing a phantom carriage bearing the wraith of a fine lady and her broken gambler spouse?

Despite the fashionable example set by his king, 'Farmer George', the Miser never invested in agricultural improvements on his estates and with age came inertia. He gave up collecting the income from his farms, stocks and mortgages. All lay dormant. It was said that his wealth was immense and that 'the dividends on most of his stocks [had] not been received since 1788, nor the interest on his mortgages for a long period.' And when at last he died, £20,000 in banknotes was found in his London house at 10 Grosvenor Square and £50,000 was stashed – 'in case of emergency' – at Child's Bank, along with £100,000 worth of South Sea stock, and a key to a chest which contained priceless gold and silver plate, sacks of guineas and rolls of banknotes, promissory notes and indentures that had not been seen for nearly four decades.

Meanwhile, his high-spending cousin, Charles Jennens, had dissipated his fortune in pursuit of culture, earning himself the nickname Soleyman the Magnificent. Charles was a vain popinjay who lived in princely style in his Brobdingnagian mansion, Gopsall Hall in Leicestershire, surrounded by dozens of servants dressed in ornate equipage. The landscaping of his park alone had cost eighty thousand pounds. In London he covered the short distance from his house in Great Ormond Street to his publishers in Red Lion Court in a carriage drawn by four grandly caparisoned horses, preceded by four lackeys who swept the oyster shells off the pavements before he descended to the street. But

Charles Jennens's foppish appearance was deceptive. He is now remembered principally as Handel's patron and librettist. Music scholars opine that, between 1738 and 1744, none surpassed his poetic talent and mastery of scripture. His libretti included *Saul*, *Belshazzar* and, most memorably, *Messiah*, an idea which he suggested to Handel and of which the original score is covered in notes in his hand – evidence of his close collaboration with the composer. This pompous if unexpectedly gifted man was critical of the composer, suggesting while collaborating over *Saul* in the autumn of 1738 that his head was 'more full of maggots than ever'. Like the Miser, the bachelor Charles Jennens died childless.

Under English inheritance law, which distinguished between 'personal' and 'real' property (meaning lands), most of the spoils were amicably divided, according to the Statutes of Distribution, between the Miser's nearest relations, all cousins-once-removed, grandchildren of his aunts Ann and Esther. A Jennens bride had co-incidentally been proposed for an earlier William Lygon, son of the Correspondent. She had actually married William Hanmer, scion of an established family who owned two estates, one near Acton and the other on the Welsh borders. Their sixth child, Susanna, was born in 1711 and married the Worcestershire squire Reginald Pyndar Lygon of Madresfield. This is how in 1798 Reginald Pyndar Lygon's heir, William, became one of the three beneficiaries of Jennens's fortune, sharing the personal estate with Lady Andover and receiving the equivalent in today's terms of forty million pounds. The real estate was inherited by the Curzon family. At this stage, some of the estate remained unallocated. The legacy would not be un-contested but those battles lay in the future. Now, William Lygon, with his extraordinary new fortune, set about transforming Madresfield.

Within a year of the death of the Miser, William commissioned the architect George Byfield to extend the manor house and its gardens. Since Queen Anne's reign, long avenues radiating out from a focus and marching over the countryside in defiance of its contours had been an obvious way of topographically insisting upon the authority of the great house – what Wordsworth would call putting 'a whole country into a nobleman's livery'. Smaller roads and smaller estates followed the trend, and it was at this time that Madresfield was ennobled with the Gloucester Drive: an arrow-straight avenue one mile long.

For two decades and goaded by Catherine, William Lygon had been pressing ministers to revive the medieval Beauchamp title, established in 1447 but extinct within two generations. The couple chose to revive the Norman name redolent of ancient lineage, though the link was remote and through the female line. Emboldened by their inheritance, Catherine and William pursued this goal with new vigour.

Now the Lygons were rich enough to compete in the highest echelons of Society and so they moved to a large house in the more fashionable St James's Square –

number 14, which is today the premises of the London Library – and commandeered Pitt to procure their ennoblement. Pitt received three letters requesting a peerage from 'Mr Lyggon [*sic*]'. Perhaps it is significant that Pitt's paternal grandmother, a Villiers, came from Waterford, a county adjacent to Kilkenny. Had the Villiers family benefited from the sequestered Denne lands and was Pitt discharging a moral debt? In recommending the Lygons' elevation, Pitt had to choose an appropriate moment. It arose during a reshuffle of Admiralty appointments. Sir Benjamin Bloomfield, Secretary to the Sovereign, agreed to include Lygon in the preferments and the initiative was referred to in a letter from Bloomfield on 22 April 1805 and diplomatically worded to suggest rather more lofty considerations had weighed in his favour: 'The King thinks that it would be advisable . . . to advance Mr. Lygon, Member for The County of Worcester, whose excellent character, steady support of Government, and very large fortune, place him in a situation without just competitors.' It is rumoured that in 1806 the title of Baron Beauchamp of Powick cost the Lygons eight hundred pounds. Cash for peerages was not uncommon at this time. The Exchequer's coffers were empty owing to the Napoleonic wars: a contemporary of Lygon, a Peter Raiment (1741–1808), bequeathed ten per cent of his property for the reduction of the National Debt in return for his title.

Though William and Catherine remained meticulous and careful about money, they began to spend on a considerably larger scale. A letter from Catherine to William at Madresfield, concerning the preparation for a London dinner party, illustrates not only her precise housekeeping but her intention to impress. In the early nineteenth century a pineapple, the fruit so beloved of Richard Ligon in Barbados, cost about £80 (£5,000 in today's money) to plant and rear over three years by attentive and knowledgeable gardeners in a heated pinery:

If you can send up the coach by next Saturday, not an hour before, 1 good Pine[apple] and plenty of Garden stuff [vegetables] and some pigeons, it will be acceptable here next Sunday but the weather is so hot, don't send the basket before Saturday. No fowls. Take great care of the swan's mate. Please write me word about what painting is doing. Are the coals and the bricks come? Is Jackson at Leigh? Have new Iron barrs put in the coppers in the Scullery, have them done now. I will write when I will have them done up by Jackson. Ever Yrs. CB [Catherine Beauchamp].

Like his benefactor, William began to lend money, though at Catherine's urging he was at pains to shield the fortune from unreliable debtors. He was punctilious; on noting in his ledger a one shilling and ninepence overcharge on a three-thousand-pound loan, he swiftly reimbursed the client. Almost immediately the *ton* sought his company and in some cases pursued his new-found fortune. The Prince of

Wales's sister-in-law, the Duchess of Sussex, for example, wrote ingratiatingly to William in 1803:

> The Duchess of Sussex sends her Compliments to Mr. Lygon [and trusts] he will pardon the liberty she takes (not having the advantage of either His or Mrs. Lygon's acquaintance) if she requests him to have the goodness to call upon her, any hour most convenient for Mr. Lygon will equally accommodate the Duchess, if he will only let her know it, so that she may take care to be at home.

On being elevated to a barony in 1806, William resigned his seat in the Commons and stood down from the Board of Agriculture, despite its President Sir John Sinclair's fawning hope that he would continue to serve on the Board: 'Your visiting London occasionally, and amusing yourself with that sort of business which the Board of Agriculture furnishes, I am satisfied would be highly conducive to your health, to which nothing contributes more than a change of scene, and useful, without exhausting occupation.'

But William had to disappoint Sir John. With vast estates to purchase and administer, numerous London houses to run, Madresfield to enlarge in a style that befitted his station, sons to send on the Grand Tour and into seats in Parliament and daughters to launch on to the marriage market, he was fully occupied. The 'marriage market' was an apt expression; from the seventeenth century dowries were even advertised in newspapers. Yet how different was William and Catherine's experience from that of the Correspondent who tried to marry off his plain, disabled and undistinguished sons, William and Corbyn. Numerous suitors stepped forward to be assessed and dispatched by William and, more particularly, by Catherine. A letter written by Lord Redesdale suggests the feeding frenzy that surrounded the Lygon heiresses. 'I believe an union with the Beauchamp family is a sincere subject of congratulations', he wrote to the Earl of Longford following Louisa Catherine Lygon's engagement to Thomas, the future second Earl of Longford.

It did not take long for Catherine to decide that a mere barony was too modest a title for her family and, once again, she began to court the 'Crown's favour', something not frowned upon so long as one was subtle and had reasonable grounds for advancement. She wanted an earldom, the third highest degree in the British peerage, and on 13 January 1809, William applied for one to the king, claiming a growing income of over forty thousand pounds. A letter written in 1816 by Francis Townsend, the Windsor Herald at the College of Arms, to Lygon reveals the extent of Catherine's role in her husband's elevation to the rank of first Earl Beauchamp.

My dear Lord . . .When your Lordship says you don't believe that ten years ago [when the Barony was granted] you would have given any Woman credit for so much perseverance and success, I think you forgot, for the moment, that I have been near <u>thrice</u> ten years acquainted with the Countess. I will admit that I don't <u>now</u> know any <u>other</u> Woman to whom I could give that Credit; But I have repeatedly said, and in the whole course of my professional Life (of more than 44 years duration) I never met with any one, male or female, who could more clearly explain, or more dextrously secure, (I had almost said seduce,) Attention to Business in hand in which she took an interest. – Permit me the pleasure of adding, that no one can more sincerely rejoice in her success than I do . . .

Thomas Creevey, a radical MP and Secretary for the Board of Control in Lord Grenville's ministry of 'All the Talents', possessed nothing but his wits and the clothes on his back. His diaries of Pepysian candour recalled that it was Catherine, not William, who gave Sir John McMahon, chief equerry and private secretary to George III, '£10,000 for getting her husband advanced from baron to earl'. It had taken nine years. The sum was promptly paid to a severely depleted Exchequer. The Lygons had secured an ancient and illustrious title.

William died a year later in 1816 but Catherine out-lived him by twenty-eight years and proved a formidable dowager. Eleanor of Aquitaine married two kings and was the mother of another three; Catherine bore three earls and two generals (one of her sons achieved both ranks). Once widowed, she left Madresfield for her own dower estate, Spring Hill, centred on a handsome Georgian house which still stands, perched on a hill overlooking Broadway in Worcestershire. Preferring the distractions of London and Paris the wealthy Catherine shopped on a grand scale on the Continent to embellish Madresfield for her son and heir. She was attracted to Paris by the rich pickings that were being sold by, or had been pillaged during the Revolution from, the aristocracy of the *ancien régime*. Having been isolated from the Continent throughout the Revolution and the Napoleonic Wars, the British élite were so starved of contact and stimulus that once they could travel in safety again they did so in great number, with over a third of the House of Lords visiting Paris at this time.

Though not all her purchases, particularly the paintings, suggest an informed eye – several copies found their way into the collection, such as optimistically attributed 'Holbeins' – Catherine showed prescient taste. Wishing to assert the family's Norman descent and the grandeur implied by such a lineage, she set out to acquire French historical portraits. There were few people doing this at the time, aside from the Marquess of Hertford who gathered together the treasures of the Wallace Collection, and the Wellingtons. Certainly the French had no interest in artefacts of the *ancien régime*. They favoured the modern.

Catherine wanted to purchase objects with a Bourbon provenance and acquired, for example, 'Madame de Pompadour's note-book' which is chased in gold and mounted with thirty-four medallions of Dresden china painted by Watteau; and Boucher's portrait of the same lady applying rouge and wearing on her wrist a portrait miniature of Louis XV. Fakes notwithstanding, Catherine procured an impressive haul of paintings by Salvatore Rosa, Tintoretto, Bellini, Bronzino and Nollekens, many of which were bought at the sale in the Hôtel Crawford in Paris in 1822, along with some handsome objets d'art. Containers of fine French furniture were shipped home, including rosewood and kingwood parquetry tables and cabinets, heavily burdened with ormolu details and stamped by the famous French cabinetmakers Boudin, Roussel and Montigny; from the master guild, torchères bearing carved images of nymphs and bacchanals; engraved brass and black tortoiseshell cabinets by Boulle and gilt wood *fauteuils* upholstered with Gobelin tapestries. The haul featured one of the greatest collections of portrait miniatures in Britain, dwarfed only by those owned by the monarch, the Buccleuchs and the Portlands, and including important examples by the English masters Hilliard, Smart, Cooper and Cosway as well as leading Continental ones.

The widow Catherine continued her social manoeuvring on behalf of her sons. A letter in the Muniments from Sir Benjamin Bloomfield, in response to one she wrote to the Prince Regent regarding her two youngest sons, Henry (1784–1863, the fourth earl) and Edward (1786–1860), reads:

Sir Benjamin Bloomfield is commanded by the Prince Regent to assure Lady Beauchamp that his Royal

Highness felt particular gratification in acknowledging the Merits of Her Ladyship's Sons, and His Royal Highness, in manifesting His Estimation of those two young Officers, has derived Satisfaction from the Communication of Lady Beauchamp. Lady Beauchamp quite overrates Sir Benjamin Bloomfield's attention, in which he hopes never to be deficient where the wishes of Her Ladyship demand his humble service.

Both sons would become generals. Henry, a veteran of the Peninsular Wars, during which he was injured at the battle of Busaco, eventually succeeded to the title after his older brothers. The bullet that passed through his windpipe and was removed without anaesthetic by a surgeon in the field is displayed in a glass case in the Long Gallery and a portrait of him astride his charger and entitled 'Handsome Lygon' hangs in the Staircase Hall today. His younger brother Edward also had a distinguished military career and was made Knight Commander of the Order of the Bath.

When the first Earl Beauchamp resigned his commons seat on becoming a baron in 1806, it passed to his eldest son, William (1782–1823), who was elected to represent the county at the age of twenty-three. An amiable and worthy man, he was listed amongst those campaigning for the abolition of the slave trade; perhaps he had read his ancestor Richard Ligon's accounts of the life of a slave in *A True & Exact History of the Island of Barbadoes*. A mischievous ballad, sung by the political opposition, gives some idea of the controversial local election and Catherine's domineering role in her son's victory.

> *There was a rich man tho' 'tis not very common*
> *If People say true, he was rul'd by a Woman*
> *Who lectur'd so often on hoarding up pelf*
> *That he soon became stingy and mean as herself.*

> *Now it happen'd one day he was made a great Lord*
> *But no light of as how does my listing afford;*
> *Most People suppose, tho' it must not be told*
> *That the principal actor, was one Mr Gold.*

> *He the County of W— having thirty years led*
> *Was resolved to place his sweet son in his stead*
> *My Lady most wisely fix'd on a Day*
> *That Billy his sweet pretty face should display.*

> *But sad to relate, when they came to the Town*
> *They found that sweet Willy could not be cram'd down,*
> *Without strong opposition from all ranks of Men*
> *Who ne'er wished to see Billy L— again!*

But in the end Billy proved to be a political nonentity; he died childless in 1823 and the earldom passed to his brother John.

On William's becoming the second Earl Beauchamp in 1816, Catherine had steered her third and favourite son, 'Handsome Henry', into his brother's former seat in Parliament. The Honourable H. B. Lygon, a Tory,

A THIN PIECE of PARLIAMENT.

'A Thin Piece of Parliament': Henry Lygon, the fourth Earl Beauchamp, MP for Worcestershire.

represented Worcestershire loyally but dimly until 1831, when he lost his seat as the constituency boundaries were redrawn. Catherine would have none of it. From Spring Hill, she masterminded Henry's infamous Reform Bill contest. It was a raucous fight. The seventy-one-year-old dowager made it clear that she – and her son – overtly opposed the Reform Act's extension of the franchise, its abolition of 'rotten boroughs' and its curtailment of electoral bribery. As the puppet master behind Henry's campaign, she invested fifty thousand pounds in regaining his seat and drafted in the family's bailiff, a Mr Jarvis Arnold, who knew all the electors on the Madresfield estates, as electoral manager. Many of her traits were immortalized in members of Trollope's de Courcy family in his Barsetshire novels. The pro-Act reformers selected Captain the Honourable Frederick Spencer (brother of Earl Spencer) to stand against Henry and a Pickwickian battle ensued. Aristocrats and the populace brawled in the Worcester streets. While canvassing in the Corn Market, Henry was attacked by the rabble and forced to retreat to a tavern from where, on learning that the show of hands favoured his opponent, he demanded a formal poll. The riotous election lasted seven days. While his supporters tossed port decanters, the only missiles to hand, down from the Committee Room windows on to the crowd in Broad Street, Henry attempted to voice his objections to the Act above the din of the electorate below, but they were not interested in his reactionary views. Lygon polled the lowest number of votes and it was not until the following year that he won a seat representing the new constituency of Worcestershire West. In time, both his son and grandson would succeed to that parliamentary seat. Two wooden truncheons hang on the wall of the Entrance Hall at Madresfield commemorating Lygon election victories.

Catherine's political fights were minor skirmishes compared to the battle, spanning the reigns of seven British monarchs, which generations of the family waged in the High Court of Chancery against claimants to the Jennens Inheritance. Curiously, it had taken more than a decade after the original settlement before the first challenge was presented in court. In April 1810, three Yorkshire yeomen, Jonathan, David and Stephen Jennings, claimed to be more directly related to the Miser than the beneficiaries of the estate. Their contention probably arose because in the seventeenth century the Jennenses of Birmingham had adopted the Jennings of Ripon coat of arms to embellish their social credentials. This claim was thrown out of court. Following the first Earl Beauchamp's death in 1816 and spurred on by Catherine's attempts to rake in the remainder of the Miser's unallocated estate, through which she won yet more 'considerable sums of money in stocks and dividends', a Joseph Martin of Colchester began a fight on behalf of the most tenacious claimants of all. In his wake, a long queue of hopefuls formed, including a Mr and Mrs William Andrews of Harborne who asserted that they were *both* related to Jennens. They filed their case in the Court of Chancery in 1827 and it was only finally defeated ten years later, principally owing to the defendant's delaying tactics.

In the nineteenth century, ghoulish members of the public seeking cheap entertainment could either pass the day gawping at the shackled inmates of a lunatic asylum or pack into the public gallery of a court of law to watch desperate claimants in a contested probate case, hidebound by the complications of High Chancery and the rituals of its pettifogging officials. Chancery procedure was so notorious that in Regency times the expression 'in Chancery' was used in boxing to describe a pugilist locking the head of his opponent under his arm and mercilessly pummelling him while his victim was unable to retaliate. Probate cases often hinged on complicated lines of descent that were hard to unravel because so many births were unrecorded, often for reasons of illegitimacy, or incompletely recorded, arising from the tradition of using a family Christian name for the eldest son of each generation without a middle name to distinguish him. Church records and even gravestones were falsified and the College of Arms' habitual openness to bribery only deepened the confusion.

The court cases contesting the notorious Jennens Inheritance drew large crowds. Claimants and witnesses were cross-examined by formidable lawyers retained by the defence. One elderly lady, a Mrs Davenport, became so confused about who was who in the Jennens genealogy that she kept referring to a 'Lord Jeremiah Smith', who did not even exist. The crowd loved it. Case after case was defeated by both reasonable and unreasonable rulings: for example a judge's assumption that a woman could not have given birth in her late fifties/early sixties; or the fact that neither a disputed inscription nor a signature in a family bible resembled the hand of either Humfrey Jennens or his illiterate daughter. Exhaustion also took its toll. One Taunton family, for example, who had to sign legal papers before their case began, trudged every morning to meet the Honiton coach in case it was transporting the documents requiring signature. On the day the papers were finally put on board, the family failed to reach the rendezvous and, as there was no one present to pay the postage, the packet was returned to London and vanished.

By the 1840s – Catherine died in 1844 – an industry had developed around the Jennens Inheritance as agents provocateurs, lawyers and impostors offered, for a fee, to pursue claims against the Lygons, the Curzons and the Andovers. A Jennens Society was founded in Birmingham to unite potential plaintiffs from Britain, Ireland, France, America, Nova Scotia, India and Australia. Catherine's grandson Frederick, the sixth Earl Beauchamp, dubbed this a 'blackmailing organisation' in the 1860s. Hopes were raised in anyone who bore the same or even a similar name, which included the spellings Jennens, Jenings, Jennings, Jenyngs, Jenyng, Jenyns, Jennins, Geneings and Gennens – to name but a few. An advertisement placed in *The Times* in 1858 promised that anyone interested in the Jennens case could gain valuable information if they sent

J. H. Fennell five shillings for a copy of *Researches Respecting Family History*. In 1860, in anticipation of the introduction on to the statute book of the small and crucial 'Beauchamp Clause' to establish a time limit of twenty years for claims to intestate succession, three new cases entered Chancery. All were defeated. Nevertheless, the claims kept coming and dragged on, enriching only lawyers and reducing some claimants, such as Isaac Martin, to bankruptcy. Plaintiffs began to form Family Associations in the belief that numbers and pooled resources would strengthen their hand. A concerted effort was made by a group who published a paper entitled 'The Jennens Case, 1874', now in the Muniment Room at Madresfield. It lays out the arguments challenging the allocation of the Jennens Inheritance between the three original families. It began: 'It is strange that a family [Jennens] which had been so wealthy through several generations, could only produce three claimants to this estate – each of them belonging to the aristocracy and each of them descended through the female line.'

Why, it continued, was the division of the spoils so rapid? Why hadn't sufficient time been allowed after the intestate's death for the different branches of the Jennens family to look up their genealogies? The document challenged the Lygon claim on two specific points: Susanna Hanmer's lineage and Catherine Lygon's actions. It questioned Susanna Hanmer's status at birth. Why was she entered in the church baptism records as the daughter of just William Hanmer and not both William and his wife Esther? Was she illegitimate? Why was no marriage certificate found between Susanna and Reginald Pyndar Lygon? And why was she not mentioned in the family wills?

The second challenge was directed at the now late Catherine, Countess Beauchamp. She had been required to give bonds for the performance of her trust as Administratrix of the Beauchamp estate and had selected a 'victualler', Robert Dennis of Great Carter Lane, London, and a 'fruiter', Challoner Kimshead of the same place, each 'being bound in the sum of £66,000'. Why had a countess selected lowly men rather than 'men of position in London' to act for her? Why did their names not appear in the London directory for 1817? 'We leave it for others to say how it was that Lady Beauchamp could get none but men of straw to become security for her,' it concluded. But is it surprising that Catherine chose two grocers as her guarantors? After all, her own husband's family had only recently emerged from the trade – the first earl's great-grandfather had made a good living from it. Perhaps Catherine calculated that these tradesmen were more trustworthy than the society figures who had recently made their acquaintance, possibly with ulterior motives.

A second document in the Muniments entitled 'Memorial for Public Information: The Great Jennens or Jennings Property – now in Litigation in the High Court of Chancery, 1876' introduced the controversial subject as follows:

The above is well known to those conversant with the domestic history of our country for the last seventy-eight years as a *cause célèbre*. From time to time this case – so fruitful in mysteries – has agitated public opinion. Its appearance and disappearance in the Courts of Law have successively amused, astonished, instructed and dismayed observers. The defeated have been succeeded by the newly-resolute and the sanguine. Evidence in the restless hands of diligent explorers has come to light. Claimants bearing any one of the numerous variations of the original name of this very ancient family have presented themselves – coming from the ends of the earth. The temptation has been princely wealth – fabulous wealth – wealth for generations – wealth beyond idea and computation.

The Central Committee for the Jennens' Family Association had branches listed in America, Australia and the Cape of Good Hope and claimed 'a global family tree of interconnectedness'. It was working on behalf of the 'true heirs' and somewhat disingenuously stated: 'Let this be perfectly understood . . . It is Right and Justice the present plaintiffs . . . seek. It is acknowledgment, and not the ten millions, (nor any millions) which they specially desire. It is reversal of the wrong and the restitution of the right at which they aim.' The Association argued that the three families – the Lygons, the Andovers and the Curzons – which had shared the Jennens Inheritance had done so by circumventing, or obliterating, evidence of closer descendants.

The battles raged in High Chancery and lesser courts for an astonishing 170 years as clockmakers, stockmen, railway guards, émigrés, impoverished gentry, aristocrats and adventurers stepped forward to stake their claim. More than 130 years after the Miser's death, an American from Virginia, Mrs Elizabeth Barnett, began proceedings against the seventh Earl Beauchamp. She believed that Humfrey's son, William, had emigrated to the colony and that through him she was the true heir. Though her case was dismissed, in an article published in a magazine in 1943 she stated that she had now turned her sights on Lord Curzon who, according to her, owned nine castles that were rightfully hers. In the end, however, as far as the Jennens Inheritance was concerned, it was 'finders keepers, losers weepers'.

A mythology grew up around the Jennens Inheritance. Unexpected legacies were the stuff of Victorian dreams, promising unparalleled social advancement. Since the State Lottery, an idea hatched in Venice and introduced into England in 1694 as 'The Million Adventure', had closed in 1825 and football pools were yet to be invented, many hung their hopes on such pipe dreams and were encouraged by the plots of Victorian novels by Thomas Hardy, Wilkie Collins and lesser writers – a sub-genre which was dubbed 'the fiction of probate' – in which lives were transformed by a vast inheritance or wasted in the expectation of one.

Fog everywhere. Fog up the river, where it flows among green aits and meadows; fog down the river where it rolls defiled ... Never can there come fog too thick, never can there come mud and mire too deep, to assort with the groping and floundering condition which this High Court of Chancery, most pestilent of hoary sinners, holds, this day in the sight of heaven and earth.

Thus wrote Charles Dickens in *Bleak House*, published in instalments in the popular magazine *Household Words* between March 1852 and September 1853. Dickens bore a grudge against the law, having experienced its cruel and corrupt ways. When he was a boy, his father had been imprisoned for a minor debt in the Marshalsea debtors' prison. Aged fifteen, he had begun his career as a legal clerk and at eighteen he had been hired as a legal reporter. Dickens suffered in person the iniquities of High Chancery when, in 1844, he attempted to defend his copyright for *A Christmas Carol* from plagiarism. With his legal costs mounting to over seven hundred pounds and the realization dawning that the pirates were bankrupt, he abandoned the suit. 'The one great principle of English law is, to make business for itself,' he commented bitterly after the case collapsed, convinced that the legal system had become 'a by-word for delay, slow agony of mind, despair, impoverishment, trickery, confusion [and] insupportable injustice'. This was a view shared by many. As Jennens probate cases dragged on through the courts, a campaign was launched in *The Times* at the beginning of the 1850s against the 'inertia of an antiquated jurisprudence'. Reform was demanded. Dickens began his own campaign for legal reform in the pages of *Household Words*, which he edited and for which he wrote signed and unsigned editorials. In late 1851, for example, he penned two biting pieces, entitled 'The Martyrs of Chancery' and 'The Last Words of the Year', in anticipation of the new session of Parliament, scheduled to open in February 1852. Action was finally taken when a commission recommended urgent reform. It led to the Chancery Procedure Acts being introduced in March 1852.

To what extent did the battle over the Jennens Inheritance inspire Dickens's story of 'a house that got into Chancery and could not get out'? In the preface to *Bleak House* the novelist explains: 'The case of Gridley is in no essential altered from one of actual occurrence, made public by a disinterested person who was professionally acquainted with the whole monstrous wrong from beginning to end.' Though, unlike the Gridley case, the Jennens Inheritance was not trapped in probate as, on Jennens's death, it had been dispersed between three families, it nevertheless trapped hopeful claimants in its web for 170 years. The use of the surname Jarndyce, not so dissimilar to Jennens, also gives us a clue to Dickens's sources. When he started the novel in the second half of 1851, Mrs Dickens was suffering from violent headaches and severe nervous depression and was under the care of Dr James Watson, a 'hydropathic practitioner', at Malvern Spa, just four miles from Madresfield. Dickens regularly visited her there: the small town would have gossiped about their local grandees, the astonishingly rich Beauchamps, whose share of the Jennens Inheritance was being contested so frequently in High Chancery.

From the portrait hanging over the fireplace in the Saloon, young Jennens surveys the treasures of the *ancien régime* financed by his fortune. Cushioned by great wealth and adorned with their elevated title the Lygons too had become *vrais talons rouges*.

Chapter Seven

THE BREVIARY

When the Wastrel extended the original manor house he had made the fashionable addition of an oak-panelled Long Gallery on the first floor. Such a fine, high-ceilinged room, over 150 feet long, erected for no particular use, implied that this was the home of a Tudor gentleman of substance. On inclement days, when his pleasure gardens were inhospitable, he would have strolled down its Turkish rug-strewn wooden floor and looked out across his lands towards Bredon Hill. Today it is furnished with many of Madresfield's oldest pieces of Jacobean and Continental oak – gatelegged tables, settles, coffers, benches, cradles, cricket tables – which are interspersed with display cabinets filled with memorabilia associated with the family. Two grand pianos were added in the nineteenth century. It is not a cosy room, not even a comfortable one, but it effectively communicates a sense of bountiful space.

The ebony piano stands in the bay window and is

flanked by plain bookshelves. Alongside the hymn books, missals, philosophical tracts and early Middle European works on psychology that stand on these shelves are several first editions, dated 1858, of the *Day Hours of the Church of England*, a translation of the Roman Breviary. It is curious that a publication still in daily use by Anglican worshippers was anonymously compiled – but such were the times.

Nearly thirty years earlier, on 2 February 1829, from far across the frozen flats of the Vale of York, an onlooker would have seen that the medieval cathedral, York Minster, was ablaze. The roof of the central aisle, the organ, its screen, the tabernacle work, the stalls, galleries, bishop's throne and the pulpit were destroyed. The fire was the spectacular result of one of the most successful acts of arson in British history, committed in God's name by Jonathan Martin. This tongue-tied tanner, like many others at the time, believed that the Church of England had become corrupt. If the clergy did not change their ways and rekindle the nation's spirituality, fire and damnation awaited them. His protest could be regarded as the first – if somewhat inarticulate – act of defiance in what became known as the Oxford Movement.

Two hundred miles to the south-west of York, at Madresfield, a different, more cerebral expression would be penned on behalf of that same movement by William and Catherine's grandson, the sixth earl, Frederick (1830–1891). His *Day Hours* was a controversial publication not least because during the

Victorian era *all* religious matters were politically charged – hence the anonymity of authorship. Even seemingly straightforward administrative issues relating to the church, such as a grant to the Irish Catholic seminary, Maynooth, could threaten to topple a government. A heightened sensitivity – the direct consequence of the Repeal of the Test and Corporation Acts in 1828, the emancipation of the Roman Catholics in 1829 and the Reform Bill of 1832 – intensified religious debate since Parliament was no longer made up exclusively of Anglicans. In an atmosphere in which the Anglican establishment felt threatened, political actions and acts of personal devotion were now judged according to their implied allegiance: to the established Church or otherwise.

Matters came to a head in Oxford, when on Sunday 14 July 1833 the gentle John Keble, Professor of Poetry at the University, stood in the pulpit of the University Church of St Mary's and declared 'National Apostasy'. He criticized the government's attempt to suppress ten Church of Ireland bishoprics. The Church of England was a divine institution, he argued, and not a department of state whose rulings could be tampered with by politicians. His sermon, later published as one of the *Tracts for the Times*, launched the Oxford Movement. Keble, together with Dr Edward Pusey, Regius Professor of Hebrew and Canon of Christ Church, and John Henry Newman, vicar of St Mary's, was joined by a growing band of followers, variously dubbed Tractarians, Puseyites or Ritualists. Though Frederick was only three years old when the Movement began, in time he became a keen supporter and a friend of both Keble and Pusey.

The Movement's objective was to revive the religious life of the Church of England which, they felt, had ebbed since the Dissolution of the Monasteries and the break with Rome. Rituals had been abandoned and the sacraments debased. The poor were herded into 'free seats' labelled to announce their humble status and situated in poky cold corners, while the rich sat in customized pews warmed by fires. Coats of arms had replaced the crucifix on the walls of churches. The altar was mistreated and even reduced to being 'such a rickety, unworthy piece of furniture that no gentleman would have tolerated it in his kitchen,' as one diarist observed. The ancient vicar of Bloxham in Oxfordshire, though he remembered to put a loaf of bread and a bottle of wine on the table, realized during the consecration that a vital detail was missing. Did anyone have a corkscrew? he asked the congregation. With such examples in real life, it was not hard for Jane Austen, a clergyman's daughter, to mock two parsons in her novels: Mr Collins in *Pride and Prejudice* and Mr Elton in *Emma*. Many vicars enjoyed a tranquil sinecure in a well-endowed rural parish, while others absented themselves in pursuit of comforts and society elsewhere. With little regard for the problems of the working man, such misfits in their mahogany pulpits seldom inspired spirituality in their congregations. William Ewart Gladstone, who would become one of

England's greatest statesmen, and who turned Tractarian himself, regarded the situation as 'dishonouring to Christianity [and] disgraceful to a nation'.

Newman, Pusey and Keble, in what Newman called 'the almost hopeless endeavour' to reignite spirituality within the individual and the church, recommended that the church return to their notion of its medieval roots and restore the rituals and decorations that had fallen slowly into disuse since the Reformation. These Christians deplored the brutality and secularism of the French Revolution and the scepticism of the Encyclopédistes. Their creed formed the bedrock of Frederick's strict upbringing, which was supervised by his Tractarian nurse, Eliza Marks.

It is no surprise that Walter Scott's *Waverley* novels and the writings of Goethe and the Lake poets can all be found in the Madresfield Library. The Tractarians shared the Romantics' belief in the power of the imagination and the priority of faith over dogma. Poetry encouraged an understanding of, and more importantly a *feeling* for, the sacraments. Keble was a widely read poet himself. In 1827, he published *The Christian Year: Thoughts in Verse for the Sundays and Holy Days*, a volume which recalled the mysticism of Catholicism. By engaging the imagination rather than the intellect, Keble, as Newman acknowledged, 'did for the Church of England what none but a poet could do: he made it poetical'. Ninety-five editions of *The Christian Year* appeared before his death. It was a Victorian bestseller and several copies can be found at Madresfield.

Though the Oxford Movement was born in the quads of Oxford University, it was an anti-intellectual and, above all, a pastoral movement. The Tractarians looked to the common people for support and in return provided them with pastoral care. They attempted to offer spiritual guidance and practical help to the slum-dwellers of the cholera-ridden inner cities of industrial England – London, Liverpool, Glasgow and Manchester. Two generations of Lygons committed themselves to the reforming works carried out in these cities' slum settlements.

In the wake of the Tractarians, social-reforming novelists depicted the wretchedness of this underclass to stir the readers' consciences. Week by week in the pages of the popular magazine *Household Words*, Charles Dickens and Elizabeth Gaskell unfolded tales of pathos for their sentimental and God-fearing readership. The lonely crossing sweeper Joe in *Bleak House*, for example, was shown by Dickens to be so ignorant, so neglected, that in his dying moments he could not even recite the most essential supplication in the Christian canon, the Lord's Prayer. Though change was being demanded in some enlightened circles, much of Victorian society held attitudes of 'crippling narrowness'; and religious sectarianism intensified following the conversion to Catholicism of Newman and other prominent Tractarians and hundreds of their followers. Since they came from the educated and influential classes, the established order felt further threatened.

It is difficult to appreciate now the threat that the

Oxford Movement was seen to present to the Church of England and the establishment in general at the time. Sympathy with Rome still smacked of treason. Even a man's dress could advertise a treacherous leaning towards Rome or a patriotic stance behind Anglicanism and, by implication, the state. A vicar in a chasuble and crucifix announced his Tractarian sympathies. The height of a layman's starched collar, the breadth of his whiskers or the crucifix embroidered on his scarf end were read as Puseyite indicators.

Anthony Trollope made much of this symbolic language. In *Barchester Towers*, the soul of Mr Slope, the Bishop's chaplain, 'trembles in agony at the iniquities of the Puseyites. His aversion is carried to things outward as well as inward. His gall rises at a new church with a high-pitched roof; a full-breasted black silk waistcoat is with him a symbol of Satan; and a profane jest-book would not, in his view, more foully desecrate the church seat of a Christian, than a book of prayer printed with red letters and ornamented with a cross on the back.' Frederick, Earl Beauchamp, would certainly have provoked Mr Slope's wrath. Here was a wealthy and politically active peer, who built Gothic churches with spires reaching towards heaven; who venerated Holy Communion; who fraternized with Jesuits in Rome; who savoured Gregorian chant and commissioned gilded crucifixes and altar reredos which he generously donated to churches on his estates. A photograph of him in the National Portrait Gallery, entitled 'Church of England Layman; Politician;

Author', provides – at a glance – the measure of the man. This is a buttoned-up and grave Victorian. The hair on his head is flattened across his high brow; the hair on his face is clipped into Tractarian whiskers of walrus proportions. He is the very model of a Christian of the High Church and of high seriousness.

Since the founding of the Oxford Movement high churchmen had discussed the merits of publishing a version of the Roman Breviary. Frederick was approached to select prayers and edit this important prayer book and he took considerable trouble over it, consulting his extensive liturgical library and quibbling with leading religious figures – both Catholic and Anglican – in pursuit of doctrinal exactitude. Frederick avoided all sentimentality in his choice of prayers for the breviary, steering the reader into accepting one fixed, specific and appropriate piece for each day of the week, which took no account of the state of mind in which a reader came to prayer on any given day. His audience's subjective needs were irrelevant. This reflected Frederick's asceticism – and indeed intolerance. If he considered a hymn in a service to be doctrinally doubtful, he would make a point of snapping shut his hymnal and standing frostily silent at his pew while others continued their 'fancy' song. 'He hated anything "fancy". If he liked ceremonial it must be that of the Church. He did not approve of half-and-half ritual; a cope without a mitre, a pastoral staff without either, gave him no satisfaction.' His views would remain intransigent throughout his life. In 1876,

The high-minded high churchman Frederick, the sixth Earl Beauchamp.

halfway across the Channel to France with one of his greatest friends and fellow Tractarians, Charles Lindley Wood, second Viscount Halifax, he commenced an extraordinary ritual. He was carrying a brown paper parcel which, he confided to his companion, was 'an improper book he had confiscated out of the porter's chair in Belgrave Square three years before'. Since that time he had worried about how he should properly dispose of the 'vile' publication. It should, he concluded, be drowned at sea and he gravely cast it to the waves, much to Halifax's amusement.

Frederick made a private arrangement with the publishers that the *Day Hours* be sold at a heavily subsidized rate; resulting in, according to Halifax, 'a deficit which Beauchamp himself had to make good'. The Muniments hold many letters of congratulation to Frederick on this anonymous publication. Sumner, the Archbishop of Canterbury, 'could not help putting two and two together though I have said nothing to anyone'.

Frederick's grave personality was forged during a dour childhood. His elderly father, General 'Handsome Henry' Lygon, who was to become the fourth Earl Beauchamp, had been Catherine's favourite son. It was noted that Henry 'had a good deal of the martinet in him and his sons were somewhat rigidly brought up'. He had married Lady Susan Eliot, the daughter of the second Earl of St Germans, a gentle woman who died in childbirth leaving behind her five children: Henry, Frederick, Georgiana, Susan and Felicia. Frederick was just five. Since their estranged uncle, John, the third Earl

Beauchamp, lived at Madresfield, the children grew up at Spring Hill, their grandmother's home, which had become a house of grief. Henry locked himself away in mourning and remained a widower, leaving his children to the solemn servant-turned-governess, Eliza Marks. She took her new duties seriously and was a stickler for ritual. In her opinion, her elevated position demanded a suitable title; she was no longer to be addressed by her charges as 'Markey', she was 'Miss Marks' now.

Miss Marks was a stalwart soldier in the Oxford Movement and determined to instil its tenets in these children, particularly Frederick who, as the second son, was destined for the church. When in town at their Brook Street house, she took them to the few Tractarian churches. On Sundays, they had to attend church seven times and, when not praying, each child was required to write a précis of the day's sermon. Every weekday, their waking hours began and ended with chapel. In 1844, once he had been steeped in church lore and ritual, Frederick went to Eton where he began to collect antiquarian books, particularly religious texts and medieval manuscripts. It was from these that he gained his exceptional command of Latin and his feeling for ecclesiastical *incunabula*.

While Frederick was at school, his sister Felicia married Charles Cavendish, the grandson of the Duke of Devonshire. In October 1847, she began married life as a cleric's wife in the parish of Little Stamford in Lincolnshire, which was in the duke's gift. Frederick approved of her Tractarian improvements to the unadorned church there, though many in the congregation were aghast. She reintroduced ritual, decorated the altar with flowers and High Church adornments and arranged for Holy Communion to be celebrated twice a week. Her three domestic servants were expected to attend. She trained a choir and was so prescriptive with the parishioners that the overwhelmed Charles nicknamed her 'my High Priestess'. On the eve of their first wedding anniversary, Felicia went into labour and was delivered of a stillborn daughter. By dawn she too was dead, aged just twenty-one. Frederick was forbidden by his father to attend the funeral as he was due to go up to Oxford on that very day.

Given his upbringing and bereavement, it is unsurprising that Frederick, as he entered Christ Church to read Greats, chose, above that of other contemporary undergraduates, the company of Henry Parry Liddon, a disciple of the college's Tractarian canon Dr Edward Pusey, and a future cleric. Lygon and Liddon became lifelong friends and bundles of letters at Madresfield chart their enduring relationship in which ecclesiastical discussions were the keynote. Born into a Low Church family, Liddon made the long journey to High Church ritualism now, lighting his rooms with candles and strictly adhering to the Roman Breviary. While some in college scoffed, Frederick approved. Being rather humourless and singularly reserved, Frederick did not let his head be turned by the pleasures of undergraduate life. Instead, he passed his time with church-minded men and became an authority on ecclesiastical music, rites, doctrines and liturgy. Like Liddon, he took a vow of celibacy and set about preparing himself for a contemplative cleric's life.

Aside from the Church, another of Frederick's preoccupying interests as an undergraduate was the Oxford Union Society, a debating chamber for students and embryo politicians. He was elected its President in 1851 and it was here that he befriended and worked alongside Lord Robert Cecil, the Union's Secretary, who became the Marquess of Salisbury. In later years, Frederick would hold office in two of Salisbury's cabinets. During his time at Oxford, however, it was Church matters, not political ambitions, which preoccupied Frederick. In 1852, he was elected a fellow of All Souls. Soon after, in January 1853, his childless uncle John died, and his father acceded to the earldom.

So high were Frederick's Church views that he made a pilgrimage to Rome in the spring of 1856 to study its architecture and ecclesiastical history and to visit his cousin Charles Pakenham. Son of the second Earl of Longford, Pakenham had converted to Catholicism in 1850 and was studying at the English College in Rome. There, Frederick, Liddon and Pakenham prayed for the reunion of Canterbury and Rome. Alarm bells rang among members of the Lygon family when rumours reached home that Frederick had been seen several times in the company of Monsignor Edward Howard, a Jesuit and scion of England's premier Catholic family, the Fitzalan-Howards, Dukes of Norfolk.

A dozen or so letters from Monsignor Howard to Frederick and some replies drafted by Frederick on to scrap paper have survived in the Madresfield Muniments. Through three soul-searching months between April and June 1856, in Rome, the two men were locked in an intense doctrinal debate as Howard endeavoured to guide the twenty-six-year-old Frederick into the Roman Church. Howard lent him books and together they read crucial texts. The intensity of their conversations is reflected in the physical expression of the script; some letters are penned in haste to sub-stantiate a position argued face to face earlier in the day; some contain underlinings as the priest attempts to drive home a point. Frederick was clearly facing the greatest decision of his life.

Frederick's staunchly anti-Catholic father was horrified. Was his son about to convert? Conversion was an act of great moment which many regarded as betrayal. It could lead to lifelong division between father and son, between brothers and between close friends. But, though Frederick teetered, unlike his cousin Pakenham he never actually jumped. Emotionally wrung out, he retreated from Rome. On 1 July from his home on Grosvenor Place, Frederick finally wrote to Howard. He admitted to 'putting off from day to day telling you what I thought you would not like to hear': he had decided that he could not make the conversion. 'I should always have regretted having taken such a step in the excited state in which I then was'. Frederick had irrevocably withdrawn from Howard and from Rome.

His Christian mission continued in his political career and in 1857, Frederick entered Parliament as MP for Tewkesbury. He rose rapidly, being made Lord of the Admiralty within two years. He found time, however, to produce the first edition of his *Day Hours* in 1858. Once his brother Henry had succeeded to the title in 1863, becoming the fifth Earl Beauchamp, Frederick replaced him during the next three years as MP for West Worcestershire. Frederick could out-pettifog any opponent, debating through the night until the other side lay exhausted in submission. His tenacity extended beyond the House and into the parliamentary constituencies. In the General Election of 1865, for example, he so effectively galvanized support for Gathorne-Hardy, who was standing for the Oxford constituency and who shared Lygon's High Church views, that the newcomer defeated the great Liberal candidate and future Prime Minister, Gladstone. Benjamin Disraeli, then Chancellor of the Exchequer, wrote to Frederick congratulating him on his contribution to 'an historical event which I believe to be mainly, if not entirely, owing to your resolution and energy'.

Frederick was a man of exactitude – in debate, administration, protocol, social hierarchy, ritual and even in dress. E. W. Benson, a future Archbishop of Canterbury, described him as 'a very smart, bright man, a little chimerical, gaily dressed and brushed, and beneath a most loving son of the church'. *The Times* singled him out in a review of the decade in Parliament:

> Mr. Lygon . . . his dress is perfect, and his neckties are
> the admiration of the House. His appearance one night
> as he stood at the bar was, from the Reporter's Gallery,
> quite dazzling, for he sported a capacious scarf of
> brilliant scarlet, which covered his breast, and, con-
> trasting as it did with his white waistcoat, and flashing
> in the gaslight, made him look quite meteoric.

Frederick focused his efforts on Church-related matters, earning the sobriquet 'the Ecclesiastical Layman'. He wrote all Disraeli's speeches on religious matters and confidently suggested that Disraeli should publish these, offering himself as editor. Disraeli agreed to the project, flattering the editor: 'No one but you could be the editor, as you know my innermost mind, and there is entire sympathy between us.'

While Frederick worked tirelessly on political and ecclesiastical matters, his older brother Henry passed his time dressing up and travelling for pleasure. Since childhood he had traded on his 'delicate health' to elicit indulgence for his idleness. After serving briefly in the Life Guards, he sold his commission and went abroad on a permanent Grand Tour, initially of Europe and then of the Americas, staying, where possible, in the local officers' mess. Henry was homosexual. His letters home – complaining to his father or issuing instructions to his brother – reveal a prosaic man compared to his high-minded sibling, yet one who was perhaps more human. He reported on the weather endured, meals eaten and barracks frequented. In the autumn of 1853, for example, while touring America and Canada, he moaned:

> The American hotels I consider all 'humbug', nothing but show, all flash, and to anyone who has an Englishman's idea of comfort almost unbearable. The system of chewing in this country is something too odious, and I do not exaggerate at all when I say that it alone would prevent a Lady [appearing] among such a filthy society but no! Pull up, I could go on for an hour in this strain . . .

When in Worcestershire, Henry bred horses and purchased more land. On his accession to the title in 1863, he initiated the great building programme at Madresfield carried out by Philip Charles Hardwick, the architect of Charterhouse, which was so extensive that it continued until 1888. Hardwick pulled down most of the twenty-five-roomed old building, save for the Elizabethan façade, and erected an enormous neo-Gothic extension – an irregular trapezium – which wrapped around the back of the court and covered virtually all the two-acre plot inside the moat. The works incorporated the medieval foundations and the original wattle-and-daub walls as well as the cellars and the lower part of the walling along the north-west and south-west sides. The project – which Henry would not see completed – transformed Madresfield from a squire's manor house into a 160-roomed Victorian stately home more befitting an earl.

By 1864, Henry's tuberculosis had forced him to retire to Brighton for the sea air, leaving Frederick to run the estates, oversee – and hone – the building works and exhibit patience and tact when his demanding brother assailed him by letter with instructions and criticism. In March 1866, aged only thirty-seven, Henry died of consumption and Frederick succeeded him as sixth earl.

Frederick's devotion to God was bound up in the Gothic rebuild. Though in ecclesiastical matters he was nit-picking and academic, his architectural instincts were sentimental and idealized. The Gothic was the Tractarians' preferred architectural style. Their romantic imagination associated it with the medieval: the chivalric knight, the medieval monk, the artisan. Inspired by nostalgia, these modern crusaders turned their backs on classicism, a style they associated with the decadence of Ancient Rome, the godlessness of Georgian England and, worst of all, the barbarity of French Republicanism. Gothic revivalism – conveniently rinsed of its violent associations – suggested to them high-minded poetry, an undivided and true church, Plantagenet nationalism and, for those so inclined, a sense of ancient lineage. As utilitarianism and materialism took their grip in the mid-Victorian England depicted with precision by Mrs Gaskell in her portraits of the factory magnates, so aristocrats 'Gothicized' their homes in emblematic protest. The

'Medievalism at Madresfield Court': an unnamed guest's illustration in a commonplace book of 1873.

An ivy-clad Madresfield, photographed in 1862.

Catholic convert and architect A. N. W. Pugin then
seized on this style and turned it into the *only* Christian
style of architecture: the reproduction in stone of the
branches of a forest – God's first, primitive church. In
Pugin's hands the Gothic smacked of Papism but once
Ruskin, a staunch Protestant, had purged it in people's
minds of these associations and linked it to his programme of worthy social reform, the Tractarians could
adopt it.

Ruskin was a persuasive advocate. In April 1864, he
delivered a lecture entitled 'Traffic' in which he stated:

> I notice that among all the new buildings which cover
> your once wild hills, churches and schools are mixed in
> due, that is to say, in large proportion, with your mills
> and mansions; and I notice that the churches and
> schools are almost always Gothic, and the mansions
> and mills are never Gothic. May I ask the meaning of
> this? For, remember, it is a peculiarly modern
> phenomenon. When Gothic was invented, houses were
> Gothic as well as churches; and when the Italian style
> superseded the Gothic, churches were Italian as well as
> houses . . . But now you live under one school of archi-
> tecture, and worship under another. What do you mean
> by doing this? Am I to understand that you are think-
> ing of changing your architecture back to Gothic; and
> that you treat your churches experimentally, because it
> does not matter what mistakes you make in a church?
> Or am I to understand that you consider Gothic a pre-
> eminently sacred and beautiful mode of building,

which, you think, like the fine frankincense, should be mixed for the tabernacle only, and reserved for your religious services? For if this be the feeling ... it signifies neither more nor less than that you have separated your religion from your life.

Frederick, of course, never a man to separate his daily life from his religion, was living, on Ruskin's terms, a 'unified' life, having Gothicized Madresfield. Towers, spires and great halls were built by devout fellow countrymen across Victorian England. Half of the churches standing today were built by devout fellow countrymen during the nineteenth century and half of those were neo-Gothic in style. In civic architecture, the tower, such as Pugin's clock tower housing Big Ben, was used to suggest wise authority, while in domestic architecture the tower asserted superiority (now that crenellations were deemed too militaristic). On a more practical level, a tower could house modern water tanks. Interpretations of the medieval great hall were intended to evoke the idea of chivalric hospitality towards every man, woman and child welcomed to the modern knight's table. Frederick included all three – a spire, a tower and a great hall – in the extensions at Madresfield. The result was a peculiar building and architectural historian Nikolaus Pevsner judged that 'the young Hardwick was not ... known for his light-ness of touch.' Hardwick later completed the new chapel in 1867 and the bell turret in 1875. A new storey was added to the left of the Great Hall in 1885.

Mercifully, however, despite its enormous size and aspirations to grandeur, Madresfield remained almost cosy.

Frederick's ecclesiastical ambitions had died with his brother. Once he had inherited the earldom, aged thirty-three, he was expected to marry and produce a family. In December 1866, he sought advice from his trusted friend, Liddon. Had he not taken a private vow of celibacy? Surely this was incompatible with marriage. Liddon consulted their mentor, Pusey, who opined that, as it was only a private vow, Frederick did not need dispensation. He must now assume his duties as a good husband and a Christian landowner.

Frederick lost no time in finding a wife. He spent Christmas with the historian Philip Stanhope, the fifth Earl Stanhope and founder of the National Portrait Gallery, at his house in Kent, Chevening. On 6 January 1867 he wrote to Stanhope's only daughter, Lady Mary, who was an exceptionally clever woman, 'My dearest, I went to Holy Communion this morning at 8.30 a.m. to thank God for giving you to me . . .' They were married the following year. The new Countess Beauchamp spoke seven languages, painted beautifully and was a keen scholar. Her family loved to tell of her precociousness. At the age of six, she was sitting on the Duke of Wellington's knee in male company when the old soldier began regaling his friends with a bawdy tale. On noticing that the girl understood he switched to French. Nevertheless, she giggled at the punchline. In 1851, Macaulay had dedicated a poem entitled 'Valentine' to her. It included the lines:

The loveliest lass of all is mine –
Good morrow to my Valentine!
Good morrow, gentle Child, and then
Again good morrow, and again
Without one cloud of strife or sorrow.

Mary and Frederick began a happy, though brief, marriage, sharing their High Church convictions. Various commonplace books lie about Madresfield in which Mary painted delicate and accomplished watercolours: still-lifes within and vistas from her new home, along with sketches of her children and their pets. She died in childbirth in 1876, aged thirty-two, having given birth to five children in eight years.

Despite having handsome estates, Frederick was not by national standards a great landowning magnate. A survey taken in 1878 records that his lands stretched over 16,899 acres, and lay in the counties of Worcestershire, Lincolnshire, Gloucestershire, Warwickshire and Leicestershire. They were valued at £23,886. But his landholding was modest compared to those of the great magnates elsewhere in Britain; for example, the Duke of Beaufort held 51,085 acres, the Marquess of Bute 116,668 and the Duke of Devonshire 198,572.

Between 1885 and 1914, one-third of the senior administrative posts in cabinet were given to peers of the realm and so it was not unreasonable for Frederick to seek high office. In line with this trend, he was proposed by Disraeli, now Prime Minister, for the honorific position of Steward of the Household (a post held by his ancestors, the medieval Beauchamps), but Queen Victoria considered his Tractarian views to be politically divisive and would only accept him if he camouflaged them. He served the royal household between 1874 and 1880, but was eventually dismissed because of his haughtiness towards the servants. However, in recognition of his services, he expected to be raised to the rank of marquess. Writing to the queen on 10 April 1878 on the subject of Beauchamp's elevation, Disraeli explained that the earl would not be fobbed off without a marquessate but the queen refused. Disraeli concurred that Beauchamp was 'a disagreeable man' but had he not conducted for four years the business of the Home Office in the House of Lords with sustained ability? he suggested to her. 'It is impossible to throw such men over if you wish to keep a political party together. Such men must be rewarded and if they have fancies for Marquisates, it is better that they should be Marquises than Cabinet Ministers.' But Frederick did not get his way.

In 1878, Frederick married for a second time: Lady Emily Annora Pierrepont (1853–1935), the twenty-five-year-old daughter of the third Earl Manvers. It was a marriage which alienated the elder children by his first marriage, Mary, Susan, William and Edward, who did not like their stepmother and felt increasingly estranged from their father.

Between 1885 and 1887, Frederick twice served as Paymaster General in Lord Salisbury's administrations. On being offered Post without Portfolio, Frederick was peeved, complaining to his Prime Minister that 'hereditary peers are to be held excluded from efficient duties.' He resigned in a huff, riling his old Oxford companion Salisbury by pointing out that he had not 'sufficiently regarded the claims of hereditary peerage' in his appointments and promotions.

Despite being lofty and inflexible, Frederick was an enlightened landlord. He conscientiously modernized and extended the estate, built cottages for employees and tenants and in 1864 carried out the wishes of his uncle John, the third earl, in memory of John's first wife, by spending her sixty-thousand-pound dowry on building almshouses at Newland for 'decayed agricultural labourers'. He provided retired tenants and estate workers with pensioners' flats for which he charged subsidized rents, built a post office, shop and working men's club, built three Gothic churches on his estate and donated substantially to the restoration of the Priory at Great Malvern. Unlike Dickens's character in *Bleak House*, Mrs Jellyby, the Victorian Lygons focused their charitable works at home and, cleanliness being next to godliness, Frederick's sister Lady Susan Lygon set up a laundry in one of the villages on the Madresfield estate, to provide work and a home for young women rescued from the streets. Frederick's aunt, Lady Louisa Lygon, introduced a savings scheme for domestic staff at Madresfield and donated land near her London home in Chelsea for the Lygon Almshouses, which still stand.

Frederick considered the provision of education to be

John Keble (far left), William Gladstone (far right) and Dr Charles Blomfield (centre), the Bishop of London, at Fulham Palace with other Tractarians.

a duty and, on a national and local level, he worked hard for religious education and voluntary schools. He founded and endowed an unusually large school at Madresfield, and helped found Malvern College and the Alice Ottley School for Girls in Worcester. He composed glees – compositions for unaccompanied male voices – for the church and established a choir school at Newland. But perhaps it is the creation of Keble College, Oxford, in 1870 that stands as his enduring memorial. He was not someone who articulated sentiment: instead he expressed his love of the Church and his admiration for John Keble in his substantial funding of the building of this college – the first new one for over 150 years. This extremely controversial project dominated the last thirty years of his life.

There had been mutterings about founding an Oxford college among Tractarians since the 1840s. Keble died in 1866, and as Christianity appeared to be increasingly vulnerable in the light of Darwin's theories of evolution, they wanted to found a college in his memory and to run it on strictly High Anglican principles. It should be small and aim to educate candidates for Holy Orders. A frugal lifestyle would offset the reputation that the university had acquired as an expensive club for the sons of the aristocracy. However, it must not be a poor man's college since that, it was feared, would attract only those of inferior social position and it must 'counteract Rugby and Balliol', Frederick stressed to Liddon.

An eminent group of Tractarian sympathizers,

including Frederick, Liddon and Pusey, launched the appeal to raise fifty thousand pounds, and it attracted important benefactors, including Gladstone, Samuel Wilberforce, Bishop of Oxford, and the Rt. Hon. Gathorne Gathorne-Hardy, MP. Frederick immediately subscribed five thousand pounds himself and continued to donate both publicly and anonymously, doubling his gifts to the college, fighting for its charter and seeking to secure its favourable consideration by the Liberal Cabinet. William Butterfield, known for his Anglo-Catholic churches, was selected as an appropriate architect. Tuition fees per term were limited to four pounds. The small rooms – built off corridors rather than the grander and more typical Oxford 'sets' constructed on staircases – were designed to maximize supervision and were sparsely provided with austere college furniture, rather than the student's own. A modest three pounds a term rent would be charged. Battel bills (food, lighting, etc.) would be capped at ten pounds, no debts would be tolerated and servants were not to be tipped. It was stipulated that students attend a morning and evening service in the chapel and the college gates would be shut at nine p.m. They were expected to continue this quasi-monastic existence in college all year round rather than leaving on vacation. Its 150 students were to be given 'a Christian training based upon the principles of the Church of England'. Counter to Oxford tradition, the college was to be run by a council and not by the fellows. Many of the benefactors stipulated that the scholarships they endowed be confined to members of the Church of England.

After much debate, Gladstone granted the new college a charter in 1867 and the foundation stone was laid on 25 April, St Mark's Day and Keble's birthday. Butterfield took his inspiration for the college from the upper chapel of the basilica of St Francis of Assisi in Italy. His interpretation was a red-brick and polychrome building, striped blue-black, red and off-white, and topped with a riot of chimney stacks and gables, dubbed by one newspaper as 'holy zebra style'. Not surprisingly, in its Gothic style, Keble bore a remarkable resemblance to the rebuilt Madresfield and some rooms in college were named after the Earls Beauchamp.

In 1870 the college opened – and how it invited derision! A bargee in the town referred to it as 'that new place near the Parks what's going to stop us all from saying, "Damn"'. (Frederick assiduously gummed the press cuttings – good, bad and indifferent – into a scrapbook.) Criticism ranged from the look of the college to its purpose. How could Oxford's honey-stoned elegance be blighted with this egregious red-brick monstrosity? *The Times* attempted to be positive when it wrote on 26 April 1876 that the chapel 'may tone down still more in time, especially if relieved by ivy and other creepers' and while it admired the interior of the chapel it loathed the Gregorian chants of 'droning sameness'. Other reporters scoffed that 'rumours of evolution should never reach them [the students]' within 'its painfully ugly walls' and that Keble men could not 'make use of the virile pleasure of running into debt'. They feigned horror at the new boating jacket colours which were spoiling the sartorial traditions of the Isis. The final brickbat came on 3 May from *The World*:

It was designed as a protest; it stands there, for all men to see, as an eyesore. Keble College was founded as a purely and rigidly sectarian college, just at a time when those tests which were the bulwarks of sectarianism were swept away. And the curious thing is that the Minister who was responsible for the abolition of tests is the statesman who was the chief patron of the college established for the special purpose of retaining tests. Mr Gladstone combined in his own person the leadership of the Liberal and anti-clerical party in Parliament with the political leadership of the High Anglicans.

Though feelings ran high, the college did achieve its aim; within the first twenty years, 879 students matriculated of whom 450 took Holy Orders. Frederick had left an abiding mark on his era.

To the end, Frederick and his old Oxford friend Henry Liddon corresponded regularly on the minutiae of ecclesiastical matters. Just months before he died, on 22 March 1890, Liddon wrote to his friend promising to lend his copy of the Prayer Book of 1627. The shy Liddon, whom Frederick had unsuccessfully advised to accept a bishopric and the headship of Keble College, died five months before Frederick himself collapsed suddenly and died of apoplexy on 19 February 1891 while carving the meat for the Nursery.

Even beyond the grave he disdained the 'fancy'. His last will and testament, dated 25 March 1890, states that his funeral was to take place at Madresfield and 'I hope that a leaden coffin may not be necessary, I expressly forbid the use of all flowers at my funeral and I also expressly forbid the erection of any tribute or monument whatsoever.' His unmarked grave lies between those of his two wives, Mary and Emily, on the site of the altar of the original Norman church at Madresfield. The only monument is a tall cross which bears the date of his death but no name. Incorporated into this cross is a part of the tympanum of the door-way to that church. In his mind, it would have connected him to his Norman ancestors. Later, the architectural historian Nikolaus Pevsner noted, 'the tablets to the Earls Beauchamp are exemplarily unassuming'.

Chapter Eight

THE ILLUMINATION

Frederick liked to read his folio-sized books at a
mahogany cylinder bureau in the Library, where he
sat with his back to the window overlooking the Moat
Garden. This bureau was so tall that, save for his velvet-
shod feet peeking out from under its wooden skirt, he
would have been entirely hidden from the view of anyone entering the room. One can imagine him seated
before his prize possession, the Madresfield Book of
Hours, which is illustrated with highly coloured and gilt-
bordered illuminations which stand proud from the
ancient vellum pages. This medieval manuscript, which
took its name from the place where it would be housed
for over 150 years, is one of the great English medieval
manuscripts produced before the dawn of printing. The
book's provenance – creation, suppression, recovery –
encapsulates several centuries of the spiritual history of
the English people.

The fragile, 188-page prayer book dates from

approximately 1320 and is a quarto manuscript, 252 millimetres high and 155 wide. It is protected by a thin white deerskin slip-on cover known as a chemise, and fastened with two pink-stained straps buckled in brass. The binding dates from the fifteenth century and is of tawed deerskin drawn tight over the oak boards and stained pink with kermes, a vivid red dye extracted from crushed beetles which live on the kermes oak tree. A century after the prayer book was made, pages featuring illuminations were removed from a psalter and inserted into this Book of Hours to embellish it. The illuminations – jewel-coloured double miniatures – were crafted by layering vivid dyes and gold leaf on to a raised gesso ground. Each one depicts a miracle of the Virgin; the pages provide a daily progression of devotional prayers to her. One spread illustrates the Miracle of the Roses: in the left miniature, a monk's prayers turn into flowers as the words fall from his lips and are gathered by an angel who strings them into a chaplet or rosary; in the right-hand miniature, the monk crowns a statue of the Virgin with the floral wreath. Even the plainer pages feature an exuberant arabesque of foliage and tendrils around the margins. Whereas the themes of the miniatures are heavenly, the marginalia of the prayer book are as down to earth as the country pleasures of the passing seasons. A Chaucerian ploughman furrows his way across a field; a wimpled woman, skirts hoicked high, scythes through wheat; a hunter flies his hawk; a peasant treads grapes and another beats acorns out of an oak tree for the hungry swine.

The illuminated prayer book originated in the Dark Ages and gave its final flourish during the Renaissance when, despite the invention of printing, wealthy families continued to commission hand-decorated books. Books of Hours first appeared in England in the mid-thirteenth century and approximately eight hundred English examples survive, though few are as ornately decorated as this. Joan de Braci would have used a Book of Hours or a psalter to teach her children to pray and to read.

The Madresfield Book of Hours was probably commissioned by Maud de Tilliol of Scaleby in Cumberland, from whom it passed to a succession of owners – the Scropes, the Nevilles, the Constables and the Lascelles – who added their family crests. Sometimes crests and signatures of notable people – a monarch or a dignitary – known to the family were added together with marginalia, souvenirs, family anniversaries and even recipes. As a result of the disestablishment of the Church under Henry VIII and the iconoclasm that followed, few such manuscripts survived in England in comparison to the Continent. References to saints, the Virgin Mary or the Pope were anathema to the authorities of post-Reformation England and since possession of such texts implied treason families were forced to hide or destroy artefacts that might betray their allegiance to Rome. This book's survival is even more remarkable given that devotion to the Virgin and prayers for her intercession smacked of Papism in Tudor England.

In the mid-sixteenth century, when the Reformation forbade its practical use, the Madresfield Book of Hours went missing. It did not reappear for centuries, and then was bought by Frederick. The binding was found to contain dried blades of grass, seeds and animal hair suggesting that it might have been hidden or abandoned in an agricultural building for some time.

Ownership of this exceptional manuscript and other rare volumes gave Frederick entry into reputedly the oldest and the most exclusive club in the world: the Roxburghe Club. This takes its name from the great eighteenth-century book collector John Ker, third Duke of Roxburghe. It admits only forty members at any one time, typically drawn from the highest ranks of the British nobility. The club was founded by a curate and neighbour of the Lygons, Thomas Dibdin.

Dibdin had served in a parish near Madresfield, where he had made the acquaintance of another neighbour, living across the border in Gloucestershire. This was Dr Edward Jenner, the physician who discovered the vaccine for smallpox – the disease which may have killed Corbyn and Jane Lygon and their three children. To Jenner, Dibdin acknowledged, 'I owe in good measure, my fixed passion for Bibliophilism', and he set about compiling his first bibliographical work, entitled *An Introduction to the Knowledge of Rare and Valuable Editions in Greek and Latin Classics* (1802). The book proved to be a tool of social advancement for Dibdin, who moved to fashionable Kensington in London and established himself as bibliophile to the aristocracy. The second

Earl Spencer, an ancestor of Diana, Princess of Wales, became his patron and Dibdin began cataloguing his library at Althorp in Northamptonshire.

Members of the Roxburghe Club first gathered over a dinner at Adelphi Terrace, in London, the home of Mr (later Baron) William Bolland, on 17 June 1812. They were all keenly interested in the sale at auction of the late Duke of Roxburghe's collection, then in progress. The most important lot, a first edition of Boccaccio's *Decameron*, said to be the rarest book in the world, was to be sold the following day. Bolland invited other enthusiasts to discuss the founding of a club to celebrate and advance book collecting. The next day, the auction reached a climax in the late Duke of Roxburghe's dining room. Among the bidders for the *Decameron*, or 'practitioners in the black letter craft', as Dibdin dubbed them, were the Duke of Devonshire with his magnificent income and a 'cluster of Caxtons', the Marquess of Blandford (heir to the Duke of Marlborough), Lord Spencer, Sir Mark Masterman Sykes and, it was rumoured, Napoleon Bonaparte's agent seeking to bag the prize for his emperor.

Dibdin's high-flown account of the day reads like a duel between knights of old. Mr Evans, the auctioneer, stood at the top of the room, while to his right, the Earl Spencer leaned nonchalantly against a wall and further

It is the only surviving complete copy of the Venetian 1471 edition of the *Decameron* printed by Christopher Valdarfer (fl. 1470–88). It was sold in the Roxburghe sale for £2,200 to Lord Blandford. On his bankruptcy sale soon afterwards (in 1819) the volume was bought by Lord Spencer, the underbidder at the Roxburghe sale, for considerably less.

down the room stood the Marquess of Blandford. The cleric refers to these 'champions . . . clad in complete steel for that contest' whose determined bidding had forced other knights to replace their swords in their scabbards. The gavel eventually fell at £2,260 to Blandford. It was an astonishingly high price – the equivalent of £1.7 million today. In celebration, that evening Dibdin organized a gastronomic dinner in the St Alban's Tavern, St Alban's Street (now Waterloo Place), attended by eighteen important bibliophiles. Spencer was elected President and Dibdin was appointed Secretary of the Club. No Lygon was present. The Club's rules were laid down: membership was to be by invitation only and each member 'should reprint some scarce piece of ancient lore to be given to the members, one copy being on vellum for the Chairman and only as many copies as members'.

The Lygons came relatively late to serious book collecting and it was not until 1866 that Frederick was elected to the Roxburghe Club as its 103rd member. Apart from the Madresfield Hours he had amassed an impressive library of ecclesiastical books, though the Roxburghe Club history records inaccurately that 'he added little to the Madresfield Library'. In fact, he took great joy in seeing the face of his lifelong friend Liddon beam with sympathetic satisfaction on seeing another treasure – liturgical, Shakespearian, medieval – newly added to the collection.

An inventory of 1899 listed the highlights of this twelve-thousand-book collection. It itemized an illuminated English manuscript dated 1370, entitled *Horae, B.V.M.* (Hours of the Blessed Virgin Mary), and another dated 1420. The medieval missals included one with elaborate borders and illuminations dated 1460 from the Low Countries; one from Mainz in Germany dated 1483; and another from Nuremberg from 1485. There were bibles dating back to 1568, as well as the first missal printed in Rome in 1475 of which there were only three copies in the world, which would have been of particular interest to Frederick. Political documents included three original Acts of Parliament passed during the reigns of Edward VI, Queen Mary and Elizabeth I. Inevitably a copy of *The Vision of Piers Plowman* of 1550 was collected as it is set in the Malvern Hills. Frederick also bought a first edition of Dante's *Inferno*; a second edition of Shakespeare's *Comedies, Histories and Tragedies* dated 1632 and a fourth edition dated 1685. Royal bindings from Windsor Castle and the French court, twenty volumes of Loddidge's *Botanical Cabinet* and a spectacular series of volumes of Redouté's elaborate flower book, *Les Liliacées*, hand-coloured and published at the beginning of the nineteenth century, added visual flourish.

It is recorded that Frederick only attended one dinner of the Roxburghe Club but he honoured his commitment to print privately a rare manuscript and give one copy to each member of the Club and one for its library. In 1870, he presented the Roxburghe with its 93rd publication, entitled *Liber Regalis; seu Ordo Consecrandi Regem et Reginam*, a text not from the

Madresfield collection but from the Chapter Library at Westminster. The title can be loosely translated as the *Coronation Book*. This is a detailed account of early coronation ceremonials and was possibly a source book for the coronation of Richard II. It was written in clear bold hand between 1350 and 1380 on thirty-four pages of thick vellum. In his introduction, Frederick stated that the manuscript was 'one of the most precious to lovers of ancient state, and admirers of the faith and dignity of their fore-fathers'. It is not surprising that Frederick chose such a manuscript. He was a committed royalist; as Steward of the Royal Household he oversaw the minutiae of royal entertaining and ceremonial; as a pedant, no detail, however small, would have missed his discerning eye. He also proudly presented a copy of his Roxburghe volume to Queen Victoria, even though she was not a member of the Club.

Liber Regalis informs us that 'the earliest coronation of a Christian prince within the limits of Great Britain and Ireland is generally supposed to be that of Dermot or Diarmid, supreme monarch of Ireland, by his relative Columba.' This consecration ritual remained essentially unchanged from the time of Ethelred to that of George IV. The book also provides fascinating details about the weight and composition of the royal jewels. The Imperial crown, for example, weighed 7 pounds and 6 ounces and contained 320 jewels, while the Queen's crown was a more modest 3 pounds 10 ounces and held only 125 jewels. With the additional burden of the orb weighing 1 pound and 4¼ ounces, the silver-gilt sceptre of a similar weight and all his heavy robes, the monarch's progress up the aisle was necessarily ponderous. The Regalia of England were kept by the Abbot of Westminster until the dissolution of the Houses of Parliament but at the time of the Commonwealth they were dispersed, to be replaced after the Restoration by new regalia which are now kept in the Tower of London.

Membership of the Roxburghe Club was not entailed from father to son. Each generation had to earn its place, though uniquely, five consecutive generations of John Murrays, popularly remembered as being the publishers of Lord Byron, were elected. After Frederick's death, his heir, William, the seventh Earl Beauchamp, was elected to the Club in 1898, at the age of twenty-six. He not only added books to the Madresfield collection covering the traditional topics found in a nobleman's library – architecture, literature, botany, art history – but he also added many volumes on diverse contemporary subjects, from psychology, the political writings of Engels and Marx, trade union history, and Sidney and Beatrice Webb's study of Industrial Democracy to monographs on tattooing and Maori art. He also created a substantial collection of children's books, including volumes illustrated by Arthur Rackham and Kate Greenaway, among others.

While such acquisitions are evidence that the new earl had a modern outlook on life, it seems he was also drawn to the black letter books (in Gothic-style script) that his father had collected. The evidence at

Madresfield tells us that the Gothic held tremendous aesthetic appeal to him and the contents of such books – typically prayer, heraldry, medieval art, courtly practice and ancient lore – fed his romanticized notion of the Middle Ages, a time as he saw it when high principles of devotion and chivalry prevailed within the unified Christian church and from which his Norman lineage could be traced. In pride of place in William's library was a copy of Malory's *Le Morte D'Arthur* illustrated by Aubrey Beardsley from a limited edition of three hundred printed on Dutch handmade paper. He added visually stunning European and American bindings and handsomely illustrated books from William Morris's Kelmscott Press – he had almost a complete run of books they printed, for he favoured fine Arts and Crafts publications. His English taste is represented by tomes on English sixteenth- and seventeenth-century embroidery and carving, Pre-Raphaelite painting, and medieval and Gothic-revival architecture. Compared with his father's recondite interests, his tastes stretched wider and into more unexpected corners.

As his political reading widened, so his radicalism deepened – an evolution that can be traced along the bookshelves of the Library, which perfectly reflects the interests of a high-minded man of the time. In just one bookcase, for example, can be found *The Republican Tradition in Europe, The Condition of England, Labour and Protection, Education and Empire, Personal Liberty*, Charles Kingsley's *Sanitary & Social Essays*, Fabian essays on socialism by G. B. Shaw and the Webbs, *The Working Faith of the Social Reformer, Popular Government* and *Essays Upon Some Controversial Questions* by Thomas H. Huxley.

William deliberated carefully over which text to reproduce for the Roxburghe Club, but in the end he decided on the collection of Henry VIII's musical ballads.

At Madresfield, a red wax seal – a heavy circular disc the size of a clay pigeon – bearing the coat of arms of Henry VIII lies in a box in the Muniment Room. Henry VIII held a particular fascination for William: he was drawn to the Tudor king and his fascination with the pageantry and chivalry of the earlier medieval period, a fascination William shared. Henry, particularly in the first years of his reign, had taken King Arthur as his role model of kingship and he deployed the Arthurian legend to legitimize the Tudor dynasty. The Arthurian revival took two forms in the nineteenth century: during the first half it was a moral crusade for church, king and the chivalric return to principle over expediency, but by the end of this century it had evolved into a romantic and aesthetic movement, reaching its apotheosis in the Pre-Raphaelite and Arts and Crafts movements. While Frederick had inclined towards the earlier interpretation of medievalism, his son was drawn to the later one.

As a prince of the Renaissance, Henry received a careful education in the principal fields of learning, which included music. He became an accomplished musician and prolific composer, and it was these skills that William, Earl Beauchamp, would celebrate four hundred years later in his private publication for the Roxbughe Club in 1923. *Songs, Ballads and Instrumental Pieces Composed by King Henry the Eighth* includes an introduction, all of the monarch's extant musical compositions – scores and lyrics – and a record of the musicians of his court and their instruments, such as single and double regalles, virginal, clavichord, lute, flute, recorder, cornet and gitteron.

The editing project, which took nearly ten years, was undertaken on William's behalf by his oldest sister, the fastidious and musically gifted Mary, who was serving as lady-in-waiting to Queen Mary and was granted access to the Royal Archive. She wrote the pithy introduction to the collection in which, for example, she discriminates between 'charming' and 'archaic' pieces, and contrasts Thomas Cromwell's fawning comments on the king's compositions with the more robust opinions offered by Erasmus or the Venetian ambassador, Falieri. The views of the scholar and the diplomat should, she advises the reader, be given more weight as they 'are not inspired by loyalty, but are candid expressions of admiration from men who are not English subjects'.

One of William's other notable contributions to his fellow members – who included at the time three dukes, two marquesses, seven earls, one bishop, five lords and a future prime minister – was an exhibition, in 1931, of modern American printing, organized in conjunction with the San Francisco Roxburghe Club.

After William, the third member of the Lygon family

to join the Roxburghe was William's son, Viscount Elmley, later the eighth earl. In 1975, he chose to print a facsimile of the Madresfield Book of Hours for the Club members. It was the only Lygon publication for the Roxburghe to be reprinted from an original in their own library. James Stourton, now a member of the Roxburghe himself but seventeen years old at the time, recalls meeting the eighth earl at Madresfield soon after his host's Roxburghe edition was published. The grand gentleman sitting behind the high bureau eagerly enquired of the boy, 'Have you seen my new book? I wrote it.' He was pointing to *The Madresfield Book of Hours*. The earl was no scholar and, as his obituary in *The Times* diplomatically expressed it, he possessed 'a rare simplicity of character'.

All three Lygon publications for the Roxburghe were decidedly English in their subject matter. Rather than offering facsimiles of Continental scholarship or literature, they selected texts which illuminated an episode, a trait or a ritual in England's history.

The Roxburghe Club members still regard it as the 'most exclusive club in the world' though today membership can be roughly divided into one-third aristocrats, one-third scholars, such as the Keeper of Manuscripts at the British Museum, and one-third wealthy but non-aristocratic individuals, such as the late Jean Paul Getty, who have created unique libraries.

Over a century after Frederick's death, the Madresfield Book of Hours was sold to Jean Paul Getty. Today it can be found one hundred miles away from

Madresfield at Wormsley in Buckinghamshire, the home of Mark Getty, son of the great book collector. Behind Getty's Georgian home stand a stack of rough-hewn rocks balanced high into the sky. This modern purpose-built galleried library is a masterfully realized fantasy entered by pushing through a curtain of sixty-foot-high creepers hanging from the roof of a rock tunnel. It conjures up the entrance to the secret headquarters of an Ian Fleming villain. It is in this neo-Gothic library lined with Arts and Crafts-style oak bookcases that Frederick's treasured manuscript now resides. Its loss to the Lygon family is compensated for by the fact that the proceeds were used to repair one-third of Madresfield's two-acre roof.

Chapter Nine

THE TUNING FORK

For two decades the piano tuner W. H. Elgar, whose carefree charm had won many county clients including the musically discerning Beauchamps, had come out from Worcester twice a year to service the three grand pianos, two spinets and the Chapel organ at Madresfield Court. In contrast to the run-of-the-mill tradesman in a horse and cart, Mr Elgar usually rode out to his appointments on a thoroughbred and made a day of it. On one June morning in 1867, however, he travelled to the Court in the family cart, pulled by Jack, a white pony. He was accompanied by his son, Edward, who was absent-mindedly blowing on the ivory whistle chained to his father's waistcoat. It was his tenth birthday. As soon as the vehicle turned into Madresfield's smooth gravel drive, Edward Elgar fell silent, gazing up at the mansion's jagged roofscape set against the Malvern Hills beyond. The cart had passed along the Back Drive, which skirted the orchards, entered the yard and scattered chickens as it pulled up alongside the Bridge of Sighs. Crossing the bridge, the tuner and his son were admitted into the tradesman's entrance of the 160-roomed mansion and, passing through the Servants' Hall, they were escorted up the black-painted oak staircase and into the Long Gallery. There Mr Elgar carefully placed his tool bag on the parquet, walked towards the piano standing in the bay window overlooking the park, laid his tuning fork down on its polished ebony lid and inspected the keys.

Meanwhile, the young Edward – mindful of the liveried footman standing motionless, like a Nutcracker, in the shadows – circled the piano surveying the different views of the enormous room, sixty paces long, in which he stood. Huge Kangxi-blue and Emperor-yellow Chinese vases stood proud against the dark oak panelling, brass jardinières threw back at him his distorted reflection and the plasterwork ceiling formed a giant draughtboard high above his head. On the far wall, sabres and épées hung in geometric groupings and beneath his feet lay rugs from the Orient. He sidled along the panelling towards an ebony and brass display cabinet. Beneath his gaze lay curios labelled 'a lock of Mr Pitt's hair', 'a lock of the Duke of Wellington's hair' and 'a white bullet from the neck of Captain The Honourable H. B. Lygon'. The boy might have appreciated their relevance to the Lygons: Pitt the Younger had sold the family an earldom to help finance the Napoleonic Wars and Henry Lygon, the fourth earl, had fought under the Iron Duke in the Peninsular Wars and was shot in the neck at the battle of Busaco in September 1810. A second, satinwood cabinet was arranged with the booty of colonial adventures: marble-sized jewels embedded in the jade and rock crystal hilts of Indian daggers; an Indian jade hookah; an ivory elephant whip and a pair of eighteenth-century Persian ivory flintlock pistols. For the Lygons, they recorded two brothers defending the Empire. For the boy, perhaps they reminded him of the cuttings on Indian art that his mother pasted into her scrapbooks.

Looking out from the windows overlooking the Moat Garden, Edward would have witnessed the architect Hardwick's work in progress and possibly the finishing touch being hoisted up on to the water tower: a massive lead gargoyle of a dragon, which seems to creep stealthily down the tiles towards the unwary sitting a hundred feet below in the Moat Garden.

Once the piano had been tuned, the boy ran his skinny fingers adroitly up and down in some arpeggios, paused, took a deep breath, and began Beethoven's First Symphony, his favourite. He played with precocious aplomb. It would be more than a decade before he returned to the Long Gallery, where he would find a slim-waisted girl with a serious air practising her scales. She was Lady Mary Lygon, the musical eldest child of Frederick, sixth Earl Beauchamp, and she was to become one of his favourite pupils.

Elgar's father had served a musical apprenticeship at Coventry & Hollier in Dean Street, Soho, and then in 1841 had moved to the small but musically important city of Worcester, attracted by the renowned Three Choirs Festival, and had opened a music shop in the shadow of the cathedral. The piano tuner played on some of the finest pianos in the county and was a violinist in various amateur orchestras and at the Three Choirs Festival. Though an Anglican, he had been appointed organist for St George's, the city's Roman Catholic church, and his wife Ann converted in 1852. Ann Elgar was an unusual woman. The busy wife of a modest tradesman and the mother of seven children, she was well read and thoughtful, finding time to write poetry, paint and study the natural world. The landscape in which she raised her children was intrinsic to their sensibilities; she had taught them to savour its details and seasonal changes.

City life did not suit her. Yearning for the countryside, just before her fifth child Edward was born in 1857 she persuaded her husband to load up their pony and cart and move to an idyllic cottage of six little rooms at Broadheath, just ten miles from Madresfield. On weekdays Mr Elgar boarded in Worcester, and at the end of each week his children strained to hear the high pitch of his ivory whistle calling from the lane to announce his homecoming. Within two years, however, the family had returned to live above the shop. Nevertheless, Mrs Elgar maintained her links with the hamlet and holidays were spent back at Broadheath. The journey out of the city and over the iron-railinged bridge which spanned the River Severn became an abiding memory for young Elgar. There at Broadheath he played summer music on makeshift stringed instruments cobbled together from lengths of gut from the shop. As he grew older, he made solitary visits to that countryside across the river.

When young Elgar could escape duties behind the counter or play truant, one of his favourite pastimes was to borrow a score, stuff his pockets with bread and cheese and head out to the banks of the Severn or the silent churchyard of St John the Baptist at Claines, just north of the city. Sitting amongst the bluebells and cow parsley, he would scrutinize the music he had brought. The Worcestershire fields were his conservatoire. From the age of ten, about the time he first visited Madresfield with his father, he began composing. Like his mother, he was moved by the wonder of nature and strove to capture her sounds. Composing became an open-air activity for him. He practised fixing the 'music' of the countryside – perhaps inspired by the staccato strike of the woodpecker's beak against a tree, the king-fisher's halcyon trill, the thrush's vibrato song, the hypnotic adagio of summer breezes pushing though riverside reeds, the momentous crescendo of a waterfall.

On his father's piano-tuning rounds he had glimpsed the aristocratic world and yet as he entered adolescence this 'most miserable-looking lad', a Catholic son of a tradesman, felt the full weight of social condescension. Anti-Catholic prejudice had escalated in England in the middle of the nineteenth century as waves of Irish Catholics, fleeing the potato famines of the 1840s, settled in England. The month that the ten-year-old Edward had accompanied his father to tune the instruments at Madresfield, June 1867, an anti-Catholic meeting in Birmingham, just twenty miles east, had degenerated into rioting which was eventually broken up by sabre-wielding police. But the conservative cathedral city of Worcester, where the established Anglican Church coloured social and, more particularly, musical life, was a spur to Elgar's ambitions.

Elgar left school in 1872 and pieced together a sheaf of musical jobs: helping in the shop, standing in for his father in the organ loft at St George's and playing in provincial orchestras. He also tutored violin and piano students, a task he later compared to 'turning a grindstone with a dislocated shoulder'. Aged twenty-two, he successfully applied for a more challenging post as bandmaster of the Worcester City & County Pauper Lunatic Asylum. Every Friday, from 1877 to 1884, he travelled the four miles from Worcester south to Powick, on the Madresfield estate, where he conducted the asylum's orchestra and composed small pieces for the staff to play. This enlightened programme for the entertainment of the inmates was ahead of its time.

In the Victorian home the piano, or 'the household god', was as common an object as the dresser, whether it was a grand piano in the imposing drawing room of a country house or an upright in a modest parlour. It was regarded as an object of gentrification – even moral edification. Genteel and musically minded Worcestershire had no shortage of young ladies who wished to burnish their charms under Mr Elgar's musical instruction. Elgar counted Mary Lygon amongst his private pupils. She was twelve years his junior and, according to her niece Sibell, he enjoyed coming 'out from Worcester twice a week to give her lessons. He was devoted to her.' Though initially the relationship was formal, she was never condescending to him and a lifelong friendship began, based on their shared passion for music.

From an early age, Mary had shown herself to be both authoritative and diplomatic. When her brother William, Frederick's heir, was born, a family friend observed that though the three-year-old girl was no longer the centre of attention, she showed every sign of keeping 'him under her slipper' for many years to come. A few years later, she and her four siblings had to adjust to the premature death of their mother in childbirth and in time the arrival of a stepmother and four half-siblings. While William and his brother Edward intensely disliked their stepmother and retreated together into their own world, Mary, who was as uncomfortable with the situation as they were, managed to steer a more tactful course. She found solace in music and during her adolescence she harnessed this love to her developing organizational skills and philanthropic instincts and founded one choir at the village church and another at the Industrial School for Girls which her stepmother had established in the village. At home, the poised and serious-minded Mary marshalled her siblings – eight in total – into plays, concerts and mini-operas and organized them together with the servants in a twice-daily sung service in the family chapel. Guests dining in the Great Hall were entertained with Mary's musical concerts performed in the minstrels' gallery above by the family choir, who would be joined by any musical servants – once they had finished serving dinner. They sang from sheet music ordered from their local music shop, that of Elgar's father, and the programmes, now in the Muniment Room, show that Mary shared her music teacher's love for the Continental compositions of, among others, Bach, Brahms, Delibes and Gounod.

Elgar periodically descended into depressions – what he called his 'black dog' – which were prompted by concerns over money, social status, professional recognition and the relentless treadmill of teaching. Fortunately, another pupil had stepped into his life in October 1886. Miss [Caroline] Alice Roberts, a thirty-seven-year-old spinster, was nearly nine years older than Elgar. Every week, she travelled to Malvern from Redmarley d'Abitot in Gloucestershire to take music lessons with him and it was not long before the coachman suspected there was more to the relationship than music. Perhaps Elgar recognized some of his mother's qualities in Alice. Both women were passionate amateur poets and utterly convinced of his genius. Alice's had been a rigidly class-conscious and patrician upbringing. Her father, the late General Sir Henry Gee Roberts, was a hero of the Indian Mutiny of 1857, the year of Elgar's birth. Like many India hands of his day,

General Roberts had amassed a collection of Indian memorabilia – weapons, trophies and carved ebony furniture inlaid with ivory – which Alice, his sole heir, brought to the marital home. Perhaps they reminded Elgar of the glass showcase of Indian treasures he had seen as a boy at Madresfield. For Elgar, Alice offered companionship, love, advancement and a focus for his ambition. She also enjoyed private means.

Elgar's in-laws spurned him while Alice distanced herself from his family since their rank in society did not accord with her ambitions for him. In May 1889 they were married, on neutral territory, at the Oratory in London. The couple had one child, a daughter called Carice, and Alice devoted herself to her husband's advancement.

As the daughter of an earl, his pupil Mary's own marriage prospects were extremely promising. Photographs of this clever, attractive young woman suggest a disciplined, almost prim character. Her firm-set mouth and erect carriage hint at an independence of mind. Eschewing marriage proposals, she committed herself to a demanding position at court and to the needs of her unmarried brother, William, for whom she acted as confidante and organizer of his busy social and political schedule. Though suitors came and went – including a proposal in December 1893 from Lord Digby – Mary preferred her independence.

Mary was now moving in royal circles. In 1895, aged twenty-six, she was appointed a lady-in-waiting to the Duchess of Teck, and then to her daughter, Princess

Devoted brother and sister: William Lygon, the seventh Earl Beauchamp, and Lady Mary Lygon, Elgar's Thirteenth Enigma *and lady-in-waiting to Queen Mary.*

Victoria Mary, who was married to Prince George, the Duke of York. Princess May, as she was known, had first met Mary in the autumn of 1891 in Malvern while visiting the spa and surrounding country houses. In 1901, after the death of Queen Victoria, May became the Princess of Wales and moved to Marlborough House; in 1910 she became Queen Mary on the accession of her husband as George V. Mary served her for thirty-two years. Court life was rigidly hierarchical. As lady-in-waiting, Mary had been permitted to travel around in a single-horse brougham provided by the royal stables. Her promotion to Woman of the Bedchamber was registered by an upgrade in vehicle: a two-horse brougham. As the princess's companion, Mary dealt with her correspondence, organized her appointments, played the piano for her and read to her. In a constant migration with the royal household between the many royal residences in England and Scotland and on state visits or holidays abroad, Mary could not be at Madresfield as often as she wished. In the spring of 1896, for example, the Yorks (as they were then called) represented the royal family at various family weddings on the Continent. They left England on 14 April and did not return for a month. From Coburg, Mary wrote to her mistress's mother, the Duchess of Teck: '. . . the [German] Empress [Queen Victoria's eldest daughter] wore a flame-coloured velvet dress, embroidered in gold. Her Royal Highness [Princess May] wore a pink dress embroidered in silver: and her diamonds looked magnificent.' Prince George and Princess May upheld the custom of always dining with an equerry and a lady-in-waiting in attendance and, consequently, were rarely alone together. Mary's tact and devotion proved invaluable to the couple's private life as well as to their public duties. This role took her deep into the heart of the court for the last years of Victoria's reign and the whole of Edward VII's, a connection from which her old music teacher was to benefit immensely.

Mary had matured into a handsome woman of strong opinions. Devoted to her brother and writing to him almost daily – she was known to compose up to eighty personal and administrative letters a day – she communicates the tedium of being 'in waiting' to the royals. She had as little as two hours a day to herself which explains why one letter in January 1896 'is being written from HRH's dentist!' On 8 January 1897, for example, she tells 'Dearest Willie' that she spent the day 'sticking 160 bookplates into some of the Duke's books', and that there was 'absolutely *no* news!' Another day was passed reading to Princess May for three hours. Longing to be by her brother's side at Madresfield, she confessed that 'I am really becoming sentimental in my old age but I really do miss you horribly! There's an admission . . . wish that you were either here or that I was at Madresfield – the latter by Choice!' She was concerned if he was alone for more than two days and wished that she had wings so that she could fly to his side for a couple of hours.

From afar, she took great interest in Madresfield's

redecoration, ordering samples for him from William Morris, advising him on colours and budgets. 'How does the maple furniture look?' she asked him in a letter from Sandringham on 26 October 1895. 'Is the oak panelling outside Eddie's room yet? What a posse of questions!' She discussed servants' wages, guest lists for house parties, ways to economize and to circumvent their stepmother. Planning a house party for the Duke and Duchess of Connaught at Madresfield, Mary wrote to her brother:

I think it excellent, especially as Arthur [the Duke] (who went to White Lodge yesterday) says they are longing to get away somewhere. I will do my very best to urge it. If expense is Mamma's objection, and you still wish to do it, I don't see why you should not agree to refund her for it, next year. It would be much better for the servants than doing nothing all the time.

Throughout the 1890s Mary had continued to organize concerts, as she had done when she was a child, but now she invited the public to them; in November 1890, for example, she had hosted one for the Church of England Working Men's Society. They provided a showcase for the ten choirs she had gathered from their estate villages – 230 voices and 29 instruments – conducted by her with considerable skill.

It was in these Worcestershire circles that Elgar continued to encounter his former pupil, despite her peripatetic life. Mary was adept at persuading people to contribute their time and talents to her concerts, determined as she was to provide a good musical education for the local people: at her request, in 1893, Elgar conducted two of his own compositions for one of her programmes. Some years later, Mary wrote to Elgar saying she was glad that 'In country districts . . . standards of taste in matters musical does improve each year a little.'

A silk picture embroidered by Mary hangs in William's bedroom in the Tudor part of Madresfield. It is entitled *Madresfield Musical Competition*. The collage features a satin ribbon held up by finches and warblers which is embroidered with the statement, 'Music is a great and glorious gift of God'. It was from a concert in 1896 that she evolved the annual Madresfield Musical Competitions which soon developed into a countywide event. Mary was a pioneer of the musical festival movement in Britain but Elgar confided to a friend that initially her competitions had infuriated him because he was not consulted over music to be played, despite being a leading musician in the area.

The programmes for the various Madresfield concerts and entertainments that she organized show that, as well as promoting music amongst the members of the community, she was concerned to raise money for her good causes. For example, a garden party was planned for 15 April 1898 at Madresfield in honour of the National Union of Teachers, featuring the Civil-Military Band of Worcester directed by Elgar's younger brother, Frank. On 3 April 1898 Elgar replied to Mary from his home, Forli, in Malvern:

Dear Lady Mary Lygon, The whole of my northern expedition is put off & so I am free on the day of your Concert & will come, if you still wish it, to conduct the two trios. I would prefer to have the largest number of voices you can feel confident in: & <u>all</u> the violins possible. (In London we had 15 vios: to 30 voices). As you are kind enough to ask my opinion I think the lady who plays for you – Miss Burley – wd. render the accompts better than anyone else here. Believe me, very faithfully yours, Edward Elgar.

She replied by return:

Dear Mr Elgar, Thank you for your letter. I am VERY glad that you will be in Malvern on the 28th and it is most kind of you to say that you will help us at the concert by conducting the trios. I will try and get as good a choir as I can . . . I should also much like, if I may, to go over the trios once with you first. I could come any morning (except Thursday) next week – at any time that would suit you – or on Monday or Tuesday afternoons . . . unless it should be more convenient for you to come here – as we should much like to show you and Mrs. Elgar our garden which is rather nice just now – with all the spring flowers out. In that case will you come to luncheon next Thursday or Sunday?

To open the garden party, Elgar's 'March Imperial' was performed, followed by a selection of Continental compositions by Schubert, Gounod, Strauss and Boccherini. Part One was played 'In the Rocks' – the rock garden to the west of the house – and Part Two took place 'Near the House', overlooking the moat filled with geese, mallards, mandarins and wood duck followed by their newly hatched ducklings. The programme described to the guests the structure and planting of the gardens, based around a triangle of avenues: one cedar, one elm and one of *Picea glauca*, 'an avenue unique in this country'. Where the cedar and spruce avenues met, a clump of cottage garden flowers, called crown imperial (*Fritillaria imperialis*) were planted by Mary's brother. As the son of a leading figure in the Oxford Movement and a devoutly religious man, William, now the seventh Earl Beauchamp, would have been aware of the legend surrounding these modest flowers. They were said to be the only ones in the Garden of Gethsemane not to bow their heads in reverence as Christ passed by. They subsequently repented of their pride and bow their heads in perpetual shame, tears of regret hanging from inside their orange petalled bells. The teachers were invited to explore the maze, laid out in celebration of William's succession, and the wild garden. The rose garden was set against a semi-circle of pleached lime and adorned with a small marble statue and a sundial, placed there the previous year and carved with a motto: 'That day is wasted on which we have not laughed'.

As a prominent member of the Worcestershire Philharmonic, a choral and orchestral body founded in

1897 as a vehicle for Elgar's conducting, Mary regularly met him there. Their first concert was held in May 1898, and Mary suggested to Winifred Norbury, the joint honorary secretary, that 'it would be rather nice to do something of Tchaikovsky and with that and Dvorak, Dr. Penny and Mr. Elgar on our programme, we shall be very advanced.'

In the autumn of 1898, Mary prevailed upon Elgar to compose a piece for her Magpie Musical Society. 'We only sing unaccompanied madrigals – from Palestrina . . . down to modern times: and Mr. [Lionel] Benson [the conductor] very much wishes to have something from you, and if possible, a five part song – with two soprano parts – you will be surprised to hear – we have more women than men!' In her tactfully persuasive manner, she added that the society was a 'favoured body' since C. H. H. Parry, Charles Stanford and George Henschel had all written pieces especially for it 'and it will be very kind of you if you will also confer this distinction upon us'.

Elgar, now living at Birchwood Lodge, near Malvern, replied on 14 November 1898:

Dear Lady Mary Lygon, We are at our cottage & I am 'doing' much music which is <u>contracted for</u>. I hope however to find time to write the part song for your society: words are a difficulty – if you could suggest some I shd be glad: I have piles of poets, major & minor, but I have found nothing which suggests music – 5 pt music – yet.

Plaintively, he added, 'It is very sad that the philharmonic must continue to miss you – we <u>do</u> miss you very much indeed.'

Elgar's charm attracted many other women, who flocked about him: Winifred Norbury, her sister Florence, Isabel Fitton and Dora Penny, who helped him correct proofs or accompanied him on walks and later, once he had learned to ride a bicycle, on cycle rides too – up to fifty miles a day. Conscious of being almost a decade older than her husband, Alice indulged his friendships with other women, including Mary Lygon. It is clear from correspondence and musical programmes that Elgar devoted considerable energy to Mary's musical events. Perhaps he was a little in love with her.

Even now, in 1898, the forty-one-year-old Elgar was still dependent on teaching, which distracted him from his true calling: composition. He was so frustrated that his compositions were not earning much money that on the bottom of his score for *Cockaigne* he quoted from *Piers Plowman*: 'meatless and moneyless on Malvern Hill'. On returning home from his round of musical duties, Elgar would stride about his study, placing sheets of a manuscript around the room, propped up against chair backs or balanced on the mantelpiece. Periodically, like a fencer jabbing at his opponent, he would step forward to make a correction or an addition to the score. One October evening that year when he came home from a day's teaching, Alice noticed that he was particularly low. She gave him dinner and suggested that he relax with a cigar. In a little while, lost in a trance of exhaustion, he started to run his fingers over the piano keys.

'Edward, that's a good tune . . . play it again, I like that tune,' Alice urged him.

'Tune, what tune?' he asked.

Alice retrieved her husband from his reverie. 'What is it?'

'It's nothing, but something might be made of it,' he conceded. He replayed the 'nothing' and it pleased him. It would become the 'Enigma Variations', the first piece that earned him enduring fame.

The Variations were Elgar's tribute 'to my friends pictured within'. Elgar loved riddles and pranks and this score began as a pleasing in-joke to be shared amongst his intimates. Each of the thirteen variations conjured up a mood or an incident associated, in his mind, with a friend. Number one, 'C.A.E.', for example, was a 'romantic and delicate' tribute to his wife, Alice; number six, 'Ysobel', was inspired by his student Isabel Fitton, as she worked to master the viola; the Malvern architect Arthur Troyte Griffith's maladroit piano playing was parodied in variation number seven, entitled 'Troyte'. Number eight, 'W.N.', recalls his friend Winifred Norbury and her gracious eighteenth-century house. Elgar's publisher, August Jaeger, is present in a remembered conversation about Beethoven: the opening bars call to mind the slow movement of Beethoven's Eighth Sonata, the 'Pathétique'. His variation, number nine, is entitled 'Nimrod' because *Jaeger* is hunter in

German. Elgar was an inspired miniaturist; these exquisite snapshots of each character are as precious and precise as the portrait miniatures hanging in the Drawing Room at Madresfield. The identity of the friend portrayed in the last variation, number thirteen – cryptically marked *** in the manuscript – would remain a mystery until the work became so famous that the asterisks began to excite considerable speculation. Elgar later revealed in a letter to Jaeger, without naming anyone, that they 'take the place of a name of a pretty lady who was, at the time of the composition, on a sea voyage. The drums suggest the distant throb of the engines of a liner over which the clarinet turns a phrase from Mendelssohn's "Calm Sea and Prosperous Voyage"'.

Elgar joined the waving crowds that stood at Worcester's Foregate Street station on 10 April 1899 to wish the local grandee Earl Beauchamp and his sister Lady Mary Godspeed to New South Wales where he was to serve as Governor. As they stepped up to their private train to the cheers of local well-wishers, the composer presented Mary with a farewell bouquet of wild spring and hedgerow flowers: cyclamen, meadow saffron, pussy willow and tiny daffodils.

During her five-month stay in New South Wales Mary played hostess for her brother at Government House in Sydney. She continued to spread her belief in the power and importance of music and opened the Governor's residence to people from all walks of life for musical evenings. The Australians recognized Mary as 'no mean musician' as she took the piano part in a quartet 'with taste and excellent tempo' and they saluted her efforts to reinstate music as a regular feature of life in Government House. 'Every girl with a voice, or a touch, goes up to warble, or execute to Lady Mary, whose amicable opinions, alas!, are just a little too uniformly commendatory for the good of the people who only listen and pay', read a rather sniffy report in the *Sydney Daily Telegraph* of July 1899. As at Madresfield, she organized choirs, sponsored competitions and wove music into the fabric of daily life at Government House. She endeared herself to the press by making it clear that she was neither a cyclist nor a believer in women's suffrage. Asked by a lady journalist in Sydney whether she cycled, she replied in a decided tone, 'No. I am old-fashioned in that respect. I don't like it.' 'This will', another journalist predicted, 'ensure her popularity with many people in Sydney, where it is said to be quite refreshing to discover a young lady who is free of any yearning to make the pace either with a bicycle or a political pamphlet.'

By the time she departed on 29 September 1899, the Australian press unanimously acknowledged that she had conducted her duties with tact and elegance and devoted herself to charitable works, with true Lygon conviction, 'without distinction of sect'. She had also underwritten the expense of the Schools' Musical Competition held in the Town Hall. 'These are the things which will make us miss Lady Mary Lygon.'

Soon after Mary returned from Australia, Elgar took up boomerang throwing, a pastime he shared with his lady friends. The sight of a party of tweed-clad Victorians tossing an Aboriginal weapon must have been arresting. Who had introduced the composer to it? In her account of another voyage to the Antipodes, Mary wrote, 'An additional interest here is given by the Aboriginees, a weird, stunted race, who are slowly dying out. They gathered together in a "corroborree" and gave an exhibition of boomerang throwing, a dangerous mode of warfare, and one almost inexplicable to the modern scientist.' While in Australia, her brother – echoing their ancestor Richard Ligon's concern for the Negro on Barbados – had taken up the cause of these people, founding a society for their protection. Today, on the wall of the minstrels' gallery in the Great Hall, behind the fraying regimental banners that hang from flagpoles over the balustrade, there is an unusual decorative device: a group of boomerangs. Like many objects at Madresfield, these plain wooden circumflexes accent another episode in the Lygon family history.

On Mary's return from Australia, Elgar wrote to her on 25 November 1899, about another work entitled 'Three Characteristic Pieces', which he had dedicated to her.

Dear Lady Mary Lygon, We are so very glad to know you are safely back & please do not begin to talk of returning to NSW or even to think of it. Regarding the MMC [Madresfield Musical Competition] I need not say that I shall be really delighted to be of any service in the good cause & will, of course, be honoured by a place on the Committee being found for me . . . I am so very glad that you like your little pieces: they are being played but the <u>full scores</u> are only now printing – this retards their progress.

He would have been frustrated at the delay in printing: in a letter to Jaeger, dated 24 March 1899, he had urged his publisher: 'I want to know if you get the *title* done *very* soon as Lady Mary is going away & I should like her to see it first . . . She is a most angelic person & I should like to please her.' Mary had just taken tea with him at his new house, Craeg Lea, on that day and he had sought her permission for the dedication. He had then written to her from Craeg Lea on 31 March but the letter had not caught her before she sailed. It read: 'Dear Lady Mary Lygon, I felt so guilty after asking you about the dedication the other day that I have made the printer send a proof so that you may see it before you leave: please tell me if you wd: prefer anything altered. I need not repeat what I said as to the extreme pleasure it gives.'

Elgar's phrasing in both letters is warm, even unguarded, yet he had been discreet over the identity of the inspiration for the thirteenth enigma variation and while Mary had been abroad, controversy had raged over the three asterisks. On 22 February 1899, shortly before the Variations' publication and her departure for Australia, Mary had written to her brother: 'My dearest William, I . . . then went to see the Elgars who are most pleasant. He has written some big orchestra theme and

The swan from the Beauchamp family crest, a nineteenth-century oil painting that hangs in the small Dining Room.

The twelfth-century outer doors to Madresfield, which do not have handles: the house has never been left unattended.

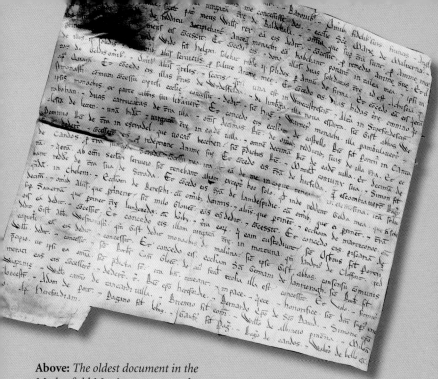

Above: *The oldest document in the Madresfield Muniments – a parchment charter issued in 1121 by Henry I, the Conqueror's son, granting land for the foundation of Malvern Priory.*

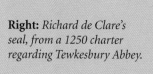

Right: *Richard de Clare's seal, from a 1250 charter regarding Tewkesbury Abbey.*

MADRESFIELD COURT, THE SEAT OF THE EARL OF BEAUCHAMP.

Thou nurse of my manhood how oft have I strayed ,
O'er thy lawns, and thy meadows, in sun and in shade ;
And though I no longer am domiciled here ,
To my heart will sweet Madresfield ever be dear ;

And with joy through my life I could wander about ;
'Its gardens, its shrubberies, its walks and its moat ,
Till with aid of my fancy, loved nymph, I could feign ,
The days I so valued, were with me again .

The red heels: William Jennens, whose
legacy endowed the Lygons with a
fortune, c. 1710 by Charles Jervais.

The ambitious Catherine Denne,
wife of the first Earl Beauchamp,
fashionably dressed à la turque.

Madresfield viewed from the moat, with Philip Hardwick's neo-Gothic tower complete with gargoyles and dragon.

The Long Gallery, sixty paces in length, where Elgar's father tuned the pianos.

C. R. Ashbee's Guild of Handicrafts carved the bookends and doors of the Library with biblical themes.

One of the two dozen flame-stitch bargello *chairs embroidered by the seventh earl in exile.*

LORD I AM NOT WORTHY THAT
YOU SHOULD ENTER MY HOUSE

*The stained-glass window outside the Chapel shows a penitent
Beauchamp kneeling before Christ: this image, commissioned
shortly after his marriage, is a premonition of his later disgrace.*

The Chapel, one of the greatest rooms of the Arts and Crafts movement and a tender paean to family life. This fresco detail shows Hugh and Elmley as children, and the model for the angel was their nanny.

Evelyn Waugh often sat at this Nursery window to write in the early 1930s.

The Staircase Hall is three storeys high and crowned with three glass cupolas. A stanza from Shelley's Adonais is carved into the frieze.

UNTIL DEATH TRAMPLES IT TO FRAGMENTS THE ONE REMAINS, THE MANY CHANGE AND PASS:

variations and each of the latter portrays a friend. I am called "Incognita" but I only heard this today – as he is too shy to tell me and he would not play them.'

The 'pretty lady on a sea voyage' whom Elgar had referred to in his letter to his publisher, Jaeger, was clearly Mary. His close friend Dora Penny considered that, in his mind, the asterisks stood for 'My Sweet Mary'. Why was he so bashful about the dedication? Did he consider it to be too private to reveal to the public? The wording 'My Sweet Mary' is a surprisingly intimate acknowledgement of his friendship with his former pupil and benefactor.

After much cavilling by critics, Elgar finally put the matter effectively beyond doubt in his manuscript notes of 1927 for the pianola roll issue of the Variations. He specified that 'the asterisks take the place of the name of Lady Mary Lygon', his thirteenth enigma. This revelation made his Variations a shade less enigmatic but undoubtedly more prestigious.

Jaeger was alert to the significance of the Variations and, through his recommendation, Hans Richter agreed to conduct its premiere on 19 June 1899 in London. Mary had been at Elgar's house on the day that the score was sent to Richter's agent. Richter's endorsement secured a mass audience for Edward Elgar as it had achieved thirty years earlier for Wagner's *Tannhäuser*. The critics were unanimous in their praise. Here was an English composer of rare distinction. Gustav Holst commented that '1880 is usually given as the date of the "Modern Renaissance" in English music.

For me, it began about twenty years later when I first knew Elgar's Enigma Variations. I felt that here was music the like of which had not appeared in this country since Purcell's death.'

Alongside a first-edition copy of the Variations in the bookcase in the Staircase Hall at Madresfield there is a leather-bound edition of Elgar's oratorio *The Dream of Gerontius*. It is inscribed in the composer's exuberant handwriting to Mary's brother William and his new wife, Lady Lettice Grosvenor: 'To Lord and Lady Beauchamp with every good wish, from Edward Elgar'. Elgar had been working on *Gerontius* between 1899 and 1900. It is hauntingly beautiful and arguably his greatest work, written 'from his very *soul*'. The mystical *Gerontius* is a journey from this world to the next. It takes our story back to the period when the Oxford Movement – a movement in which, as we have seen, Mary's father Frederick played his part – was challenging the Church of England establishment. Elgar based the libretto on Cardinal John Henry Newman's monumental, nine-hundred-line poem of the same name. Newman, one of the movement's leaders prior to his conversion to Roman Catholicism, had written the poem in the 1860s, following the death of a close friend. It imagines the point of death at which the soul departs the body to meet its maker and learn His Judgement. A copy of this poem was given to Elgar and his bride on their wedding day by their parish priest.

Elgar gave expression to Catholicism in a way that no English composer had done since William Byrd three

Edward Elgar in 1903 with his bicycle, 'Mr Phoebus' (a pun on Sunbeam, the manufacturer).

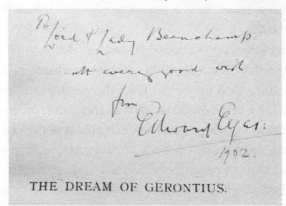

First edition of The Dream of Gerontius *inscribed by Elgar to the Earl and Countess Beauchamp.*

centuries earlier. He could create this convincing evocation of suffering because he himself was deeply depressed. His 'black dog' had returned. After much hard work, and despite critical acclaim, he was 'at the end of [his] financial tether'. He had failed to achieve the recognition that he craved. The Elgars remained uneasily in social limbo and his friend Rosa Burley, headmistress of the Mount School, detected an 'ungovernable resentment' in him. During 1900, Alice was so alarmed by her husband's state of mind that she steered away from any conversations about death, particularly suicide, for fear of exacerbating his depression. Physically exhausted, Elgar finally finished *Gerontius* on 3 August 1900 and, realizing that it was his masterpiece, he added a quotation from John Ruskin's *Sesame and Lilies* to the score: 'This is the best of me; for the rest, I ate, and drank, and slept, loved and hated, like another; my life was as the vapour, and is not; but *this* I saw and knew: this, if anything of mine, is worth your memory.'

But *Gerontius* received a disastrous début in October 1900 – on hearing it, Stanford opined that it 'stinks of incense' – and it was not until the piece was played in 1901 and 1902 at Düsseldorf that it won recognition. *Gerontius* soon became one of the most popular choral works in Britain, though it was not acclaimed in London until it was heard in June 1903 at Westminster Cathedral. Mary was present and wrote to congratulate Elgar. 'How splendid Gerontius was at Westminster. And the most gratifying thing must have been the inability of the audience to applaud at the end: they just went away quietly and reverently.'

Mary had been travelling again. She set sail from Portsmouth on 16 March 1901 on her third trip to the Antipodes in as many years, accompanying Prince George, the Duke of York, and his wife May of Teck, who had been invited to open the first Federal Parliament at Melbourne. She spent the next five months serving as lady-in-waiting and travelling via Gibraltar, Malta, Port Said, Colombo and Singapore, to Australia and New Zealand and then on to Mauritius, South Africa and Canada. They sailed on the P. & O. liner *Ophir*, temporarily commissioned by the Royal Navy and entirely refurbished for the royal party. At each stage as they circumnavigated the globe they were met by squadrons of ships from the Royal Navy. 'A great many of us do not realize that the ships of the English Navy form a huge belt round the Empire, and therefore round the world,' Mary wrote in a four-part account of the trip which was published in the *Madresfield Agricultural Club's Quarterly* on her return nearly eight months later. '. . . and as in turn we met, and were escorted by the different squadrons, we could realize why for many centuries this Service has been one of the great glories of our country.' The royal party was in mourning for Queen Victoria and consequently could not attend state balls or dinners and was instructed to wear black at all times. An exception was mercifully made in the tropics and on board ship, where a more informal mourning palette of grey and white was permitted. 'Toques', Mary had explained in a letter to her sister Margaret, Lady Ampthill on 26 February 1901, 'are a great difficulty – as there is so little variety in *all* black ones.'

During this trip, the Duchess of York rose to her royal duties with charm and confidence. 'Her Royal Highness has quite got over all her shyness abroad and almost enjoys a procession,' Mary wrote to her sister. 'Her smile is commented on in every paper and her charm of manner; in fact, she is having a "*succès fou*" especially as no one was prepared for her good looks all photographs being caricatures.' Perhaps the Duke was now the shy one, she suggested. By the time the party reached Albany in Western Australia, the Duchess's charm outshone her husband's: 'She took the whole of Australia and New Zealand by storm . . . and every state has successively fallen in love with her looks, her smile, and her great charm of manner. She is at last coming out of her shell and will electrify them at home as she has everyone here.'

In 1891, Elgar had moved from London back to Worcestershire, exclaiming, 'I can't work anywhere else.' He now moved again from his home Forli to a new house, south of Malvern and set well up in the hills, called Craeg Lea. Three days after the move to Craeg Lea, Mary came to tea. Throughout the early years of the century she and Elgar continued to work together. On 29 April 1903 he conducted the *Coronation Ode* at the Madresfield Musical Competition. Later that year she wrote to thank him for the photographs of 'your marsh [Longdon Marsh, below the Malverns] . . . I can quite see from them what its fascination must be: and to you it must be very much what the bush in Australia was to me – excepting that my bush produced no inspiration – but that was not *its* fault!' It is clear from these letters that they now enjoyed a relaxed and humorous intimacy. In anticipation of the Madresfield Musical Competition for 1902 she wrote from York Cottage on the royal estate at Sandringham on 10 January asking him to conduct *Emmaus* and the *Coronation Ode*: 'Firstly it will give the concert much needed *éclat* and secondly it will fill all the competitors with great pride – and pleasure – to sing under your baton!' On 5 September 1903 she wrote from the family home in Belgrave Square regretting that she could not come for tea: 'My dear Mr Elgar . . . what is even more sad is that I shall miss the Birmingham Festival. I suppose there are to be no rehearsals of *The Apostles* in London, to which one might ask very humbly to be admitted?' The following year, when he dined once again at Madresfield, he was introduced to Edmund Gosse, man of letters and librarian at the House of Lords. Through this introduction, Gosse granted Elgar permission to set some of his words to music (his translation of 'After Many a Dusty Mile', the third of Elgar's 'Five Part Songs from the Greek Anthology').

A row of variously sized, morocco-bound and gold-tooled visitors' books stand on a shelf in the Madresfield Library. The one spanning the early years of the twentieth century shows that Elgar and his wife were frequent guests at Madresfield. Elgar's father may have used the tradesman's entrance but the composer now entered through the front door. And, at last, the forty-six-year-old composer was famous. Dressed in his fur-lined coat, he cut an impressive figure with his military moustache and proud bearing – an iconic Edwardian image of a creative genius, as enduring in the nation's mind as those of the impresario Serge Diaghilev and the poet D'Annunzio. Like many romantics of his generation, Elgar shared with Mary's brother a fascination with medievalism, reflected in the novels of Sir Walter Scott and the poetry of Tennyson, the Gothic revival, the work of the Pre-Raphaelite movement and the writings of critics and social reformers such as John Ruskin and William Morris. These Edwardians longed to return to the imagined world of chivalry and high principles and to reinstate what they felt to have been the honest and fulfilling life enjoyed by peasant craftsmen and farmers in the Middle Ages.

On 6 May 1905, Mary married Lt. Col. the Hon. Henry Walter Hepburn-Stuart-Forbes-Trefusis, MP (a surname she immediately shortened to Trefusis), the younger son of the twentieth Baron Clinton, and went to live in Porthgwidden, near Falmouth in Cornwall. The 'thirteenth enigma', who kow-towed to no one, had finally, aged thirty-six, agreed to settle down. Her stepmother was shocked that Mary wore black stockings under her white wedding dress. Over 4,400 Worcester people contributed to a wedding present, nearly half of whom were children from elementary and Sunday schools. It was a testament to her commitment to her local community.

Despite marriage, her bond with Elgar never loosened. Mary continued her work with music, founding the Cornwall Music Festival and being appointed President of the English Folk Dancing Society in 1912. Alice Elgar, keen to maintain useful connections, ensured that they came to stay with the Trefusises in Falmouth. After one visit in July 1910, Elgar wrote to a friend advising him that the visit was 'heavenly . . . Lady M. is as of old and always "nice" & dear and rather severe'. It was during this stay that he broached the idea of dedicating a future symphony to the memory of King Edward VII. Alert to an opportunity, Elgar wondered whether Mary would act as an intermediary with the palace.

Through her good offices as lady-in-waiting to Alexandra, the Queen Mother (Mary continued to serve the royal household but her duties had been transferred from Queen Mary), Elgar was granted permission to dedicate a number of his compositions to various members of the royal family. In March 1911, Mary pursued the idea, raised by Elgar in Cornwall the previous year, to dedicate his Symphony No. 2 in E flat to the memory of Edward VII. She sent Sir Arthur Bigge, private secretary to King George V, a précis of a letter she had received from Elgar:

Encouraged by King Edward's interest & kind enquiries about his Compositions, he intended to ask permission

to dedicate a recent symphony (a big orchestral work) to
H.M. before his death. Would His Majesty sanction its
dedication to the Memory of King Edward – in some
such form as: Dedicated to the memory of King Edward
VII by gracious permission of H.M. King George V.

She pointed out to the king that, in her opinion, 'As
Elgar is the greatest living composer in any country, the
work would be worthy of such a dedication.' Permission
was granted.

Elgar's reputation was further burnished when the
Prime Minister commended him for a knighthood and
in June 1911 he was awarded the Order of Merit, a
tribute that, to the composer's delight, placed him
higher up the pecking order than his late father-in-law,
who was merely a KCB. Carice observed that her
mother was delighted because 'it puts her back where
she belongs'. After the 1911 coronation, Elgar boasted in
a letter to his old friend Ivor Atkins: 'Worcester people
(save you!) seem to have little notion of the glory of
the O.M. I was marshaled correctly at Court & at the
Investiture *above* the G.C.M.G. & G.C.V.O. (the highest
Lord Beauchamp can go!) – next G.C.B. in fact. Such
things as K.C.B.'s &c are very *cheap* it seems beside O.M.'
Clearly, the full weight of the English class system still
sat heavily on Elgar's shoulders. Despite the Lygons'
patronage, this letter shows he had not overcome his
social insecurity. He never did, despite being appointed
Master of the King's Musick in 1924. Nor, despite
fame and recognition, did he ever lose his slight

Worcestershire burr. Fifty-five of his seventy-six years were spent in that county and its countryside was essential to his creativity. His attachment to place was symbolized by the purchase, in the early 1930s, of several feet of the railings from the dismantled old iron bridge that had spanned the Severn and over which he had crossed so often as a boy to take him back to Broadheath. He had them erected in his Worcestershire garden.

Elgar's music is a curious mixture of the minutely local and the pan-European; those vignettes of nature captured along the Severn Valley became part of the canon of Continental music. It does him a disservice to pigeonhole him as an intrinsically English composer. Citing his patriotic marches, rowdy imperialism and royal set pieces to the exclusion of his subtler, graver and more experimental works, the Little Englander attempts to claim Elgar as one of his own, a claim which – unwittingly perhaps – limits the great man's scope and reputation. He was, above all, a European composer in the central European symphonic tradition and admired his contemporaries, Saint-Saens, Chabrier and Delibes, on the Continent where modern music was being composed. And the recognition that he craved for so long initially came not from his fellow countrymen but from Continentals such as the German conductor Hans Richter, Richard Strauss, and his German publisher, August Jaeger.

Mary shared Elgar's love of the Continent; she was multi-lingual, well-travelled and well-versed in its cultures. Like him, she treasured her roots in the Worcestershire countryside. When palace duties permitted, she returned to Madresfield; when absent she had a corsage of snowdrops or violets sent to remind her of home. She died in 1927; Elgar outlived his pupil by seven years. He died at his home in February 1934 and he was buried at St Wulstan's, the Roman Catholic church at Malvern Wells. No music was played at his small funeral. Instead, at the memorial service held at his beloved Worcester Cathedral three of his thirteen 'Enigma' Variations were played: one recalled his wife who had died in 1920; another, August Jaeger, and the last, the 'Romanza', evoked 'My Sweet Mary'.

Eighteen months before his death, Elgar had addressed the Friends of Worcester Cathedral: 'Having spent my life, with absences, in the shadow of the Cathedral, having been born close to it and having come back as a truant to die under its shadow, nothing would give me greater happiness than to know that its future improvement was assured.' Today, at Madresfield, a stack of flyers and a small basket lie on the hall table opposite the front door. Guests can leave a contribution for the renewal of the organ pipes on which he played and for the choir which he conducted in the cathedral. Mary's grand-niece is chairman of the present-day fundraisers. The last visitor left a twenty-pound note in the basket, a note on which Elgar's portrait is printed.

Chapter Ten

THE WEDDING PRESENT

The Chapel is a relatively small room, twenty-five feet square, which is situated at the side of the Library and extends into the Moat Courtyard. Intended for a private place of family worship rather than a public statement of religious allegiance, the decoration centres on a dreamy Pre-Raphaelite fresco of powdery softness which, over time, has faded to become diaphanous and almost other-worldly. The young seventh earl and his countess are captured kneeling at the altar and facing one another, and each blond child born to them was added to the fresco. Gradually, the walls were covered with children playing among flowers with angels (modelled on their nurses) in attendance. A roseate light illuminates them all through the stained-glass windows.

Can a chapel be described as Prelapsarian? Could fallen man have created a room of such loveliness, such a tender paean to family life and the pleasures of the

Garden of Eden? It is a room of such sweetness and repose that it takes your breath away.

The abiding influence of Frederick on his son William was the importance of the Church, England's Church. While the father broadcast his unbending views on the Church of England, the son chose to venerate his God in a private way and saw merit in many religions.

Eleven years after his father's death, Mary's beloved brother William, who had learned the facts of life not from a parent but from the Aga Khan on a train, wrote the famous opening line of Herrick's poem into his scrapbook of 1902: 'Gather ye rosebuds while ye may'. Perhaps it was a reminder to himself that he must find a wife. The scrapbook – keeping scrapbooks was a family trait – also includes his 'pin-ups': drawings and photographs of society beauties and actresses. On Thursday 15 May this eligible bachelor was invited to dine at 35 Park Lane. The young Winston Churchill was another guest. There William met the homely and sweet-natured Lady Lettice Grosvenor – twenty-six-year-old sister of Bend'or, the second Duke of Westminster, who was reputed to be the richest man in Europe. Two days later, on 'Whitsun Eve', Lettice's diary records, 'Dearest Beauchamp came at 11 and asked me to marry him and I said yes. For ever *Laus Deo*.' William returned at lunch bearing 'a most beautiful emerald ring' and four days later showed his fiancée 'all the wonderful [Beauchamp] jewels'.

All the church bells at Madresfield rang a welcome to

its new châtelaine on the last day of May when the couple returned from honeymoon. It was a glittering match. Lettice's sister Margaret, known as 'Meg', had married Prince Adolphus of Teck, the brother of Princess May, the future Queen Mary. The Lygons no longer merely served the royal family, they were now related to it. A sense of the grandeur to which Lettice was accustomed is given by an entry in her diary for a shooting party held at her family home, Eaton Hall in Cheshire. It reads, 'Lord Essex took me into dinner. We are in the State Rooms – so cosy!' Observers remarked that William and his bride made a shy, even awkward, couple. After the wedding, the estate workers and tenants were invited to admire the lavish and numerous presents – canteens of cutlery, silver candelabra, jewels – and the wedding cakes were sent to the local orphanage, St Agnes, and to the Beauchamps' Industrial School for Girls in nearby Newland on their estate. Lettice was so happy that her diary confesses, 'I cannot remember what we did.'

The new countess brought an enormous dowry. She was singularly devout and her diaries are peppered with Latin praises to God, the recording of particular saints' days and accounts of church-going – often several times a day. Since she regarded their marriage as a sacrament, it was appropriate that she chose to finance a redecoration of the Madresfield chapel as a *memento matrimonii*. The work took two decades to complete and the designs were fastidiously chosen and overseen by William.

Turning the pages of his scrapbooks, it is plain to see what he loved. He included postcards and press cuttings that exemplify his abiding love of the Arts and Crafts movement: Walter Crane and Kate Greenaway's nursery images; the honest, wooden furniture of Mackintosh and Voysey; Pre-Raphaelite Madonna lilies; aesthetically dressed maidens portrayed by the pioneer photographer Julia Margaret Cameron; Beardsley's etiolated, monochrome illustrations for *The Yellow Book*; Lalique's glass curlicues and Koepping's sinuous vases, as iridescent as beetle's wings; an obituary of Ruskin; William Morris's tapestries of wildflower glades and Burne-Jones's sketches of soft-cheeked maidens with tousled hair pinned at the nape of their long necks. A principled socialism added backbone to these artists' and craftsmen's endeavours which appealed to William's sense of justice. There was nothing hard-edged about William's keen and tender taste. Though it ranged across continents, from the spare and academic delicacies of the Japanese and the joyous sensualities of the Persian, to the cottagey vernacular of the European crafts movement, the keynote was a preference for a gentle and idealistic way of life.

It is this keen and tender taste that distinguishes the Chapel at Madresfield. The Pre-Raphaelite frescoes and stained-glass windows that adorn it were carried out by Henry A. Payne, assisted by three men, the youngest being only fifteen: Joseph Saunders, Dick Stubbington and Harry Rushbury, later Sir Henry Rushbury, RA. The furniture was crafted by the Birmingham Municipal

School of Arts and Crafts, a school based on the precedent set by C. R. Ashbee's pioneering Guild School of Handicrafts in London's East End.

The walls were specially prepared in lime plaster mixed with marble dust. The frescoes were applied in egg tempera made up of powder colours – buttercup and saffron yellows, briar-rose and candyfloss pinks, duck-egg and clear-spring blues – which were ground into egg yolk and loosened with water.

Payne's vision is quintessentially English. He created a Garden of Albion rather than Eden. In a letter to William, dated 16 June 1903, he suggested that two realistic, kneeling figures of the earl and his wife should be painted on either side of the altar. They are guarded by St Michael, the Virgin and Child and St Elizabeth flanked by guardian angels. These characters do not rest in a formally laid out, Italianate garden nor a grand Capability Brown sweep of parkland. Instead they are placed in a simple English cottage garden planted with the common flowers of a Worcestershire meadow. A trellis circles the garden to form a *hortus inclusus*, an enclosed garden, a reference to the Song of Solomon – 'a garden inclosed is my sister, my spouse'. Briar roses ramble up the trellis and against it Madonna lilies – *the* Pre-Raphaelite flower – loll in profusion. The grass is strewn with an idealized floral array, ranging from January's snowdrops to December's crocus, growing side by side in this dreamy seasonless corner of England.

A clue to the choice of 'planting' in this painted

garden lies in William's library where several shelves on botany include works by the garden writer William Robinson as well as by his disciple Gertrude Jekyll, showing that William, a forward-thinking liberal, preferred the modest and subtle cultivation of a 'wild' garden, randomly and informally strewn with quiet native flora, rather than the imported exotics bedded out in ordered ranks in many Victorian gardens. Each flower is so perfectly realized in the fresco that it is not surprising to learn that the artists regularly plundered the grounds for specimens, much to the annoyance of the gardeners.

Two young saplings, emblems of the future, stand sentinel either side of William's glade. On the right of the altar grows the oak, an allegorical representation of longevity, and on the left a lime provides a perch for a green woodpecker. The laughter of woodpeckers is a familiar sound in the grounds of Madresfield. A lace-like intricacy of minuscule decorative detail runs over the whole chapel. Scarlet, forest green and golden stripes band the woodwork, swallows swoop through rose bushes set in panels across the Gothic-arched ceiling, honeysuckle tendrils coil through harebells along the organ casing, and biblical images – the Crucifixion, the *Pietà* and the Resurrection on one side, Joseph the carpenter, the Betrayal in Gethsemane and the ploughman on the other – are stained across little glass window panes. In spite of the profusion of intense detail, there is an abiding sense of calm in this room.

Though the decorative methods and skills in this

chapel are those of the Arts and Crafts movement, the actual style of the figurative painting – the people and the flora and fauna – owes less to the taste of the Grosvenor Gallery Pre-Raphaelites, Leighton or Burne-Jones, and more to the early Italian Renaissance painters, Botticelli, Piero della Francesca, Fra Angelico and his pupil Benozzo Gozzoli.

The head of the family, William, kneels in his coronation robes to the right of the altar, his new wedding band clearly adorning his finger – a Continental rather than English custom. His crested shield is laid to one side in the branches of the briar rose. To the left, his countess kneels, dressed in her wedding gown and modestly bejewelled with an amethyst crucifix swinging from a seed-pearl girdle and an emerald ring. Lying beside her on the grass is her prayer book opened at the tenth Psalm. The illuminated letter B of 'Blessed are those that fear the Lord' is decorated with a miniature scene of her wedding.

The frescoes evolved as each of their seven children was born; an evolution which is anticipated in the countess's diaries. With Edwardian coyness she records, for example, in February 1904, 'cosy evening with Will'; three months later she writes, 'Lovely. Met my Darling at M.L. [Malvern Link] 1.15. Delicious afternoon on my sofa', and in quick succession their children were born. It may be speculative but she periodically adds the footnote *Laus Deo* on certain pages and they coincide with days that William was home. On others she simply entered 'St Paul to the Ephesians, chapter 4, verse 13'.

This reads: 'And so we shall all come together to that oneness in our faith and in our knowledge of the Son of God; we shall become mature people, reaching to the very height of Christ's full stature.' Did these entries indicate days on which the couple made love?

Their two eldest children, William, Viscount Elmley (b. 1903) and his brother Hugh (b. 1904), were the first group to be added. Hugh is playing with the petals of a pink while his older brother, with his straw hat tossed over his shoulder, kneels by his guardian angel stretching his fingers out to pluck the harp in her lap. On the opposite wall, guarded by an angel who was modelled on their nanny, two toddlers are seated on the grass. Mary (b. 1910) is stroking a white dove while Dorothy (b. 1912) admires the toy kitten and box of marbles laid out before her. Further back from the altar two older sisters, Lettice (b. 1906) and Sibell (b. 1907) read from an illuminated prayer book, and finally the youngest, Dickie (b. 1916), was added to the wall in the organ loft, a tiny child inspecting a pink and balancing unsteadily on podgy, slippered feet. As each child arrived or an anniversary passed, Lettice recorded being given a jewel. 'I walked with my Darling and he gave me a wonderful fire opal' on 22 February 1904; and on the anniversary of their engagement day, 17 May 1904, she received from him 'a lovely star sapphire ring'. For Christmas Eve 1905 she entered the simple observation: 'All so happy and beautiful.'

Other loved members of the family were commemorated, without hierarchy, in minuscule panels along the balustrade of the organ loft of their chapel: from the Shaftesburys and the Grosvenors to friends such as the Tractarian cleric the Reverend Percy Dearmer, and his wife; and servants: 'G. H. Martin 1864–1925, for thirty years a skilled carpenter in this house', and the house steward, 'F. A. Love, 1857–1927, for forty years a faithful servant'.

Payne put all his creative energy into the frescoes and it exhausted him. But other artists were also hard at work: the theme of the altar paintings by Charles Gere is the sacrament of the Eucharist; it attests Beauchamp's Anglo-Catholic loyalties – Christ is flanked by four angels swinging incense burners. The triptych, designed by the architect William Bidlake and painted by Charles Gere, depicts Christ holding up the chalice in readiness for communion. To his left, a barefooted peasant scythes the wheat for the bread, and to his right, another harvests grapes for the wine. The small silver altar cross, decorated with *champlevé* enamel, and the candlesticks are important examples of Arts and Crafts metalwork and were created by Georgina Gaskin, an illustrator, and her husband Arthur Gaskin, who in 1902 became the head of the Victoria Street School for Jewellers and Silversmiths in Birmingham. While the Gaskins designed the crucifix and made the cross itself, the Christ figure was cast in Paris 'as it is almost impossible', Gaskin wrote to Lord Beauchamp in the spring of 1903, 'to get fine casting done in England'. It was a long-drawn-out process because the French craftsman drank, but Gaskin insisted on using him because 'unfortunately English casting is so "trashy" and poor that I am quite in the man's hands'. The Gaskins charged a hundred pounds for the cross and eighty pounds for the pair of candlesticks. At the time the average workman's wage was £1 8s a week.

What is striking about the correspondence in the Madresfield archives between the master craftsmen and their client is how confident they were in their views and how elegantly they expressed them. C. Napier Clavering, one of the Birmingham Guild metalworkers, for example, wrote:

> Dear Lord Beauchamp, I looked in and saw the dove and am afraid I am still unconverted to your view – I think it is too realistic and considering the symbolism intended it seems to me to be objectionable to make it a medium of support, with a hook screwed into its back! I am sorry to be obstinate on this point, but really I had rather not let my Guild's people make them; and I believe it is, as you suggested, only the force of habit and association which makes you take the other view.

In a tense letter dated 5 September 1905, Payne wrote to Beauchamp:

> I feel some difficulty in answering your letter as it shows such entire misunderstanding and want of sympathy. Next to my desire to let the work be of my best has been my wish to finish it as soon as possible – it involves too much discomfort all round to make me

waste one unnecessary moment. Self-interest alone would prompt me to work as hard as possible myself and to make my assistant do the same; for I have had to leave my house unoccupied for six months this year and also to leave my workshop with its heavy rental – the charges of a workman. I have left many pressing commissions which would be far more lucrative than this present work and this present work has been more fatiguing and trying than you can possibly understand. There have been days when to escape has been one's only thought and for all this I get a bare £200 a year [equivalent to £15,000 today]. That one should prolong wilfully this state of affairs is entirely absurd . . . I would far rather abandon the work altogether than to be subjected to such minute and unjustifiable supervision. I am responsible to no one but myself for the number of thorns and lily leaves executed *per diem*.

Payne took nearly three months to finish the kneeling figure of Lady Beauchamp alone.

I do not in the least agree with your strictures on the consistent waste of time. I have been a very hard taskmaster in the case of my assistants and as for myself I do not think I have ever worked so hard in my life as I have done in the chapel. Work is not to be measured by the amount splashed on the wall but by the value and quality of it when done. I beg you will share this letter with Lady Beauchamp.

He also corrected the earl on the required length of the candles to put in the sticks. He continued to work on the Chapel until 1918.

The theme of peace runs through the Chapel. In golden script *Gloria in Excelsis Deo et in Terra Pax* arches over Christ's head; 'The peace of God which passeth all understanding shall keep your hearts and minds through Christ' is inscribed along the right-hand wall; young Mary cradles a dove of peace; and the Beauchamp and Westminster shields are laid to one side in the briar roses by the altar. It is entirely consistent with both William's public politics and his private manner that his Chapel celebrated the state of peace. Throughout his political life he worked for peace between nations as well as between politicians within his own party and across the house.

Outside the Chapel a stained-glass window shows a soldier on his knees, begging the Lord's forgiveness. The inscription below him reads, 'Lord, I am not worthy that you should enter my house'. The sinner's face is that of the seventh earl.

Chapter Eleven

THE TREE OF LIFE

The Library is another room created by William, the seventh earl. It is an essentially English room that, despite its size – approximately sixty feet long and thirty feet wide – has an atmosphere of robust cosiness. Spurning glitter, Classicism and Rococo *boiseries*, its Arts and Crafts design evokes an old Albion, carved from her oak woods and embellished with the symbols of her Protestant bible. The shelves are stocked with the major works from the English literary canon – Langland, Chaucer, Shakespeare, Bunyan, Donne, Dryden – and the Word of God and the word in literature hold sway over decorative distraction. William was drawn to everything implied by the word 'England'.

When you enter through the Library's carved oak double doors, the room immediately invites high-mindedness. The progress of man's life is carved into the panels of the door itself: a child rolling a hoop, a knight and his maiden, a pilgrim followed by his family, a sage with his staff. Straight ahead stands the Tree of Life, carved in low relief on to the end of an eleven-foot-high oak bookcase. The inscription *Initium Sapientiae Timor Domini* – 'The fear of the Lord is the beginning of wisdom' – sets the keynote of the room. The tree's branches bear copious grapes, pomegranates, pineapples, melons, bananas and pears and the crenellated city of Jerusalem stands on the central boughs, below which the trunk and roots transmogrify into a fast-flowing, fish-filled river. The Tree of Knowledge is carved on to the second, wider bookcase end which stands to the right and bears the inscription *Folia Ligni ad Sanitatem Gentium* – 'And the leaves of the tree were for the healing of the nations'. It is flanked by Adam and Eve who are tempted by the apple offered by a human-headed serpent and surrounded by toads, reptiles and ugly beasts.

Three single and one pair of double oak doors communicating with adjacent rooms complement the bookcase ends. The door to the office shows a scholarly friar, a farmer sowing seeds, two figures studying a globe and the inscription *Vita Erat Lux Hominum* – 'Life was the Light of Men'. The door to the Chapel is carved with a crucified Christ under which sits the bibliophile Thomas Dibdin's friend Dr Jenner, the physician who discovered the smallpox vaccination. The door is marked with an inscription: *Taceant Omnes Doctores, Tu Mihi Loquere Solus* – 'Let all the learned men be silent: speak Thou alone to me'. The door to the Smoking

Room comprises panels showing the various ways in which man searches for the truth and the light: a craftsman carves the crucifix, a peasant ploughs the field, a musician plays his instrument, an astronomer in an observatory searches the skies, and a nurse watches over a dying man. Finally, 'Thou Shalt Not Steal' is carved into the third and narrowest bookcase end. Each door is furnished with a large hand-beaten – *repoussé* – pewter fingerplate stamped with three lions and six martlets: blazons from the Beauchamp coat of arms.

The redecoration of William's new Library between 1902 and 1905 was masterminded by C. R. Ashbee, one of the country's leading Arts and Crafts designers. Carved by Alec Miller and Will Hart, members of Ashbee's Guild of Craftsmen, assisted by the Madresfield estate carpenter, G. H. Martin, it was one of the Guild's finest commissions and Ashbee's most successful scheme for interior design. Ashbee and William had much in common; as sons of stern and distant fathers, they became radical idealists, romantics and reformers. Ashbee was born in 1863 into the sort of affluent, educated, urban and unhappy background that frequently fosters enlightened thinkers. In 1883 he took a place to read history at King's College, Cambridge, where he started to question the social iniquities of laissez-faire capitalism. Shocked by a report published in the popular *Pall Mall Gazette* which revealed in plain-speaking statistics that forty per cent of the population of Whitechapel, one of the poorest slums in the East End, lived below subsistence level,

Ashbee pored over the writings of the most articulate critics of industrialization, such as William Blake and Thomas Carlyle. Perhaps F. D. Maurice's Christian socialism was the answer, or William Morris's humane, low-tech, medieval-style workshops. Ashbee was particularly enthralled by the radical writings and lifestyle of the poet-prophet and social reformer Edward Carpenter. Carpenter, who lived on a smallholding in Derbyshire and became a founding member of the Fellowship of the New Life (a precursor of the Fabian Society), advocated a return to the land. He urged his followers to dress in smocks, breeches and homemade sandals, eat home-grown vegetables and explore their sexual appetites. One of his more controversial theories suggested that homosexuality could resolve class conflict. Since homosexuals are often socially promiscuous, then, his logic ran, it was expedient to encourage homosexuality as a means of fostering a greater understanding between the classes. Carpenter's influence spread and his controversial philosophy culminated in 1902 in the publication of his epic and Whitmanesque poem *Towards Democracy*. It became Ashbee's bible.

Ashbee's first step upon graduating in 1886 was to move to the East End of London and he apprenticed himself with the Gothic revivalist architects G. F. Bodley & Garner. The neo-Gothic style of architecture was a direct precursor of the Arts and Crafts style. To young idealists, the Arts and Crafts movement had fundamental moral and social purpose. They spurned the ostentatiousness of high Victorian mass production.

C. R. Ashbee, architect and Arts and Crafts designer, who master-minded the redecoration of the Library.

Ashbee turned to the imagery of English nature and ancient English decoration – the oak leaf, the Tudor rose, the trefoil – and applied them to useful, handmade objects. Creative manual work was not only more pleasing to the eye but could also, he believed, provide personal fulfilment and a moral compass for the craftsmen.

He took up residence at the purpose-built Toynbee Hall in Whitechapel, the pioneering project of the University Settlement Movement, which aimed to bridge the chasm between the rich and the poor, not simply by treating the working classes as opportunities for charity to be dealt with at arm's length but by inviting privileged young graduates to come and live among deprived workers. Initially, sixteen graduates, including Ashbee, moved to the East End, providing leadership and a stimulus to the workers and their families. They opened schools, maternity societies and penny banks; organized lectures and discussion groups, concerts and trips to the countryside.

The University Settlement Movement was the talk of the town. Not only did Carpenter visit but leading artists and writers of the day attended or gave lectures there. Less high-minded sightseers also visited to, as the modish quip had it, 'slum without tears'. Upholstered carriages from West End mansions pushed their way through the 'Mudfog' and the fashionably curious stepped into the stinking, rubbish-strewn streets outside the Hall.

Inside, the two tribes – the rich and the poor –

gawped at one another across the sparse, sensibly appointed dining hall, seated on the edge of hard benches, balancing homely refreshments on their knees as they struggled to converse.

Within weeks, Ashbee had seized the initiative and founded the School of Handicraft, offering the unemployed and itinerant from the East End streets a first-class training in modelling, carving and gilding. He also founded the Guild of Handicraft at the top of a warehouse in Commercial Street. It rekindled the medieval workshop's dual role as a place of work and of teaching. Commissions began to trickle in. A new life began.

By the mid-nineties, Ashbee had emerged as a public figure of standing. He ran a successful architectural practice, he was a respected designer and he contributed to leading art magazines. In 1894, his campaigning zeal and irrepressible energy found another outlet: the Survey of London, by which, with the help of some volunteers, he set about the recording and saving of buildings of historical and architectural note in the capital. Two years later he was appointed to the Committee of the National Trust and by 1900 he had published the first parish study, on Bromley-by-Bow in the East End, listing threatened buildings. These studies led to today's Buildings at Risk register which merged in 1999 with English Heritage and it was a movement to which Earl Beauchamp committed himself after the First World War.

In 1897, Ashbee met the nineteen-year-old Janet

Forbes, the first woman outside his immediate family with whom he could make an emotional and intellectual connection. Janet admired Ashbee's busy elegance. He was unusual. While not 'madly in love', she relished his company. For his part, he wondered, 'Do we sympathize enough to be man and wife?' He proposed, offering the caveat:

> My men and boy friends [have] been the one guiding principle of my life . . . Some women would take this, and perhaps rightly, as a sign of coldness to their sex, and they would shrink from a man who revealed himself thus . . . You are the first and only woman to whom I have felt I could offer the same loyal reverence of affection that I have hitherto given to my men friends. Will not the inference be obvious to you? There are many comrade friends, there can be only one comrade wife.

Janet agreed to become his 'comrade-wife' and wholeheartedly joined the Progressives. On honeymoon she abandoned her stays, cropped her hair and became a committed follower of the Healthy and Artistic Dress Union.

By 1887, the Guild was attracting many clients, including Mrs Holman Hunt, the Duchess of Leeds, the Bishop of London, Mrs Rudyard Kipling and the literary critic Edmund Gosse. Commissions won were crafted in the East End workshop which by the turn of the century employed forty or fifty men and boys. In 1897, the Guild was invited to collaborate with M. Scott Baillie on a prestigious project, the refurbishment of the dining and drawing rooms of the grand-ducal palace at Darmstadt in Germany. The grand duke was one of the great patrons of the Arts and Crafts movement and the Guild provided light fittings and furniture for the palace. It was this project which alerted William to Ashbee's practice. Through the pages of *Studio* magazine the earl had watched the palace refurbishment with interest, pasting cuttings into his scrapbook.

By 1901, the Guild was on the move again. Robert Martin-Holland, scion of the Martin banking family and one of the Guild's biggest shareholders, suggested that they settle in Chipping Campden in the Cotswolds, twenty-five miles from Madresfield. The Ashbees went to investigate. To Ashbee's conservationist eye, this stone-built town stood in a state of pre-industrial perfection, exquisite and intact, with rows of original Elizabethan cottages and an eighteenth-century silk mill. He had found the perfect setting in which to combine his two missions: to save historic buildings and downtrodden craftsmen. The Cockney guildsmen were understandably sceptical about the 'Great Move' but on 8 December 1901 they took a vote and by Christmas the majority had decided to 'leave Babylon and go home to the land'.

Few passers-by could have missed the caravan of bicycles pedalling west along the Mile End Road in London's East End on the morning of 2 May 1902.

These Cockneys, flat caps firmly pulled down over their brows, heads leaning purposefully over their handle-bars, were cycling out of Whitechapel and towards 'Camelot'. They rode behind the exuberant Ashbee, nattily dressed in plus-fours, Norfolk jacket and a generous cravat, which proclaimed his artistic sensi-bilities. He led his workers and their families – nearly two hundred people in all – out of the squalor of the East End to build a simple life together in the Cotswold countryside. The Beauchamps of Madresfield Court would contribute to his dream.

One thousand five hundred people lived in Chipping Camden at the turn of the century. They were agri-cultural workers, isolated from the ideas and the pace of London life. Their pleasures were simple: ale at the pub, clog dancing and shin-kicking competitions up on Dover's Hill over the Whitsun weekend. They did not take kindly to this Cockney invasion, particularly as Lord Gainsborough, the local landlord, had inflated rents to profit from the influx of Londoners. Few locals could understand the Cockney accent while their own Gloucestershire drawl, made even stranger to the ear by outdated 'thees' and 'thous', was equally incompre-hensible to the newcomers. Ashbee had not anticipated the problems as relations between the townsfolk and the Londoners became so unfriendly that the shop-keepers charged two prices: one for locals and a higher one for outsiders. Nor, insensitive to practicalities, had he foreseen how uncomfortable the guildsmen and, more particularly, their wives, would find their rudimentary dwellings. It was all very well to live in an authentic Elizabethan cottage but how would he like to cook on an antique range or use a communal outdoor lavatory? Mrs Osborn, wife of Herbert the ivory-turner, sat down and wept. Other guildsmen and their families got up and left. One homesick guildsman made a daily pilgrimage to the station to watch the train travelling to and from London to reassure himself that, if necessary, he could return.

Nevertheless, Ashbee set up his 'medieval' workshops on three floors of the old silk mill. Each studio specialized in a particular craft: silversmithing, enamelling, bookbinding. Gradually, the experimental community grew. Craftsmen made the pilgrimage to join it. John Gay, a Cockney with a family to support, had been discharged following an industrial accident. Despite the serious leg wound, he walked one hundred miles from London to Campden to seek employment with the Guild. Alec Miller from Oban in Scotland had steeped himself in Ruskin, Morris and the bible, and decided to live 'a new imaginative life in which art and history were coherent and united'. Miller arrived in 1902 to begin the Beauchamp commission.

If one was sensitive to the mellow echoes of history, there was no doubt that Campden was beautiful. I walked up Campden's one long street entranced and happy – a mile-long street with hardly a mean house, and with many of great beauty and richness. It was, after Glasgow and Scotch village architecture, as foreign as Cathay and as romantic as the architecture of fairy-tale illustrations. In a word, it all seemed unbelievable! Was I in the twentieth century or the sixteenth?

Miller, a master woodcarver, became the craftsman of Ashbee's dreams. Not only did he set himself extremely high standards but he was also hungry for beauty and wider intellectual horizons. Before carving, Miller would undertake considerable research, burying his nose in ecclesiastical histories, for example, to determine the appropriate vestments for Christ. When Miller began work on Madresfield, he found a new father figure: the earl. He stayed nearby at Malvern Link and would discuss crafts with his patron who, along with Ashbee, guided his literary tastes. Miller wrote to Ashbee on 3 March 1905: 'I have just finished reading [Oscar Wilde's] *De Profundis*. It is a tremendously impressive book and it has left me in a strangely complex mental state. I am awed by the beauty of the spirit that could write from prison and show no bitterness . . .'

On the eve of the move to 'Camelot', William had visited Ashbee's studio and invited him to Madresfield in January 1902 to discuss the commission. Ashbee was struck by his new patron's surroundings and tastes.

There was the same rustling of liveries, plush and crimson, the choosing of rooms to sit in for conversation, the sparkle of champagne and the still plethora

of port, there were precious books fetched out for fancy
and the epicurean requirements of literature, and all
these things were as the vapours that passed away . . .
they looked through the fringed film of English
aristocracy. It was an interesting two days.

Ashbee immediately recognized in William an unexpected sensitivity, 'a touch more human tenderness'.

While working on the Library, Ashbee, a keen cyclist,
regularly cycled to Madresfield, putting his suitcase on
the train from his local station, Moreton-in-Marsh, to
Hanworth Halt, from where William's coachman collected it. William worked closely with Ashbee, Miller
and Hart in the development of the panels. 'Lord
Beauchamp came down to the Court today, he seemed
very pleased with the deepening results of the "Tree of
Life" end, he is making an addition of another motto in
Greek, which I should term swank, having already one
in Latin on the end,' Hart wrote to Ashbee. There had
been much preparation before carving had begun but
by 15 January, drawings had been sent for approval.
Over the next few months, letters passed to and fro
between these two kindred educated men, exchanging
suggestions for appropriate inscriptions to carve into
the doors and bookcase ends. Inscriptions in architecture had become fashionable in the sixteenth
century when God-fearing admonitions, psalms and
biblical quotes were favoured. With the stylistic revival
of medieval, Elizabethan and Gothic architecture from
the 1830s, this decorative device was revived. William

and Ashbee spent weeks sourcing quotations and discarding them. They ranged from Ben Jonson's 'How swift is time and slily steals away', to quotations from *Faust*, though Ashbee conceded that perhaps 'Faust the Doctor is too Godless a person for you?' By return, the earl proposed *Taceant Omnes Doctores*. Ashbee countered with, 'I thought how well it fitted to Goethe's final rendering of the typical student who gets salvation in the end.' A handwritten postscript to this typed letter hints at the dismantling of formality between them: 'I have just had sent me Ewd. Carpenter's *Iolaus* [his anthology of Friendship]. Tis a pretty book – have you seen it and do his things interest you?' Ashbee had recently been to stay with Carpenter at Millthorpe and was full of his praises.

In working together on his Library, it became clear to both William and Ashbee that they were fellow visionaries. Since his days at Oxford William had committed himself to improving the lot of the poor and un-educated in the East End of London, taking them on healthy and inspiring day trips before he joined Asquith's reforming Liberal Cabinet. Ashbee too was motivated by improving the lot of the urban poor in a hands-on and practical way. William's scrapbooks are aesthetically and politically all of a piece – a marriage of Anglo-Catholic medievalism and Arts and Crafts vernacular – and they mirror in many ways Ashbee's interests and tastes. The two men shared a love not only of the arts and crafts but also of English embroidery, medieval architecture and Arthurian legend. Politically, education, democracy, peace and conservation roused their passions. Like Ashbee, William was a committed pacifist who would sacrifice his political career to this principle. The dreaming architect and the radical earl shared democratic instincts and a determination to leave the world a better place. Their encounter proved to be intellectually fruitful. And together they built a beautiful library at Madresfield. On one of the shelves stands a copy of Ruskin's *Sesame and Lilies*, one of William's favourite books. It includes this statement:

> . . . it is not religious men and thinkers but those that 'do something useful' that are probably closer to God and the Truth . . . These, – hewers of wood, and drawers of water, – these, bent under burdens, or torn of scourges – these, that dig and weave – that plant and build; workers in wood, and in marble, and in iron – by whom all food, clothing, habitation, furniture, and means of delight are produced, for themselves, and for all men beside; men, whose deeds are good, though their words may be few; men, whose lives are serviceable, be they never so short, and worthy of honour, be they never so humble; – from these, surely at least, we may receive some clear message of teaching; and pierce, for an instant, into the mystery of life, and of its arts.

Chapter Twelve

THE RED BOXES

The Ante-Room links Tudor and Victorian Madresfield. The sixteenth-century part of the house is made up of small, oak-panelled rooms hung with tapestries, armour and old weapons of hand-to-hand combat. It served as the original and more intimate home of the earlier Lygon squires, knights, soldiers and MPs. The Victorian part contains grandly appointed rooms filled with the accumulations of wealthier generations. Though the Ante-Room is small – slightly wider than a corridor – it displays the cultural aspirations and political achievements of the later Lygons. Sunlight enters it from the east, over Bredon Hill, and catches the threads of Flemish tapestries which hang from brass poles high up under the cornice and plays over the parquet floor laid with rugs from the furthest reaches of the Empire. It shines down on the marble busts of Pope Benedict XIII, Marcus Aurelius and the Emperor Nicholas I of Russia on their porphyry plinths.

Since the late Middle Ages, members of the Lygon family had represented a local constituency, requiring them during parliamentary sessions to leave the remoteness of Worcestershire and live in London. For centuries, they had served on the back benches. A group of red leather despatch boxes with brass handles and locks, which today stand on a fruitwood table in the corner of the Ante-Room, attest to their political advancement since the mid-nineteenth century. Each one is tooled in gold with the Beauchamp crest and the title of an office of state. Commissioned by Her Majesty's Stationery Office from Wickwar of Poland Street, London, they served for each government minister to transport his state papers. One, for example, is stamped 'Postmaster General' and belonged to Frederick, the sixth earl; another, 'First Commissioner of Works', belonged to his son, William, the seventh earl, who, contrary to the Tory family tradition, crossed the house to join the Liberal Party.

Of all the Lygons, William was the most distinguished politician. The humanist education and teaching in rhetoric and the classics that he had received at Eton were the traditional preparation for public service. There, he would have encountered the master H. E. Luxmoore, who was reputed to exert 'a strong influence on a certain type of intelligent and sensitive boy'. Luxmoore inspired William with Pre-Raphaelite imagery, the noble objectives of social reform and the duties of the modern knight in serving others. These ideals were encapsulated in a deeply

*'Pussykins': the seventh earl dressed as his medieval ancestor Lord
Beauchamp of Powick, for the Duchess of Devonshire's fancy dress
ball in 1898.*

romantic image that he gave his pupils, *Sir Galahad* by G. F. Watts. A photograph of William in 1898 shows him at the Duchess of Devonshire's fancy dress ball clad as his ancestor, Lord Beauchamp of Powick, in a medieval tabard and chainmail. The chivalrous knight was an image that he relished and tried to live up to in his political life.

Eton was followed by Christ Church, Oxford, where William cut a dash and was described in the student newspaper *Isis* as a 'cool, grey-clad figure in a Liberty tie that flickers pump-shod around the hanging gardens of garish Peck quad in college'. Anxious to avoid 'mothers-with-a-marriageable-daughter', he had dedicated himself to debating in the Oxford Union where his idiosyncratic delivery, beating time to his speeches with his cap on the podium, was noted. Following in his father's footsteps, he was elected President in 1893, chairing debates with 'tact and eloquence', one of the 'enlightened . . . and more advanced of Socialist peers'. This was a prescient observation by his friend F. E. Smith for, as time went by, Beauchamp gradually moved to the left of the political spectrum.

William was a precocious politician who, according to the diary of a contemporary, made a 'display' of his independent thinking in defiance of his 'Papa'. Frederick had been an intractable, fierce-tempered father. When he died in 1891 he was remembered by two fellow peers, Lords Derby and Liverpool, as 'the most strait-laced and pompous old prig', a 'bigoted and rather bitter High Churchman: of narrow sympathies and not more than moderate understanding'. I. A. Shaw-Stewart, who had been an undergraduate with Frederick, wrote to William:

I do so trust you will grow up like him and that your life may be as useful as his was. In one respect he rather failed in Oxford. He was one man to those who were fortunate enough to be within the inner circle of his friendship, but rather too stand-offish with those with whose tastes he was not in sympathy, and he showed this too decidedly. This somewhat diminished the general usefulness of his early life – I mention this in case you should have inherited any of this trait.

William took his seat in the Lords aged only nineteen as the seventh Earl Beauchamp, and, in fact, from the time of his maiden speech was seen as a pleasingly distinctive and likeable figure, one journalist observing that though his 'hopes for social regeneration [based] on a revival of Christianity' were misplaced, 'his delivery is smooth, his voice melodious, his points carefully rounded, and he has a pretty trick of gesticulation with his left hand that seems too adorable for an Englishman'.

William marked his accession to the title by planting a maze at Madresfield based on a design he found in a children's comic. It is still easy to lose one's way in it today. Subsequently, every milestone in his life was marked with a project on the estate.

William served his political apprenticeship as Mayor of Worcester between 1895 and 1896 and then as a county councillor. It was a new but common practice at the time for members of the aristocracy to serve in local politics, thereby dissipating the tension between urban and rural Britain and between aristocracy and democracy. In his role as an 'ornamental mayor', Beauchamp soon gained a reputation for being a peacemaker.

Between 1886 and 1894, in protest against Gladstone's support for Home Rule in Ireland, most of the Liberal peers, the old Whig grandees, crossed the House of Lords to ally themselves with the Conservative Party. As a result, only a handful of peers remained in the Liberal ranks, the most senior being the Earl of Ripon, Lord Houghton (later the first Marquess of Crewe) and Lord Carrington (later the Marquess of Lincolnshire). In 1897, they were joined by young Beauchamp who crossed the House in protest against the Tory support for Imperial Preference (giving preferential trading terms to the Colonies). Initially, his sister Mary was alarmed, questioning her brother in a letter. 'I *AM* distressed that you are going to join the Radicals. Why? Is it irrevocable? People will say it is because you want a post. You don't honestly think their politics are better, do you? Think of the land death duties and Mr. Gladstone's foreign policy. *Do* pause and don't do it only for ambition, which I am afraid is your reason honestly.' Beauchamp, however – in spite of his sister's suspicions – did not regard politics as a 'greasy pole' to be shinned up for personal advancement. His Christian principles committed him to social, particularly educational, reform. As she grew to understand his work and his convictions, Mary came to support his radicalism.

Having renounced the Tory Party, no one was more surprised than Beauchamp himself at being appointed Governor of New South Wales in 1899 by Joseph Chamberlain, the Colonial Secretary in Salisbury's Conservative and Unionist administration. William was only twenty-six years old and, by his own admission, 'scarcely knew where was the colony and certainly nothing about it'. The press was excited that not only was he the youngest Governor ever appointed but that he was also a peer 'with ideas of his own and a real interest in public work'. The queen mischievously expressed the hope that a sensible nurse would accompany the boy. His posting later inspired a popular cautionary tale for children from fellow-Liberal Hilaire Belloc, who, coincidentally, when he wrote it, was renting a house in Sussex called 'Bleak House'.

> *It happened to Lord Lundy then,*
> *As happens to so many men:*
> *Towards the age of twenty-six,*
> *They shoved him into politics . . .*
> *'Sir! You have disappointed us!*
> *We had intended you to be*
> *The next Prime Minister but three:*
> *The stocks were sold; the Press was squared:*

The Middle Class was quite prepared.
But as it is! . . . My language fails!
Go out and Govern New South Wales!

Mary Lygon acted as hostess for her bachelor brother for the first five months of the posting, as she had when he was Mayor of Worcester. There is a plate produced by the Royal Worcester factory commemorating Beauchamp's appointment, with Mary at his side. It hangs in the Kitchen at Madresfield. They set off in considerable style aboard the SS *Rome* with a retinue made up of a private secretary; two aides-de-camp; Mr F. A. Love, the steward, accompanied by his wife and their two children; Mrs Mileham, a housekeeper; Mr Pope, a butler; two footmen; one under-butler; one under-coachman; and one kitchen-maid. Over one hundred crates of furniture, antiques, paintings and objets d'art were transported ahead of the party to decorate the neo-Gothic Government House in a style that reflected the in-coming Governor's exacting standards of formality and aesthetics. Beauchamp printed a guide to these treasures in order that guests could fully appreciate them when they visited his residence. The bill for travel expenses incurred on the trip out, which he submitted to the Prime Minister of the colony, was accompanied by a letter explaining that it 'by no means represents the total cost' and included £292 for the transportation of carriage, linen, plate, harness, household goods and a sailing vessel; and £400 for objets d'art.

The new proconsul was installed as Governor of New South Wales on 18 May 1899 and took considerable ceremonial pride in running Government House. On formal occasions he would stand, brocaded in gold and stockinged in silk, alongside the soberly dressed though magnificently tiaraed Mary, to greet visitors. For the people of Australia, it was a rare sight to behold the Antipodean Camelot which, in an unprecedented fashion, William and his sister opened to people from all walks of life, including subsistence farmers, teachers, suburban mayors, the lower ranks of the army and children. This broad-ranging hospitality, somewhat in the style of a Buckingham Palace Garden Party today, was a much debated feature of their stay.

Taking an active interest in education, Beauchamp regularly visited schools and in December 1899 alone entertained at the residence 4,525 children, 1,200 on one single occasion. With tremendous energy, he travelled from one far-flung town to another and on into the outback, often on a train hung with huge head-lamps to scare off the wild animals as it pushed through deserted terrain to reach tiny settlements of indigenous bushmen and farmers who were eking out a living from the harsh land. He took up the cause of the indigenous people throughout the Antipodes, including the Aborigines and the Maoris. There are monographs in the Madresfield Library on both these peoples and their art.

Initially, the Australians took a dim view of their plumed and booted Governor who stood, in their minds, as a symbol of the ties with Britain that many wished to break. Australians were in the throes of a federal movement which would succeed within a year. On the eve of Beauchamp's arrival three of the Australian colonies – Victoria, Tasmania and South Australia – had agreed in a referendum to federate on the basis of a draft constitution and although New South Wales, the premier colony, had voted against federation, there was escalating pressure to do so. Nevertheless, the people of New South Wales gradually recognized the unexpectedly democratic leanings of their Governor, who announced himself to be 'an ardent federalist'. His steward, on the other hand, was less open-minded. Corresponding with William's brother, the Hon. Edward Lygon, on 13 June 1899 he wrote: 'Well, sir, here we are in the Land of Philistines and a very queer lot some of them are. I have heard a great deal of Australia, its beauties, etc., but after all give me Madresfield, with my bit of garden, there is enough beauty there for me but there we must not grumble, three years will soon pass.'

The following spring, Beauchamp received news that would break his heart and irrevocably alter his politics. His brother Eddie, who was serving in the Boer War in South Africa, was killed by a sniper while riding out beyond the confines of the British camp on the Modder River, in the north-west of Cape Colony. Eddie was Beauchamp's greatest friend; after their mother's death the two had retreated together from the stepfamily and from their strict and distant father and found comfort in each other. In the pocket of Eddie's red uniform his fellow officers found a bar of chocolate, which Beauchamp placed in a glass cabinet in the Long Gallery, a simple memento of his sweet-toothed brother. Eddie's death convinced Beauchamp of the folly of war. His pacifism was born.

The loss took its toll on Beauchamp's nerves. On her second visit to the colony, Mary observed that her brother was suffering from insomnia and eczema. How he longed for Madresfield: the cool wooded acres, the heads of cow parsley bobbing in the summer breeze, the seasons passing over its smooth lawns, the oaken comforts of his Library and the ritual of prayer in the Chapel. And so in October 1900, to widespread disappointment and regret, eighteen months into his three-year posting, he left Sydney. One of his harshest critics in the Australian press, a Miss Gouli Gull, had revised her views on him by the eve of his departure:

> Sydney is getting ready to be truly sorry for the departure of Little Billee . . . we have had a Governor who has not tied himself to stale old customs . . . [this is a man who has welcomed] artists, poets, musicians, poor clergymen – the othah [sic] class, in fact, that is not supposed to know the front Govt. House door from the back – they have nothing but regret to utter at the loss of their informal patron.

Beauchamp, a man of contradictions – a pompous progressive, a grandly formal liberal – was easily misunderstood. His buttoned-up manner and shyness were probably misinterpreted as pomposity. Furthermore, he was catapulted into a life of ceremony and formality at a relatively young age. The bachelor earl's homecoming was marked by almost feudal celebrations in the streets of Worcester and, as his carriage approached Madresfield, the tenants unfastened the six matching black horses and themselves hauled the vehicle up to the front of the great house, where they presented him with a silver casket containing their welcome address in manuscript on vellum. He entered in a scrapbook that April the ironic observation: 'Be it ever so humble, there's no place like home.' A few weeks later, he dined at Hatfield with the Prime Minister Lord Salisbury. As he got up from the table, his host leaned towards him and quipped, 'I suppose you feel quite strange when you're rising from a chair not accompanied by the National Anthem!'

Throughout his political life Beauchamp adhered to the four classical pillars of Liberal thought: peace, free trade, economy and education. Unlike many peers, he was not an absentee but regularly attended the Lords where he championed the needs of the working man (he gave many lectures at Working Men's Clubs throughout Britain), particularly educational reform, which led to his cooperating closely with like-minded radical Sir Charles Dilke, MP for the Forest of Dean. Such efforts won him the sobriquet 'the Lloyd George of the House of Lords', but it was a lonely position since 'as a deliberative assembly, the Lords was at its

*Countess Beauchamp, 1911. John Singer Sargent's charcoal
portrait reflects her sensuality.*

Margot Asquith, wife of the Liberal Prime Minister, was a frequent
visitor, and wrote this in a Madresfield commonplace book in
1909.

weakest in the field of social policy, *terra incognita* to most peers, where minimal expertise was exacerbated by maximum prejudice.' Beauchamp was an exception. He shared with Herbert Asquith, the coming man of the Liberal Party, a commitment to social reform funded by higher taxation, to Home Rule for Ireland and to the reform of the Upper House.

Beauchamp and his new wife Lettice frequently had Asquith and his wife Margot to stay at Madresfield, though they generally preferred to confine the business of politics to their London residence, Halkin House on Belgrave Square, which became a powerhouse for the Liberal Party in the first two decades of the new century. On the eve of one State Opening of Parliament, for example, the Beauchamps threw a party for nine hundred guests. The press reported:

> Lord and Lady Beauchamp shook hands ceaselessly with their Liberal confrères for about two hours on end ... Lady Beauchamp has the advantage of possessing a lovely house as a background for official entertainments and it never looked better than the other evening, when lights sparkled from myriad of [*sic*] green candles in the famous crystal chandeliers which are such an attractive feature of Halkin House; and tawny chrysanthemums in all the rich shades of autumn were arranged wherever they could conveniently appear.

Balfour's Conservative Government was defeated by

a vote in the Commons in December 1905 and an electoral landslide confirmed the Liberals in power under Sir Henry Campbell-Bannerman in early 1906. Asquith was appointed Chancellor of the Exchequer and Beauchamp's valet was heard to predict, 'We shall 'ave Hindia or Hireland but we don't know which.' In fact William was appointed a Privy Counsellor and the following year Lord Steward of the Royal Household, a role in which he could perfect his ceremonial and diplomatic skills. A number of his ancestors had served in similar positions – Sir Walter de Beauchamp, a Crusader, was appointed Steward to the household of Edward I, and William's father had been Queen Victoria's Lord Steward. William helped plan George V's coronation at which he bore the Sword of State for the king, attended by his young kinsman Sir William Dugdale, who acted as his page. The Roxburghe edition of *Liber Regalis*, the medieval account of early coronations, must have provided an interesting reference for him.

In April 1908, Asquith succeeded Campbell-Bannerman as Prime Minister and in June 1910 appointed Beauchamp Lord President of the Council, one of the great offices of state. The Lord President acts as presiding officer of the Privy Council at which the monarch formally assents to Orders-in-Council. 'This will give you a seat in the Cabinet', Asquith wrote to him, 'and will be a recognition (which I am glad to have the opportunity of making) of your invaluable services to our party and in the best interests of our country.' Beauchamp marked the occasion by planting a number of trees, which he named the 'Cabinet Wood', on one side of the Gloucester Drive at Madresfield. In November of that year, he was appointed First Commissioner of Works, responsible for a department of state where his predecessors included Inigo Jones and Sir Christopher Wren. Here Beauchamp could bring to bear his keen love of art and architecture as well as his skills at housekeeping, curating and commissioning works for all the major government buildings, royal palaces, parks and monuments. He was responsible, for example, for placing Rodin's sculpture *The Burghers of Calais* in the gardens that abut the House of Lords and for commissioning Henry Payne to work on the Houses of Parliament.

Asquith's government introduced significant social reforms, not least the reform of the House of Lords through the Parliament Act which restricted the Upper House's powers of delay and enabled the Prime Minister to get Home Rule through the Lords. Beauchamp regarded this as an essential reform, opining that 'the less this House is hereditary the more popular will be its support and the stronger it will be'. On a number of occasions he spoke in support of Home Rule, taking issue with the Marquess of Lansdowne's call for repressive measures against all instigators of unrest in Ireland, unrest that William attributed to the harsh policy of enclosures. In July 1910, for example, he asked whether 'the noble Marquess prefers punishing or stopping crime?' On 29 January 1913, he made an important contribution as a front-bench spokesman in the debate on the second reading of the Government of Ireland Bill and, echoing his support for Australian federalism fifteen years earlier, he argued that the Irish people were:

> . . . as anxious today for the right to manage their own affairs as they were one hundred years ago [when famine, disease and depopulation struck] . . . You cannot point, I believe, to a single instance anywhere, where self-government as a system has failed. The only obstacle is a small minority in one corner of Ireland who persuade your Lordships to refuse to the rest of Ireland what four-fifths of her people want. We say that such a claim on the part of a small minority is an intolerable claim and one which we cannot allow.

Beauchamp's services to king and country were recognized in June 1914 when George V made him a Knight of the Garter, the most prestigious award in the monarch's gift. Founded in the fourteenth century by Edward III, the order was introduced to increase the prestige of his knights and unite them to his cause: to seize the throne of France. It was loosely based on the romance of the Arthurian legend and its round table of brother knights-in-arms: an intoxicating provenance for Beauchamp. He would later be joined by Herbert Asquith. In celebration he planted another copse, the 'Garter Wood', on the other side of the Gloucester Drive from the 'Cabinet Wood'.

In the same year William was granted another stage

The seventh Earl Beauchamp in ceremonial dress as Lord Warden of the Cinque Ports.

on which to indulge his love of ancient ritual and pageantry when Asquith appointed him Lord Warden of the Cinque Ports, once the most powerful political and military appointment in the realm and a title dating back to the thirteenth century. Skirmishes between pirates – such as Farnando Lygon – and the men of this ancient institution had been notorious during the Tudor reigns, but this was now a largely ceremonial position. Walmer Castle, a purpose-built defensive castle erected in 1539, was the Lord Warden's official residence and Beauchamp was installed there on 18 July 1914. True to his love of historic detail, he reverted to ancient practice for the occasion. A fleet of warships, adorned with flags and insignia, filled the harbour at Dover. On shore, the town was festooned with bunting and flags and streamers hung between tall Venetian masts erected at the side of the road, in front of which passed frock-coated local dignitaries processing behind the black-robed Mayor of Sandwich bearing a thin black rod. A trumpet fanfare sounded, troops saluted and hats were raised as a motorcar bearing the new Lord Warden glided under an arch of Constable's Tower. The earl stepped out in the full costume of his office embellished with his own blue and gold ribbon of the Garter and the stars and emblems of many orders twinkling across his breast. He was attended by a pair of cream-and-scarlet-liveried footmen from Madresfield.

Though he dressed up in the apparel of military tradition, Beauchamp's defining political conviction was his hatred of war, a hatred still vividly remembered almost a century later by his daughter Sibell. Throughout the first decade of the twentieth century, he became increasingly concerned about the escalating arms race between Great Britain and Germany, which was, to his mind, a provocative folly. He also questioned the economic consequences of such expenditure encouraged by the relentless lobbying by arms dealers. The issue was also, he believed, distracting the government from the matter of Home Rule. Beauchamp had many run-ins with his colleague Sir Winston Churchill, First Lord of the Admiralty, and, by the winter of 1913/14, he emerged as 'of all people . . . by far the most aggressive and anti-Winston' of those Cabinet members who were opposed to Churchill's grandiose Naval Estimates for 1914/15. In fact, the size of the Estimates was being widely questioned within the Liberal party and in the country at large. Many believed that British naval superiority over Germany was sufficient already, negating Churchill's call to build four more Dreadnought battleships.

Following a Cabinet meeting on 27 January 1914, Asquith wrote to his wife that there had been 'much plain-speaking (or barking) on the part of the three I call beagles' (Sir John Simon, Sir Herbert Samuel and Beauchamp), and on the same day he wrote to his confidante, Venetia Stanley, about Beauchamp, whom he'd nicknamed 'Sweetheart', whose 'mellifluous' tones were much in evidence in Cabinet.

It has been calculated that at the time of the Austrian ultimatum to Serbia, half the Cabinet were known to be a 'peace party'. Asquith was desperate to prevent a schism in Cabinet for fear of becoming dependent upon the Unionists, but on 2 August, after a lunch at Halkin House, a group of Cabinet ministers including Beauchamp, Morley and Simon tendered their resignation. John Morley wrote later: 'I have seldom felt such relief, such lightness of heart – and reaction after all those days of tension. My host [Beauchamp] said he felt just the same.'

However, at a second Cabinet meeting that day, when it was learned that Belgium had rejected a German ultimatum demanding freedom of passage and it was clear that Germany would invade Belgium, Beauchamp and Simon were persuaded by Asquith to withdraw their resignations. Asquith's personal appeal for loyalty had probably weighed most heavily with Beauchamp, an appeal that he confessed to two days later in a letter to Morley: '. . . he [Asquith] is the chief figure in my political life. Always kind and considerate, how difficult to resist a personal appeal!' A pencilled note on 10 Downing Street paper, probably passed to him by the Prime Minister during the second Cabinet meeting that day, simply reads: 'I cannot say how much it means to me to have you still by my side.'

The following morning, Monday 3 August 1914, Beauchamp sat at his desk in Halkin House and, acutely aware of the historic importance of the events to which he had been witness over the past few days, he wrote:

It is very difficult to sit down calmly in the middle of a crisis and to record events as they fly by. But the decision wh. was taken at yesterday's Cabinet – in the morning – to promise France defence of her coast & shipping against Germany was so momentous that I wish to fix it.

Grey [the Foreign Secretary] proposed it as a definite step in favour of France. For that reason I & others objected. There was however the overwhelming argument that we had tacitly allowed France to concentrate in the Mediterranean in virtue of those unfortunate naval conversations wh. were to pledge no one to anything. It was obviously unfair to leave her in such circumstances unprotected. At the end of the Cabinet Burns protested in a moving speech & said he must resign. Everybody joined in a chorus of dissuasion and the PM spoke forcibly on 'deserting colleagues' etc. Eventually he promised to return for the evening Cabinet at wh. we expected a great fight over Belgian neutrality and wh. wd. end in rupture. Grey had however gained his point & avoided a conflict. A form of words was agreed to – we were all jaded and exhausted. Burns renewed his protest & was to see the PM this morn. I cannot but feel that our promise to France is a *casus belli* to Germany. Alas for this country!

There is an extraordinary, emphatically pencilled exchange on a Downing Street card in the Madresfield Muniments. Though undated and unsigned it is clearly a series of remarks passed between Asquith and

Beauchamp during the second Cabinet meeting that afternoon. It reads:

> *Beauchamp's hand*: I still think Burns was right this morning.
> *Asquith's hand*: Perhaps – but we are holding together with a good hope of keeping out of war altogether.
> *Beauchamp's hand*: I agree or I shd. join him!
> *Asquith's hand*: We *must* keep him.

Burns did resign. Ironically, it was Beauchamp, the pacifist, who was the only Cabinet minister present at the meeting of the Privy Council which, at ten thirty p.m. on 4 August at Buckingham Palace, sanctioned the proclamation of a state of war.

The change of mind over his resignation burdened William's conscience for the rest of his life. Three years later, during a debate on cotton duties in India, the regret is self-evident:

> There are a great many people in your Lordships' House as well as outside who have not agreed with every action of every Government during the war. They have often felt that the measures proposed have run counter to a great deal that they hold very dear. Yet they did not feel that it was right to oppose the action of His Majesty's Government at that time because, small and insignificant as might have been the result of their action, they were unwilling to do anything which would hinder the Government in the operations

which they thought necessary to carry on the war with success. Therefore, deeply as they felt that their political principles had been outraged, they did not think it necessary to obtrude the fact upon the notice of your Lordships' House.

In May 1915, when the first Coalition government of the war was formed, Beauchamp was not offered a seat in Cabinet. His 'peace party' credentials did not sit happily within a government at war. One former Cabinet colleague, Charles Hobhouse, described Beauchamp as 'a nonentity of pleasant manners', though he had to concede that he had 'a good deal of courage, and [is] a man of principle'. Beauchamp would not sacrifice principle to political advancement. Many more positive letters were written to him, regretting his departure, among them one from Edmund Gosse, at the time Librarian of the House of Lords.

This is a good moment, perhaps, to remind you, as I have no need to remind myself, how solid and broad is the political position you have built up for yourself in the last six or seven years. It has been my great pleasure to see it from a near point of view. No one of your age has done so much in the time. This is what I think today, when I see your name omitted, as I have known that it was your wish it should be omitted, from the Coalition list. But I do not forget that this is no defeat or decline, it is simply a provisional pause. You remain stationary for a little while, ready to start again from the same point.

Though out of office, Beauchamp remained close to the Prime Minister, lending Walmer Castle to Asquith who, finding 'the weekly change very beneficial', spent most Saturdays and Sundays there during the war. It being within easy reach of the GHQ in France, he held important conversations there with his military staff – Kitchener, Haig and others – in the congenial atmosphere that Beauchamp had created. The bossy Margot Asquith would add postscripts to her husband's letters, such as: 'Be an angel and ask your housekeeper [at Walmer] to put me into a bedroom with a bell near my bed that will reach my maid's ears clearly.'

Beauchamp was never busier, taking up what he considered to be honourable, if unpopular, causes. He travelled the country speaking out against trade protection (he was recruited as President of the Free Trade Union) and for the highly charged cause of the conscientious objector. So demonized was the German that as the war progressed not only did the British royal family change its name but even articles of clothing were rechristened. For example, Beauchamp was seen dapperly dressed in Bond Street, and the reporter was at pains to point out that the earl's attire included a 'light grey Biarritz, we no longer refer to a "Homburg" hat', which was now deemed an unpatriotic description. With patriotic feelings running so high, it was a brave man who espoused the cause of the conscientious objector.

Within the first two weeks of the war, so many British casualties and deaths were recorded that the generals began to call for conscription. Following the high death toll at the battles of Ypres and the Somme, the Conscription Bill was introduced in 1916. But compulsory call-up was unacceptable to genuine pacifists and they set up the No-Conscription Fellowship. Over sixteen thousand men in Britain claimed exemption from military service, some, such as the Quakers, for religious reasons. These conscientious objectors or COs, Lytton Strachey being a particularly well-known and articulate example, fell into three categories: the 'absolutists', who, as pacifists, opposed all work related to war; the 'alternativists', who were prepared to undertake civilian work that was not under military control; and the 'non-combatants', who would accept a call-up into the army provided that they did not have to use weapons.

Tribunals were set up to determine the fate of these dissidents and frequently these displayed little sensitivity towards the 'conchies' as they were disparagingly called. Harshly treated by their fellow countrymen, they were often excluded from employment, and many faced fines or even imprisonment. In captivity, many were humiliated, stripped naked or forced to wear khaki and threatened with the death sentence. Some were even executed. There are many moving records of these men's experiences. Sergeant C. Lippett of the Queen's West Surrey Regiment, for example, was stationed at a prison for COs and observed, 'I admired these men immensely . . . I realize that what they did in defying British military might . . . [meant] they had far more guts than we did who were doing these things to them.'

Beauchamp, known to be a pacifist, received scores of letters from COs, their families and concerned members of the political establishment. One was sent to him from the men interned at the Work Centre, Princetown, in Devon, where a large number of COs were employed under the Home Office Committee on the Employment of Conscientious Objectors. It explained that, while the inmates had expected that the work to be assigned to them would be 'of a normal civil character and under conditions approximating to the circumstances of normal industry', in fact they were 'penalized in every way'. The work was 'economically wasteful, penal in character and as such could only be devised for punishment'.

Francis W. Hirst, editor of *The Economist*, whom Beauchamp had met at Oxford, began a long and detailed correspondence with him about the issue of COs that continued throughout and after the war. Hirst encouraged Beauchamp's public support, recommending that some degree of Machiavellian politics be employed because the American press had shown 'shocked sentiment' over the alleged torturing of COs and, since Britain could not afford to lose the friendly neutrality of America, he thought 'therefore that the matter may be put on the ground of statecraft and prudence, if the rights of conscience in themselves convey no effective appeal to ministers'.

Hirst also kept him abreast of news, advising him for example that 'I am glad to tell you that the Governor of Wandsworth Gaol has been sacked for his treatment of conscientious objectors.' On 19 June 1916, Hirst wrote: 'The treatment of the conscientious objectors is so very horrible if true, and so utterly repugnant to British traditions that I am wondering whether you would be disposed either to join in a petition or to write individually to the highest authorities'. He did both. Hirst then published a letter in *The Economist* in which Beauchamp urged the nation to consider a negotiated peace.

On reading Beauchamp's letter in the magazine, a member of the public, Priscilla Albright, wrote to him on 23 June 1916 expressing her concern about the brutalizing effect on the persecutors. Another letter referred to 'the Prussianism which is besetting us'. Men of education, it seemed, were singled out for harsher punishments than the common man.

Towards the very end of the war a moving letter from Joseph Jones in Bristol epitomized the plight of the CO.

I feel keenly about this matter, My Lord, as my son, Mr. A. C. Jones, has served a sentence of over two years. I brought him up in the Christian Faith, and taught him to be true to conviction and honour. Because he felt it his duty to refuse all forms of service under a

Conscription Act, and remained true to his Faith under the most trying circumstances, the State has branded him and treated him as a criminal, while the Church has made no protest. I submit to you, My Lord, that such treatment on the part of the Government towards the purest and most moral of our young citizens is a scandal, and ought for the sake of our National Honour alone to be brought to an end.

Beauchamp continued to defend the rights of the COs right through the war and beyond. After the armistice, despite hostilities ceasing, they remained incarcerated, excluded from work and denied the vote for a decade. Beauchamp was a joint signatory, with other peers, MPs, clergy and literary and university men, to a letter to the Prime Minister, Lloyd George, which included the passage:

... a large number of these men are sincerely convinced that they have acted under the demands of their conscience and in accordance with deep moral and religious conviction. We urge that men in prison under these conditions should not be kept there during the period of national rejoicing, and that our country should not show itself slow at such a time to carry through an act of just mercy.

Beauchamp was equally caring about the fighting man and the enemy alien. He handed over both his homes to the war effort. Halkin House became a St

John's Ambulance Brigade hospital and medical supply depot and Madresfield a convalescent home. Photographs in the family albums show crisply uniformed nurses wheeling crippled servicemen or guiding blinded men, their heads wrapped in bandages, along the raked gravel paths, through the topiary arches and on to the Caesars' Lawn. To Beauchamp, any one of them could have been his brother Eddie. In June 1917, Lord Haldane visited Madresfield to offer his moral support. The two friends held similar views. The one-time Lord Chancellor, who had been educated in Germany, a country which he held in great affection, had worked tirelessly before the war to repair Anglo-German relations and to curb the arms race. Once war broke out, these German associations unreasonably counted against him and he was dropped from the Cabinet. Anti-German feeling ran so high that Beauchamp even received letters urging him to sack his children's German governess.

The topics of peace and free trade were seen as common liberal causes, especially by Hirst and Beauchamp, and both campaigners devoted the years 1915–18 to the promotion of a campaign for an early and fair peace. Eighteen months into the war of attrition, Beauchamp published a letter on 17 June 1916 in *The Economist* containing this statement: 'The cause for which we fight has been amply stated, and the time has surely come when we may consider what difference there is between our terms and those of our enemy, and whether another year of war, with its awful loss of life and treasure, will alter that difference to any appreciable extent.' It was reprinted in the *Yorkshire Post* and the *South Wales Daily News*.

Operating almost entirely outside Westminster, Beauchamp became a leading spokesman for the peace movement, urging exploratory diplomacy. In the summer of 1917 he addressed a letter to eleven peers, three bishops and his one-time Cabinet colleague John Simon, on using their positions to press for a negotiated peace, but all the replies were more or less discouraging.

By the close of 1917, Beauchamp's adversary over Irish Home Rule, the Marquess of Lansdowne, had also come to acknowledge the need for a negotiated settlement. In November 1917 he wrote a letter, rejected by *The Times* but published by *The Daily Telegraph* on the twenty-ninth. 'The Lansdowne Letter', as it was known, suggested a programme of five points which he believed would encourage those in Germany who desired peace. Beauchamp quickly wrote a supportive letter which appeared in the *Manchester Guardian* on 5 December; following publication, Beauchamp emerged as a central figure in the campaign to support Lansdowne. He travelled widely making speeches, attending dinners and lobbying the government to begin negotiations. Hirst recommended that Beauchamp 'collect the Dukes!' and, since Beauchamp's influence reached beyond Britain's shores, he was asked for a message to the American people by an American journalist. The earl replied succinctly, 'Thank God for

President Wilson', referring to the US President's constructive peace initiatives. On 6 November 1918, five days before the armistice was signed, Hirst acknowledged his efforts rather fulsomely, writing: 'You have done more, I think, than any other Liberal statesman to bring about the peace and to restore sanity.'

Towards the end of the war Beauchamp attended the Lords more regularly but chose to sit below the gangway, relishing the independence this gave him. He spoke out against the Allied intervention in Russia and the starvation blockade maintained against Germany and defended conscientious objectors, proportional representation, reconciliation with Germany and support for the nascent League of Nations. In the wake of the coalminers' strike, which escalated into the General Strike, his sympathies did not lie with the coal-owners and as the twenties progressed he moved steadily towards the left of the party.

One of the most enduring legacies of Beauchamp's public work was the enhanced effort to preserve Britain's countryside, her works of art and her historic houses. He regarded them as essential elements in the nation's heritage and was a pioneer in fighting for their protection. In the People's Budget of 1910, he had spoken up for an extension of the death-duty exemption for chattels of historic or artistic importance. As an early supporter of the Council for the Preservation of Rural England, he was in tune with the rustic sentiments of the Arts and Crafts movement and, like many others of this aesthetic bent, he considered that modern man's attitude to the country-side had become destructive, materialistic and anti-historical. Consequently, he actively supported organizations such as the Society for the Protection of Ancient Buildings, the National Trust and the Ramblers' Association.

In the last days of Lloyd George's Coalition government, the Office of Works, over which Beauchamp had presided before the war, appointed him head of a committee to consider a further extension of the Ancient Monuments Acts. C. R. Ashbee had been one of the first men in Britain to comprehend the importance of recording these buildings and preserving them. In the report, issued in 1921, Beauchamp recommended greater enactment of powers over historic houses, which included village cottages as well as grander buildings and 'the influence of contemporary architecture'.

Beauchamp was alert to the threat confronting the great estates: the agricultural crisis of the 1880s had led to the break-up of many great landholdings. At the end of the war there was yet another escalation of land sales to which he himself contributed. Beauchamp had been forced to sell eight thousand acres of the Madresfield estate to raise money and he stated: 'The upkeep of a large country house is likely to be an ever-growing burden. The State should be prepared to recognize the services of an owner who maintains on account of its historic and artistic value a structure which is ill-suited for modern requirements.' He proposed tax relief and maintenance grants for historic houses in return for an extension in preservation control. In this, he was nearly half a century ahead of his time.

As schisms developed in the party, Beauchamp increasingly identified with the Independent as opposed to the Coalition Liberals and was elected Chairman of the National Liberal Club in 1921. However, by 1926, though Asquith was still ostensibly the leader, Lloyd George was challenging his position and the Liberal Shadow Cabinet had effectively broken down. Throughout the twenties Beauchamp's most significant role was as the bridge-builder between these two men and their followers. As leader of the Liberals in the Lords from 1924 he applied his considerable diplomatic skills in trying to keep the party together. 'Lord Beauchamp's robust Liberalism and freedom from partisan bias has enabled him to play with effect the part of conciliator,' one newspaper reported. But ultimately, he failed.

In the end Beauchamp sided not with Asquith, the political mentor who had commanded his loyalty for so many years, but with Lloyd George. And as his own radicalism deepened, he even began to regret the Labour government's lack of commitment, for example wondering why it had shown 'no trace of socialism' in its budget and arguing that Keynesian measures should be taken to tackle unemployment. He began his Address in Reply to the King's Speech on 2 July 1929 expressing his regret that there were not more socialist peers on the benches opposite. One of his daughters recalls his progression towards the left.

He supported Lloyd George against Asquith and backed him when the split came. It was very interesting to me that he was as left-wing as he was. He was very radical. And when Elmley [his son and heir] grew up and went into politics and was going to become an MP, which was the automatic thing for every eldest son in those days, my father would really have rather liked it if he had joined the Labour Party . . . I remember him saying that, tactically or strategically, it would be a sensible thing for him to do because the Labour Party hadn't got anybody like that in their ranks. I think that it was quite possible that he [her father] would have crossed the floor.

The new leader of the Liberal Party, Lloyd George, believed that 'All Englishmen, except perhaps the Duke of Northumberland, are radicals, subverters, egalitarians and revolutionaries, though very many of us restrain and conceal these qualities, and in some they are altogether subconscious.' In Beauchamp's case this was certainly true.

The plasterwork ceiling of the Staircase Hall is decorated with the Beauchamp crest interspersed with the emblems of the Lord Warden of the Cinque Ports and the Order of the Garter, the two achievements of which he was particularly proud. And at one turn of the great staircase hangs a life-size portrait of Beauchamp at the height of his grandeur. Dressed in the ceremonial robes of the Lord Warden of the Cinque Ports, hung with the chain of office of the Chancellor of London

University and proudly displaying his garter, he is grand indeed. Leaving the room and passing back through the Ante-Room towards the Library, the visitor passes the walnut table bearing his red despatch boxes. In one of them, as well as an old copy of *The Times* and some farm auction catalogues, there lies a British Legion poppy, the kind sold to commemorate those who lost their lives in the two World Wars. Since the time of William Langland, the poppy has held a symbolic place in England's iconography. This paper one is a poignant reminder of Beauchamp's fealty to the cause of peace but it also provides a clue to another aspect of his psychological make-up, which in the end led to his political demise.

Chapter Thirteen

THE SCRAP OF PAPER

It was the second winter of the Great War. William sat in the Library, warmed by the heat from the vast fireplace. Outside, the wind pushed hard against the Old Hills and the weak sun skimmed the water in the moat, passed through the frost-frilled windows behind him and struggled to reach across the book in his hands. As the clock struck two, his four daughters entered the room: Lettice and her three younger sisters, Sibell, Mary and Dorothy, all plainly dressed in darned Shetland jerseys, threadbare tweed skirts, lisle stockings and well-polished lace-up shoes. After formally greeting their father, they lay at his feet, and began the daily Madresfield ritual: listening to a story read by Daddy. That particular afternoon, recalled eight decades later by Sibell, he continued reading from *The Little Duke*, a romantic fiction based on William the Conqueror's great-grandfather:

The Archbishop waited till [the little duke] rose, and then, turning him with his face to the people, said, 'Richard, by the grace of God, I invest thee with the ducal mantle of Normandy!' Two bishops then hung round his shoulders a crimson velvet mantle, furred with ermine, which, made as it was for a grown man, heavily hung on the poor child's shoulders, and lay in heaps on the ground. The Archbishop then set the golden coronet on his long, flowing hair, where it hung so loosely on the little head, that Sir Eric was obliged to put his hand to hold it safe; and, lastly, the long, straight, two-handed sword was brought and placed in his hand, with another solemn bidding to use it ever in maintaining the right.

The author of this historical novel, so popular with Christian parents, was Charlotte M. Yonge, a Tractarian who had also written one of William's favourite books, *The Heir of Redclyffe*. Her books drew upon the romance of Sir Walter Scott and the chivalry of Malory, underpinned by the moral imperatives of Charles Kingsley's 'Muscular Christianity'. William approved of these associations, which were encapsulated in that inspirational image of G. F. Watts's *Sir Galahad* which he had encountered as a boy at Eton. As Lygons, they too had a long and distinguished lineage, rooted in Norman ancestry. *The Little Duke* is set in tenth-century Normandy between warring gangs of Normans, Franks, Danes, Bretons and Flemings. Their battles raged over the same lands which, then, in that winter of 1915,

The books Daddy has read to us

Lettie   Madresfield Court Great Malvern   *Nell*

since June 1915 – to December 1916

The Tapestry Room
The Pigeon Pie
Lilian's Golden Hours
The Christmas Child
Wandering Willie
The Talisman .... and
Ivanhoe   some Poetry.
St Ives .... Theodora Phranza.
The House of Walderne
The Black Arrow
The Caged Lion
The Little Duke
The Jungle Books
The Maltese Cat
Boscobel.
Puck of Pook's Hill
Rewards and Fairies
The Armourers Apprentice

Devoted father: over eighteen months during the First World War, Earl Beauchamp read all these books to his young daughters.

were scarred with the trenches where young men in their thousands were being slaughtered.

William was committed to his seven children's education, emotional well-being and moral training. Virtually every day that he was at Madresfield he set aside one hour after lunch to read to his daughters. His older sons, Elmley and Hugh, were at Eton and Dickie, his youngest, was still as yet unborn. Lying flat on their backs to encourage erect deportment, the girls were transported by their father in imagination into medieval castles with Yonge and Walter Scott, on to mules along the North-West Frontier with Rudyard Kipling or into what Sibell remembered as an 'intoxicatingly funny' adventure down an Irish river with the story-telling vicar George Birmingham. The earl also selected Victorian novels with historical themes which echoed his ancestors' past, such as William Harrison Ainsworth's *Boscobel*, an account of Charles II's last stand at Worcester – in which Madresfield played a part – and Mrs Molesworth's edifying dramas. Mrs Molesworth's tales were illustrated by one of William's favourite artists, the Pre-Raphaelite and socialist Walter Crane. Crane's ethereal pistachio-green and map-pink illustrations evoked a romanticized children's world which could also be found on the wallpaper hanging in the Lygons' Schoolroom and across the tiles in their bathrooms. As one turns the pages of William's scrapbooks, stored carefully in the Muniment Room beneath the Library – which, in an historical sense, holds the literary foundations of both the house and the family – the greatest impression left by them is of a devoted father, savouring the milestones in his children's lives: Dorothy's christening by the Archbishop of Canterbury, Elmley's and Hugh's watercolours of snowdrops and knapweed, painted programmes for the 'Theatre Royal at Madresfield' pantomimes, Elmley's coming-of-age photographs, Court & Social accounts of his daughters' comings-out. Perhaps most evocative of all is a scrap of paper written on by two of his young daughters, the nine-year-old Lettice and her sister Sibell, and glued into one of the scrapbooks.

This list of children's books reveals as much about William as all the boxes of political correspondence stacked in the Muniment Room or accounts published in contemporary political diaries and social memoirs. It is a simple, if unconscious, testament by his daughters to his devotion to them. If fatherly love can be measured by time spent, William loved his children greatly. The list's dates fall in the middle of the First World War. During those eighteen months he spent several hundred hours reading to them, at a time when he was politically busier than ever.

His children noticed that he rarely mentioned his own childhood, school or Oxford days, and only visited his old governess, who lived in an almshouse in the village, out of duty. Despite the tight-lipped relationship that he had endured with his father and stepmother, he was determined to excel as a parent himself and set about this with energy, taking up the slack from his wife, whose delight in infants waned when they became noisy toddlers. His determination in this matter recalls the efforts of his ancestor, the widowed William the Correspondent, who similarly brought up his children single-handedly and, as his letters show, took tremendous interest in their well-being.

Tucked away behind a wall hung with mackintoshes and thorn-proof tweed overcoats, there is a pair of relatively small rooms on the ground floor at Madresfield. It was here, in the oldest, sixteenth-century part of the house once inhabited by his Tudor ancestors and now surrounded by his children's Nursery and bed-rooms, that William chose to settle himself. The rooms face west towards the Malvern Hills and though they abut the entrance on one side and the New Kitchen on the other, they are far away from the general hubbub of the house. His bedroom and bathroom are intimate, low-ceilinged and beamed. The walls are panelled in oak and hung with yards of canvas which William Morris printed with huge watery blue and green lilies. To be in this set of rooms feels like sheltering in an old chest. The only audible sound is the occasional cry of a grumpy goose disturbed on the moat bank. As in all the rooms that look out on to the moat, light dances across the wooden surfaces, reflected off the protective water below. The bathroom has small mullioned windows glazed with medieval and Pre-Raphaelite stained glass. The fireplace is set with William Morris tiles and a line of lustreware pots sits along the mantelpiece. Opposite the window hangs a large watercolour of another cabinet, the Cabinet Room in Downing Street. The interconnecting door is opened with a pewter handle hand-beaten by an artisan in C. R. Ashbee's workshop. Simple oak furnishes the bedroom: a Tudor four-poster bed, a sixteenth-century Flemish marriage chest, a Jacobean window seat, a ladder-back chair and a gate-leg table. A comfortable armchair and a jointed stool are gathered round a stone chimneybreast bearing the crest of the Knights of the Garter. William's quarters hark back to the 'hand-made world throughout' of his forebears, Joan de Braci and Thomas Lygon.

He spent time with his children here in this dark, woody world. Outside his bedroom he installed for them a line of child-level porcelain sinks and lavatories. Opposite these fittings stood a large dresser on which were stacked their chamber pots. His children were installed in the Nursery close by or, as they grew older, in one of the Tudor bedrooms above him on the Somerset landing. Like most men of his background, the earl was not physically affectionate with his children but he was modern in the way in which he welcomed them freely into his life. It was 'very un-Victorian' that he encouraged them to talk to him every morning while he soaked, like a large, pink marshmallow, with 'a sponge over his private parts', in his mahogany-panelled bath. Here, religion was discussed, cultural outings planned – the theatre at Malvern, Diaghilev's Ballets Russes or Sir Henry Wood's concerts in London – and troubles shared, whether it was the drowning of Sibell's dog in the stewes or Dorothy's fall from a new pony while out cubhunting. Curiously, politics were never mentioned as they were 'taken as a matter of course'. It was here that, like fledglings tucked under his timbered wing, they sheltered in a cosy haven of Tudor Englishness, literally and symbolically as far as possible from their mother's gilded rococo world of French grandeur on the other side of the house, at the far side of the new wing that housed the Drawing Room and her bedroom.

Within the home, both parental roles had fallen upon William because his wife was concerned with neither childcare nor household management. She was a troubled and retiring woman. Nor was politics of any interest to her and consequently she was a reluctant political hostess. 'She didn't even like visitors at Madresfield,' Dorothy remembers with regret. 'Politics meant nothing to her. She simply could make nothing of them [the politicians] and never tried to. I think it was rather a gap between her and my father because he was so very political.' Instead, she preferred to confine herself to routines of elaborate idleness, assisted by a Miss Grugham (one-time maid to the future Prime Minister's wife, Lucy Baldwin). Like Queen Victoria, the countess did not enjoy the company of children. 'Mother liked babies until they were two,' observed Sibell, 'and then she got terribly bored with them. When we were small we were each displaced by the next arrival. I had quite a long innings because I think she had a miscarriage in 1908. After that she never came into one's life, except as a vengeance; always in a bad temper.' How different William was; his sentimental carving of Lettice's infant head resting on an enormous pillow remains in the home of one of his grandchildren today. Not that his affection led him to lower standards of behaviour. In private the earl may have been relatively informal with his children but in public, as was correct, they were addressed, from birth, by their titles in front of servants and friends, and like many children of that period, they could only speak when spoken to and were drilled to file into a room after all the adults had entered ahead of them.

The Lygons grew up in that curious English aristocratic environment, a coupling of unbelievable grandeur and character-forming toughness. The family moved seasonally by private train between their three homes: Madresfield Court, which had its own station, Hanworth Halt; Walmer Castle in Kent, the official residence of the Lord Warden of the Cinque Ports; and their London residence. William always kept a hundred pounds in cash on him 'in case I have to hire a train'. Initially, when in town, the family had lived at Lower Park in Putney, then Elmley House in Wimbledon, but eventually, when the motor car replaced the horse-drawn carriage and stables were no longer required, William moved his whole establishment to his house just off Belgrave Square. This last, a white stucco mansion, had originally gone under the simple address 13 Halkin Street, but Lady Beauchamp deemed it appropriate to give it a title and so it became Halkin House.

There was no such thing as 'weekending' at either of their country homes – 'that was considered common!' Sibell remembered. Every day that the family was in residence in London, fresh fruit and vegetables were sent up from Madresfield's gardens by train.

When the Lygons were at Madresfield, they were always attended by no fewer than eighteen servants, and when there were guests, often considerably more. In the Library there is a morocco-bound 'Daily Dinner Book' in which the number of family and guests were recorded, together with the number of staff in attendance. For example, on 9 November 1903 Asquith and his family came to stay; two weeks later Their Royal Highnesses Princess Margaret and Princess Patricia of Connaught visited, along with fourteen other guests. On another occasion not only were there ten visitors' servants to be housed and fed but also two extra servants and three nursery servants were hired to help the twenty-two Madresfield servants with a large house party. In the month of July 1904 alone a total of 2,366 people were entertained at Madresfield. Then, mercifully for the staff, things would become quiet again for a while, registered in the book by 'the establishment left for London'.

If guests were expected, Lady Beauchamp would stroll through some of the sixty bedrooms with a basket containing scented soap hooked over her arm; one bar of soap was carefully placed on each Royal Worcester soap-dish and its waxed paper used to perfume underclothes in her chest of drawers. It was one of the rituals she had developed to while away the idle hours. She would religiously save other scraps of paper for the children to write out and commit to memory her mantra: TOMO, TOMO, TOMO! Tidiness, Order, Method, Organization.

If the weather was bad, Lady Beauchamp retreated to the Long Gallery where, by the fitful daylight which filtered through a curtain of foliage, she read her letters and fastidiously corrected the titles by which she was addressed on the envelopes of that day's post before throwing them into the wastepaper basket. The footmen were instructed to bring whole roast chickens up to her there, where she dined copiously and alone. Her last-born and most loved child, Dickie, was her only companion. He would be brought to her and suckled until he was a toddler and so the maids had to supplement his diet discreetly with wholesome puddings. During the war he was given all the children's sugar ration, much to his siblings' fury. During thunderstorms, she would hide in a walk-in wardrobe with Dickie, for only he, she believed, needed her protection. On sunny days, a nurse prepared Dickie and placed him in a black pram, to the front of which a groom had attached two brightly painted tin horses which rocked on springs. The countess would push the contraption round the grounds inspecting the plants.

As a child the countess had been chaperoned rather than schooled by a German governess, and was, according to her granddaughter, 'one pheasant short of a brace'. Without either sound education or inspiring parental role models, she had few resources with which to create a happy family life. The marshmallow softness that she carried as a newly-wed prematurely expanded into a matronly stolidness thanks to her greediness and her dislike of exercise. She rarely rode horses and apart from her strolls about the garden with Dickie her most vigorous activities were a gentle swim in the pool or scuttling down corridors to avoid her other offspring.

Exercise – upon the earl's insistence – was a cornerstone of the children's upbringing. Another was religion: periodically they would be summoned by their mother to be lectured on it, her favourite subject. As well as being dim-witted, Lady Beauchamp was sanctimonious, a combination which alienated her children. Her own mother's marriage had not been happy and both mother and daughter had found solace in religion. 'Everything was wrapped up in holiness. They hadn't got a hope – poor devils,' Sibell explained. The drum of Anglicanism was beaten by the countess day and night. She regarded all Roman Catholics with the deepest suspicion and banned them from the house, though William, by contrast, sympathized with them and developed a great love of the papal city. Like his father, he applauded the Oxford Movement. He was happy that the slipshod habits of the Church of England had been replaced by Anglo-Catholic ceremonies and rituals of great precision. The ornate silverware on the altar had to be set out as if for a formal banquet and acolytes were required always to light the right candle before the left. While he welcomed the *English Hymnal* in place of *Hymns Ancient and Modern*, he deprecated the Revised Prayer Book which (though he was required to defend it publicly in Parliament) the family ignored in favour of the traditional Book of Common Prayer, a text also greatly cherished by his sister's friend, Elgar.

On the front pew of the Chapel at Madresfield lie eight morocco-bound prayer books: one for each child and one belonging to William. Each cover was tooled in gold with their name garlanded by their favourite flower – a rose, a snowdrop, a vine – and inscribed from their father; for example: 'To a very darling young man, Elmley, from his loving Daddy. St. Anne's Day 1910'. William's own copy, given to him by his wife on Christmas Day 1911, was inscribed by her, 'Work thy work and in His time He will give thee thy reward'. If one of the children had been naughty they were sent up to the loft to pump the organ while their mother accompanied the hymns.

A leading exponent of this reformed Church of England was the Reverend Percy Dearmer, editor of the *English Hymnal*, author of *The Parson's Handbook* (1899), and rector of St Mary's Church, on Primrose Hill in north London. The Library contains many of his works, including *Body and Soul: An Enquiry into the Effects of Religion upon Health* (1909) and *The Truth about Fasting* (1928). Dearmer was an unequivocal Tractarian. Intent on recreating a medieval atmosphere in church, he promoted simple, unaccompanied Gregorian chant and clad

The butler's record of the number of guests, visitors' servants, and meals prepared: in July 1904 alone they entertained 2,366 guests.

himself in the vestments of Old Sarum as he recited piously from the Book of Common Prayer. He amazed Catholics and Protestants alike as he walked around his Primrose Hill parish parading his 'British Museum religion'. G. K. Chesterton observed that Dearmer would be jeered at in the streets by boys calling out, 'To Hell with the Pope!' to which Dearmer would solemnly enquire, 'Are you aware that this is the precise costume in which Latimer went to the stake?' Every Sunday, when in London, the Beauchamps took the long, inconvenient journey on public transport to worship with Dearmer.

Dressed in their finery – William in top hat and morning coat, his wife festooned in lace-trimmed silk and hung with pearls, beneath a parasol – they herded their children on to a bus, down into the newly built Underground and back up at Hampstead to begin the long walk to Primrose Hill. William bore this inconvenience as he considered that taxis were an extravagance and that the Sabbath should be a day of rest for cars as well as horses.

William insisted that his children speak impeccable French – the language of the aristocracy of Europe, and of diplomacy. To achieve this, the third cornerstone of their education, he hired a bombazine-upholstered Swiss-French governess from Neuchâtel where, he was led to believe, the best French was spoken. If lunching with their father, the children had to conduct conversation in French and take it in turns to introduce interesting topics. And after French, exercise: every day they swam. The pool at Madresfield was primitive and unsanitary – the water was never changed – and their only training was to be 'simply thrown in the deep end and told to make movements'. When the women and children had withdrawn from the poolside, William would announce, 'Gentlemen may lower their costumes,' and only then could they swim bare-chested. At Walmer Castle, the children swam in the English Channel right up to the end of November. One February, Dorothy asked for an unusual birthday present: could she be excused from swimming? Not only was her request turned down but her mother

Earl Beauchamp with five of his seven children. When at Walmer Castle, the Lord Warden's residence, they swam daily in the English Channel.

made her swim twice that day. Depending on the season, riding or hunting was used 'as a way of getting rid of us', though the girls in particular were passionate about the chase and hunted side-saddle all their lives. As children, they were accompanied by a groom who wore black worsted with silver buttons and a black silk top hat. While the girls rode over three counties, the boys, like their father, mastered boxing. Lawn tennis he also regarded as an essential accomplishment for them all.

Keen to supervise their daily programme, the earl began his day surrounded by his children. His ablutions were followed by breakfast at eight-thirty a.m. in the Schoolroom and daily prayers in the Chapel half an hour later. All the servants were expected to attend, with the exception of one kitchen maid who was excused in order to oversee the adults' breakfast. The maids sat on the left, the footmen on the right and the family at the front. The children then passed their mornings in the Schoolroom, learning French and the occasional piece of history, though they never advanced beyond Queen Anne's reign because with each change of governess the new one took them back to the beginning again. Governesses were chosen by the countess for their appearance. 'If they had their hair parted down the middle and looked like the Madonna', they were appointed. Lessons paused at eleven a.m. so that the girls, thought to be anaemic, could have a glass of port. If Father was at home, lunch was taken formally in the Dining Room with a footman behind each chair.

If he was absent, Mother escaped to the Long Gallery in the winter or the French Sitting Room in the summer where she loved to discuss religion with two equally devout women, her best friends, Princess Louise Augusta and Princess Patricia of Connaught, Queen Victoria's granddaughters.

Political demands and the children's needs aside, it also fell to William to run the household from the mahogany cylinder bureau in the Library. After chapel, the clerk of works, head gardener, gamekeeper, estate manager and cook lined up in the passage outside the Library and took turns to consult him. He organized redecorating and the moving of furniture and objets d'art, and knew everything that was going on, not only on the estate but also in the family's Industrial School for Girls in the village. He took great pride in his Madresfield duties. As he was particular about food, William also planned the menus – which was fortunate since, were it left to their mother, the family would have lived on 'cabbage, mince, puffed rice and stewed pears day after day'. On hearing of the arrival of the famous French chef Boulestin in London, William dispatched the cook to be trained by him. Mr Crump, the head gardener, oversaw the supply of first-class vegetables and was known to lecture the tenants and local farmers on the cooking of vegetables. Overcooking them, in his opinion, rendered them 'insipid'. In matters of food William was a Francophile and so, despite the fame of the local, highly spiced and popular 'Worcestershire' sauce made by Lea & Perrins, he banned it from the kitchen. He was so disgusted by it that when he visited a restaurant in Rome with his daughters and the proprietor considerately placed a bottle of it on their table, the earl got up and left.

Lady Beauchamp's indifference to the children bordered on neglect. Poor Dorothy was always being slapped because she could not read. Eventually one of the nannies suspected bad eyesight and after lobbying the countess was eventually allowed to take her charge to the optician. Dorothy was, in fact, so short-sighted that she had to wear beer-bottle-thick spectacles for the rest of her life.

If the children fell ill, stoicism was prescribed. Lady Beauchamp, infuriated by the inconvenience of it all, subscribed to her doctor's view that a glass of champagne cured every ailment. When Sibell and Lettice were taken in 1921 to Italy to celebrate their confirmation, Sibell contracted scarlet fever, but even when her temperature rose to 104 degrees no doctor was called, for fear of them being evicted from the Palazzo Hotel in Venice. The earl showed a more tender concern than his wife for his children's maladies. Mary's 'Strictly Private Diary' of 1924 records that on 30 March, 'I developed very slight measles. Daddy came and read to me,' as he did attentively over the next few days until she was allowed to 'have a bath and had my head washed . . . allowed to see family. Room disinfected.'

Though the English have traditionally dressed their children for practicality rather than for show, the Lygon children were so parsimoniously dressed in hand-me-downs from their cousins that most garments were threadbare by the time they reached Dorothy and Dickie. Dorothy remembered with glee that 'Mother didn't care a damn.' On Sibell and Lettice's trip to Italy they were dressed in such shabby clothes that they were mistaken for charity children. Occasionally, their nurse-maids – they had one each – would buy whatever was available in Malvern, the local market town. Where her children were concerned, the countess's economy was so extreme that she insisted her daughters make use of the sanitary towels 'inherited' from a dead cousin. Even the laundry maids were shocked.

Lady Beauchamp found it difficult to empathize with her children. Each birthday she just gave them another large red church candle while their father took great trouble to commission wooden trunks painted with Japanese scenes or to order a toy that they had admired in Hamley's catalogue. He was not over-indulgent; though their upbringing was a loving one, it was as we have seen strict and traditional. It was, for example, deemed to be 'unsuitable' for them to mix with anyone outside the family, with the exception of their local cousins, the Ashley-Coopers, the children of Lord Shaftesbury – though 'more dirty-minded children I have never met!' laughed Sibell. They rode with the local hunt, but otherwise the Lygon children were isolated, so that playmates were the characters from their storybooks and their imaginations. Collecting birds' eggs along the Gloucester Drive became the seizing of Moghul booty on the Silk Route; pursuing hens in the poultry yard became the re-enactment of brigands chasing galleons across the seas. When Bradford the butler's wheelchair-bound son came up from the village dressed in his fustian best, they pushed this Chinese emperor in his palanquin along furlongs of raked gravel and levelled lawns.

Their pets understandably assumed a huge importance in their lives. When Maimie's beloved Persian cat drowned, Lady Beauchamp had the corpse dredged from the moat and sent to a taxidermist. In a gesture of misplaced kindness, she then placed the stuffed creature at the foot of her daughter's bed. Maimie was so distressed on finding it that her mother attempted to take the child's mind off it by 'telling her about the curse!'

If the family was in London while Parliament was sitting, Lady Beauchamp made even greater efforts to avoid her children in the relatively cramped Halkin House. On fine afternoons, however, she would take the girls out into the Belgrave Square gardens. En route, the party passed under the windows of an insane neighbour who made a habit of gesticulating wildly and meaninglessly from an upper window. The countess would amuse herself by imitating the unfortunate woman: tossing her head back and forth, flailing her arms with mock-abandon and encouraging her girls to join in the game. Instead they would stand beside her, sometimes for as long as half an hour, heads hung in shame at their mother's tactlessness and thoughtless cruelty.

The Beauchamp family in the grounds of Walmer Castle, c. 1925: left to right, Coote, Maimie, Sibell, Lettice, Lady Beauchamp, Lord Beauchamp, Elmley, Hugh, Dickie.

William hosted numerous political events at Halkin House: informal working lunches for fellow members of the Cabinet or the Free Trade Association, formal dinners for the Liberal Party, galas, royal receptions and occasionally functions related to an official state visit. There he would stand at the top of the stairs greeting his guests from the heights of implacable courtesy, dressed up to the nines with his Order of the Garter twinkling on his breast, like a decorated pouter pigeon. While serving as Steward of the Royal Household between 1907 and 1910, he had observed the grand ritual of royal entertaining and he emulated it in his own household. He was a stickler for formality. Guests entered the dining room in strict order of precedence (royals were followed by dukes, earls and so on down the ranks). He went to painstaking lengths to oversee menus and insisted that champagne be decanted into jugs to distinguish his table from those of the middle classes. Such observances inevitably led to sneers from some guests who found him to be ludicrously grand: but he was simply a perfectionist. Care and attention to minute detail were traits that he applied to his children's upbringing and they adored him for it. 'We depended very much on father', Sibell said simply.

When at Walmer, the family attended the Sunday service at the Marine Barracks and William, who retained a boyish love of dressing up in uniforms, paraded himself in full naval costume. It was here that he acquired the family nickname 'Boom', not because of his voice but because of the characteristic sound of the foghorns warning ships off the Goodwin Sands. Before air travel, the main point of entry into Britain was across the English Channel to either Folkestone or Dover. As the king's representative, he was required to greet travellers of consequence, a role he relished. One of the first projects that he embarked upon when he was appointed Lord Warden of the Cinque Ports was to build a chapel at Walmer Castle. Official duties kept him there during the spring and early summer though the children longed to be at Madresfield. By comparison, Walmer was uncomfortable and 'so cold in our quarters that the wind blew the carpets off the floors', recalled Sibell. As the family's private section of the house was small, the children had to share just two rooms, which provoked squabbles and discontent. Among the compensations of the Kent coast were prospecting for shells along the shingle, gardening their own plot of land and, during the Great War, standing on the roof of the castle to watch the dogfights between the British and German fighter planes. The only time any of them went to sea was when Sibell, as a birthday treat, was taken out to the Sands to inspect a beached German submarine.

William's concern for his children did not stop once they had reached maturity. There is a touching correspondence between him and his wife dated spring 1923 while he was touring Italy with Elmley, Hugh and Hugh's Eton and Oxford companion, Robert Byron. During the trip William carried a copy of Augustus J. C. Hare's *Florence*, in which he had inscribed, on New

Year's Day 1898, an itinerary of his own first trip to the city. The letters illustrate his preoccupation with his young party's welfare and his affection for his wife. The four men followed an exacting and elevating study programme both of art and *l'art de vie*, and visited a variety of people: the Pope, the aesthete Harold Acton and the writer and doctor Axel Munthe. William's letters mix high culture with accounts of base teenage habits, such as sleeping-in or picking spots.

'It is going to be a fine day today,' he wrote on Monday 26 March 1923, 'but the two young men are very late – for no reason as they went to bed at ten last night and it is a waste to be in bed late on a fine day in Venice. We are going to try and find Carpaccio's Saint George. Yr. loving Will.' In Florence, a week later, he observed that while Elmley 'enjoys the pictures more than Hugh, Byron's interest in them and knowledge of them is a most excellent thing for both Elmley and Hugh'. And from Rome on 20 April he informed her that 'this morning we have to spend at the Vatican which is convenient for my audience. I am sorry not to have seen Mussolini, but one can't do everything. I cannot join Mrs Strong's enthusiasm for him but do not tell her so.'

The saga of Elmley's boil was unfolded over several days in William's generous looped script, which included the courteous habit of repeating the last word of a page on the first line of the following one, for ease of reading. From the Hotel Roma in Florence on 3 April, he informed his wife that 'Elmley had had the threat of a nasty spot on his forehead but it is passing away with the help of iodine.' The following day: 'The spot on his forehead is better this morning. Evidently, it is not going to be a boil. But he has no idea how to look after it, as you can imagine. So it looks much worse than it really is.' But it clearly lingered for weeks, for on the morning of 20 April he continued, 'Elmley, poor darling, has been rather depressed with this threatening of a boil on his forehead. It has passed away but you can imagine that it looked worse than it really was with dried blood and iodine – he had forgotten to bring the colourless with him.'

Despite their intellectual incompatibility, William and his countess cared deeply for one another. Back in 1912 she had commissioned Payne, who was decorating the Library, to make a commonplace book as a gift to her husband, bound between precious-stone-studded ivory boards. Momentous events in their marriage, such as the birth of a child or his inauguration as Lord Warden of the Cinque Ports, were recorded in jewel-like illuminations on the vellum pages. He reciprocated her affection and respect. Walking through a pine forest outside Florence on Maundy Thursday 1923, he was so struck by the vivid beauty of some violets that he immediately sent a bunch to her with his second letter of the day. On Easter Sunday, Harold Acton accompanied the earl's party to an Italian restaurant where 'we dined on native dishes' and the following day they heard mass at the Duomo. Sensitive to his wife's suspicions of

Catholicism, William assured her in his letter of that evening that she 'need not fear that I shall become Roman for our own early service seemed much more Godly and reverent'. From the cacophony of Naples, he wrote that he was 'glad to hear of all the quiet happiness of which you are the centre' and that 'you are going to the party at the Palace and I am sure you will find many friends. Which dress, I wonder, will you wear?' And he added a postscript of suggestions. Theirs was *un amour courtois* – a courtly love which over the years may have become platonic but did not die. Dotted around the house today there are many copies of a cut-out of the formal photograph taken of the whole family standing side by side at Walmer. The earl has linked his arm firmly through his wife's and clasps her hand with confident affection – an affection reiterated and amplified in these letters sent back from Italy.

William deeply influenced his young travelling companion, the adolescent Robert Byron. When they had first met, Byron – like a petulant Little Englander – had despised 'abroad'. By the time he had returned from his debut trip abroad with the Lygons, he had discovered the pleasures of 'a larger world', and after his visit to Ravenna had espoused the Byzantine. The journey was to shape the rest of Byron's short life and, as a consequence, he effectively rehabilitated the culture of Byzantium and became, arguably, Britain's greatest twentieth-century travel writer. William taught Byron to locate and study beauty and to organize purposeful itineraries. Travel was a serious matter to the earl; not for him the idle wanderings of the tourist.

Writing to William's eldest son, by then the eighth Earl Beauchamp, some years later from a hotel in America, Byron was the first to acknowledge that

> ... no one, not even myself, will ever know how indebted I was to him. Had it not been for that journey to Italy, I often wonder if I would ever have gone abroad at all. Not only did it implant in me a desire to see other countries: it laid the foundation of my delight in painting and architecture, and introduced me to that classical criterion which is the basis ... So I must express to you instead, and ask you to believe – little though it be – that such small pleasure or interest as I have been able to awaken in others through my writings have constituted, in some degree, a transmission of his beneficence. I find I am reaching an age when I look back as well as forward. Those pleasant days at Walmer, when we were all young and innocent and the world was indeed our oyster, stand out very brightly. Perhaps the gloom of an American provincial hotel is responsible for the melancholy of this reflection. But I shall always remember that some of the happiest days of my youth were passed under your father's roof.

Along with his Oxford contemporary Evelyn Waugh, who had shared his initial disdain for 'bloody abroad', Byron was not only shaped by the earl's teachings but

The beautiful Hugh, c. 1925.

also by his neo-Gothic and Pre-Raphaelite home. Both were welcomed to 'Mad' by the family. Byron would amuse the Lygons by mimicking Queen Victoria or pretending to be deaf when other visitors came to stay. Madresfield was to these young men the antithesis of the classical English country house and as such would have deeply appealed to these contrarians. Though they had been fed a diet of the classics at school and taught to admire all things Greek and Roman, they rejected the refined and 'educated' taste for Augustan marble busts, bronze obelisks and classical stone columns. Instead they inclined towards all things Gothic and Pre-Raphaelite, filling their college rooms with bric-a-brac: wax flowers under glass domes, stuffed birds in glass cases, shells arranged in intricate collages and petit point embroideries. In many ways, they were the aesthetic precursors of the hippies and it is no surprise that their contemporary Cecil Beaton could identify with, and capture in photographs, both periods with such conviction.

Learning and aesthetics aside, what struck the young who came to stay was the family spirit. While Elmley could be pompous, his siblings were amusing and loved pranks. Hugh had matured into an exquisite youth with ash-blond locks pomaded back from a face of Botticellian beauty, set with hyacinth-blue Lygon eyes. His athletic frame was flattered by close-fitting, double-breasted tailoring. Photographs and paintings of him are dotted round Madresfield. Sibell remembers him as 'a charmer and great fun. Bored at a dance we gave at Halkin House he went around telling guests that their family was waiting outside in the car and so they all made off rather quickly. He, of course, was delighted with himself.' Charm aside, Hugh was rather an airling, a flighty spirit.

Teresa 'Baby' Jungman, one of the original Bright Young Things whom Waugh caricatured in *Vile Bodies*, recalls the exceptional family life at Madresfield in a touching tribute to Beauchamp.

> There was this enormous warmth between all of them. He was a charming old boy and we [she and her sister, Zita] always sat next to him at meals so he had six girls around him [including his four daughters]. And I never remember any of them saying an unkind thing about one another or having a row, which is rather a strange thing. It wasn't the house that moved me, it was all of them.

It was clear to Diana Mosley, too, that 'he was a very much loved parent'.

As the girls grew up after the First World War, and despite their two older brothers having fallen in with a racy set at Oxford, their social lives were still restricted by their mother's snobbery and their father's political Liberalism. Lord Coventry, a rival Tory peer who lived nearby, was considered to be suitable company by their mother, much to their father's annoyance. With the exception of local hunt balls and tennis parties with relations such as the Baths, Ilchesters, Sutherlands,

Hustings for the General Election, 1929: Beauchamp; Elmley, the Liberal candidate; Coote and Maimie.

Vivians and Bathursts, and tea dances in the Long Gallery to the accompaniment of the local church band, the countess gave the girls no preparation for coming out; they were innocent of the allurements of style and coquetry. How a Continental mother would have gasped. Cleaving to her outmoded sense of propriety, their mother insisted that while the rest of society Charlestoned in flapper dresses, her girls should be attired like a vicar's daughters. She instructed the seamstress to attach droopy lace sleeves on to all their sleeveless evening gowns. And when her daughters were launched into society, they were exceedingly unsophisticated compared with their peers.

Disdaining the role of matchmaker, the countess opined that such matters 'just sorted themselves out!' though Sibell was the exception to her rule. 'Mother hoped I'd marry the Dean of Gloucester who was about seventy-two and whose wife had died. I was sixteen. She really did! She was very odd, a religious zealot. He, of course, treated me like a child, which I was.' To illustrate the rarefied nature of her Madresfield upbringing, Sibell would tell how, at one formal dinner, a pompous older man turned to her and asked, 'Have you ever eaten off gold plate before, my dear?' The matter-of-fact ingénue replied, 'Oh, not on ordinary days at home; then, of course, we just use the silver.'

A newspaper cutting in William's scrapbook introduced Lady Mary Lygon to the readership of the society column: 'As yet, she has not been seen at any large or formal function, as Lady Beauchamp believes in the custom of formal introduction . . . Lord Beauchamp', it continued, 'is a most devoted and affectionate father. He shows a personal interest in his daughters' activities, their dresses and their amusements. Like him, they all have flair for things artistic.'

A box of letters from 1927 exchanged between the earl and his children attests to the joshing and easy affection between them. In the wake of a minor illness, probably gout, William decided to grow a beard and lose some weight. 'My darling Daddy,' the eighteen-year-old Maimie wrote on the eve of her debut, '. . . I hope the beard and the waist are growing and diminishing respectively,' signing herself off affectionately as 'Maimiekinsmouse'.

Sibell, a young debutante in 1927, showed her easy intimacy with her father when she wrote to him. 'Do you like this writing or this,' she enquired, referring to her script. 'My wording', she assured him, 'is like my writing, & my behaviour. You will be pleased to hear [it] is becoming better than either – I am growing up. It is very sad, but inevitable.' He could even *parler chiffon* with his girls: Sibell not only informed her father which particular green Hartnell dress she had worn to a dance but asked him whether he would mind popping into the Elizabeth Arden beauty salon on Bond Street or Marshall and Snelgrove department store to buy her some Francis Jordan hair rollers. She enclosed a cheque for two pounds and two shillings. A few weeks later, reporting on the 'lovely time at St. Giles – very rural', she explained that they had slept out and 'I'm afraid I've got *masses* more freckles, but I'm going to Elizabeth Arden tomorrow – perhaps I shall come out without them.' Great efforts were made by the younger girls to get their father's permission to park their French governess at Halkin House or on Home Farm so that they could be alone with him and their brothers when the family gathered at Madresfield. Sibell was particularly keen to see the back of 'Mademoiselle' when her best friend, Betty Baldwin, the Prime Minister's daughter, came to stay. Mademoiselle was always an impediment to high jinks.

Meanwhile, William's eldest son, Elmley, MP for Norfolk East, and touring East Anglia on political hustings, wondered whether his bearded father now looked like Father Christmas. Dickie, now a schoolboy at Port Regis in Broadstairs, was more concerned about whether Daddy would run in the Fathers' Race.

The Lygons' happy childhood was rooted in what their friend Robert Byron called – in an expression he coined in a poem – the 'intimate content' of the countryside and the love and affection their father openly showered on them. But dark forces were stirring, threatening the orderly, aesthetic, safe and cosy world which William had provided for them.

Chapter Fourteen

THE EMBROIDERY

Through the vine-framed Library door lies the Moat Garden which is contained within two walls of the house on one side and the arc of the moat on the other. Its focal point is a tall, wrought-iron wishing well. The garden is paved in York stone and set with beds stocked with scented plants which, together with the clematis, passion flowers, jasmine and honeysuckle that climb the red-brick walls, add to the soporific scent in this sequestered suntrap. From May until September this garden serves as an outside drawing room. The faint buzz of bees hovering over pollen, the occasional splash of a heron seizing his prey or a kingfisher piercing the water's surface is all that can be heard in this peaceful place. On the far side of the moat a barricade of crenellated yew hedges planted in three concentric rows further shields this enclosed garden from the world beyond.

On a warm evening in June 1931, the fifty-nine-year-

The wishing well in the Moat Garden inscribed with the Beauchamp motto, Fortuna mea est in bello campo. *Drawing by Augustus Hare, writer and professional country house guest.*

old William sat dozing in a chair in the Moat Garden. The embroidery he was completing had dropped into his lap. He could hear, just behind him, the unripe grapes tapping against the mullioned windows in the breeze. Before him water trickled in the old iron well which bore his family motto *Fortuna mea est in bello campo* and to his right pigeons cooed under the trefoil arches of the dovecote set into the Chapel wall, its stonework carved with the saying *Ubi aves ibi angeli* – 'Where there are birds there are angels'.

Suddenly, four car doors slammed shut. A black, chauffeur-driven saloon had entered the estate, driven down the Gloucester Drive, over the cattle grid and drawn up on the gravel beyond the moat. Three formally dressed men crossed the bridge into the Court. They were not expected and it was clear from their solemnity and purposeful gait that they had come on business, not pleasure. Their ultimatum would shatter the Lygons. Bradford, the butler, showed the two Garter Knights and one peer of the realm into the Drawing Room to await Earl Beauchamp. Here, behind two sets of double doors, discreet conversations could be conducted. William left the Moat Garden and joined the visitors, who were all known to him. Lord Stanmore gravely explained that they had been sent at the request of 'the highest authority in the land'. His Majesty had been informed by Bend'or, the Duke of Westminster and William's brother-in-law, that he could provide evidence of criminal acts of indecency between William and a number of men.

When King George had heard the allegations, he had reputedly muttered, 'I thought men like that shot themselves.' He had been left in no doubt that Westminster would expose William, present his evidence to the press and have him arrested. According to the Constitution, a peer was entitled to be tried by fellow peers in the House of Lords. However, the thought of the scandal of such a trial, in which male prostitutes would be subpoenaed, billets-doux read out and low-life exposed, had so horrified the king that he had decided to intervene. The House of Lords was already seen by many as a place of idleness and privilege and there had recently been loud calls for its abolition, so such a scandal would further undermine its reputation. Furthermore, William was a friend of the king, a Knight of the Garter, who had carried the Sword of State at his coronation and who, for three years, had served as Steward of the Household. He was simply too close to the royal family for comfort. To contain the crisis, the three Knights were sent to persuade William to resign from all his official posts and to leave England by midnight.

Nineteen thirty-one was a particularly difficult year for George V. In January, his eldest sister, the Princess Royal, had died, followed a fortnight later by Sir Charles Cust, who had served as his equerry for thirty-nine years. At the end of March, Lord Stamfordham, his trusted adviser, had also died and a month later his cousin the Queen of Spain had been forced to flee Spain with her husband, King Alfonso XIII. Following the stock market crash of 1929, the country was in a serious and seemingly irreversible economic depression. And now Beauchamp.

Once the monarch's envoys had left Madresfield, William reviewed his options. He knew that Bend'or would file a writ and he was not prepared to see his children used as witnesses in a case concerning his homosexuality. The only members of his family who were at home were the twenty-three-year-old Sibell and her younger sister Dorothy. Forewarned, the countess had already fled to her brother's Cheshire estate; Dickie was away at school; the recently married Lettice was living in Herefordshire with her husband, Sir Richard Cotterell; Maimie was enjoying the London Season; Hugh was on his farm at Clevelode, near Malvern; and Elmley was in his Norfolk constituency. As was usual, at eight p.m. William attended prayers in the Chapel, joined by his daughters, their guest, Hamish St Clair Erskine, and the staff. Over dinner in the Great Hall he presented the situation to his daughters and to their horror offered what he considered to be the only solution: suicide. His death, he assured them, would not take place in England and – for the family's honour – it would look like an accident. He intended to take the overnight boat to the Continent and travel on to the German spa town Wiesbaden, where he would overdose on a sleeping draught. Though Sibell and Dorothy did their best to dissuade him, he purposefully left the room and supervised his packing, making sure he put a thousand pounds in cash in his wallet. He drew a firm line in black ink across a page of the visitors' book, and departed from his devoted family and his beloved Madresfield.

On his first night at Wiesbaden, William raised a glass of poisoned port to his lips, but the doctor on duty seized the glass from him. Gradually, as the weeks passed in the spa, he put thoughts of suicide temporarily aside. Strengthened by rest and reflection, he decided to remain on the Continent until – as he anticipated it would be – the summons for his arrest was lifted, and he could return home. Meanwhile his children, constantly fearing that he would take his life, decided that at all times one of them must watch over him. A dutiful and loving rota began as the older children took their turn – week in week out, in Europe and further afield – by their father's side. In the end, it was Hugh's persistent and supportive love of his father that persuaded him against suicide.

William's unmasking had been a long time coming. Since the mid-1920s, stories had circulated about homosexual parties at Walmer at which local youths and fishermen serviced the earl and his guests. Christabel, Lady Aberconway, a friend of Bend'or, recalled being shown into the garden at Walmer and finding the actor Ernest Thesiger stripped to the waist and slung with pearls. 'He explained that he had the right type of skin to heal pearls.' When another youth was introduced as the tennis coach, she said, 'Oh, do send me some difficult services and then tell me how to reply,' but he could not pat a ball over the net and unconvincingly explained that his wrist was sprained.

William's undoing began in Australia. In August 1930, nine months prior to the ultimatum, William had embarked on a round-the-world trip. He received an 'overwhelming' welcome in Sydney and stayed for two months, accompanied by a servant from Madresfield and a young Liberal MP, Robert Bernays, who acted as his speech writer. There was much to draw William to Sydney, where he was reputed to enjoy a varied sex life during his many visits. The earl and his valet shared a flat not as master and servant but as lovers, a domestic arrangement that did not go unnoticed. His hosts asked Bernays to inform William that on a forthcoming formal visit to Canberra, the servant would not be received. The incident was reported throughout London society and Bend'or hired detectives to gather further evidence. William had broken the Eleventh Commandment, one held dear by his class: 'Thou Shalt Not Get Caught.'

Bend'or had become increasingly alarmed by William's reputation. According to Lady Aberconway, he had never liked William. The womanizing sportsman and the bisexual aesthete had little in common. Relations between them had deteriorated further following the duke's two divorces over which he felt his brother-in-law had struck a sanctimonious pose. Diana Mosley, a friend of the younger Lygons, observed that their father could be insufferably la-di-da. She suspected that not only was Bend'or jealous of William's Order of the Garter but he may have been snubbed by him once too often; 'Beauchamp looked as if he was snubbing everybody.' The egregious womanizer was determined to bag his brother-in-law whom he saw as a hypocritical prig.

Bend'or was an angry, unfulfilled man, 'nothing but a fatuous, spoilt, aging playboy'. Despite three marriages – and he would marry for a fourth time – he had sired only one male heir to William's three. When Edward Grosvenor, the duke's only son, was just four, his father had insisted that he ride out with the hunt, despite the child's complaints of severe stomach pains. Edward died of peritonitis while in the field. Horrified by Bend'or's harsh treatment of their son, his wife left him. By 1931, Westminster was unhappily married to his third wife, Loelia Ponsonby. She claimed he got drunk every night and was unfaithful: yet while he enjoyed sexual freedom, he expected the highest standards of propriety from those around him, especially his family. 'As far as women were concerned he was a prude and he suffered from overwhelming fits of jealousy.' He frowned upon 'irregular' relationships, smutty stories and crude jokes, and any hint of homo-sexuality angered him beyond measure. Bend'or had endured a rigid Victorian rather than a more liberal Edwardian upbringing. Having lost his father early in childhood he had been strictly brought up by his grandfather and his obsessively religious mother. On acceding to the title and a vast fortune, he emerged as a spoilt young man.

Jealousy certainly played a part in his vendetta. Despite being the richest man in Europe and enjoying royal connections, Bend'or resented William's grander lineage. The defeat of his ancestors, the Grosvenors, in 1385 over the coat of arms *azure a bend' or* still rankled, to such an extent that the family called sons 'Bend'or', a name still used today. Beauchamp, on the other hand, could claim connection back to the medieval barons Beauchamp and – albeit distantly – to 'Warwick the Kingmaker', and Beauchamp in turn was keen to parade these associations. Furthermore, though as a duke Bend'or enjoyed a higher ranking than his brother-in-law, the dukedom was newly minted; it had been bestowed on the Grosvenors in 1874 by Queen Victoria. Bend'or was also jealous that Beauchamp was firmly ensconced within the royal family. For three decades Lady Mary Lygon had served the Princess of Wales – later the Queen – as lady-in-waiting, and Beauchamp had been Steward of the Household. These duties permitted the Beauchamps a level of access that Westminster could only aspire to and never gained, not least because George V disapproved of his sexual mores. While matters of lineage owed nothing to the achievements of these sparring brothers-in-law, Bend'or could not match or belittle Beauchamp's political success and capacity for hard work.

By contrast, Bend'or's own service record for his country was modest. In 1906, he had been appointed Lord Lieutenant of Cheshire, a standard position for the county grandee. To this local achievement he could add various honorary appointments: President of the National Union in Cheshire, President of the Cheshire

Dairy Farmers' Association, President of the Cheshire County Unionist Club, President of the Cheshire Liberal Unionist Association and Master of the Cheshire Hounds. It was hardly a glittering career. It would seem, as H. G. Wells observed, that in Bend'or's case 'moral indignation [was] jealousy with a halo'.

The intensity of the duke's homophobia invites suspicion. After Eton, where some experience of homosexuality was almost inevitable for a good-looking boy, he was sent to the castle of Azay-le-Rideau near Chinon on the Loire where a college had been founded to teach French to the children of affluent foreigners. After a short stay, he left abruptly and some time later the school was closed down by the police following a homosexual scandal. One wonders why Bend'or left so suddenly.

The immediate catalyst for his actions against his brother-in-law was an article published in the *Church Times* in which both his own and the Duke of Marlborough's reputations were besmirched and, as a consequence, Bend'or calculated that his friendship with George V had been irretrievably damaged. William was President of the English Church Union and the two dukes traced the article back to him. Bend'or determined to bring him down. By April 1931 Beauchamp's sexual antics had almost become public knowledge among the upper classes.

Bend'or decided that, in order to protect his sister and her children from the scandal that would surely break, he would threaten to bring William to justice, but his actions, far from shielding them, drew the spotlight on to them. Ashamed and humiliated, the countess felt compelled to place a statement in the personal columns of the newspapers acknowledging that she no longer lived with her husband but that she was well. Vicious gossip circulated to the titillation of acquaintances. Their family name now tarnished, William's children were no longer welcome in certain circles.

In the spring of 1931, some three months before the three knights came to Madresfield, Bend'or had summoned his sister and in the presence of three lawyers had laid the evidence before her. He had recommended that she leave Madresfield immediately with her children, who ranged between the ages of fourteen and nearly twenty-eight, and commence divorce proceedings. The countess, who had always been a somewhat obtuse and sheltered woman, and was now in shock, was easily swayed by her brother and, contrary to her newspaper notice that she was in good health despite the separation, she suffered a nervous breakdown and took to her bed on her brother's Cheshire estate. Bend'or had also instructed the Lygon children to testify against their father. They refused. According to Sibell, 'Bend'or was going to bring it to court which meant that all of us would have to appear to give evidence and he [her father] did not want that. That's why he went [abroad]. He could have fought it out easily and I don't think Bend'or would have come out of it very well, either.' All William's children stood by him. Dickie, who was too young to make his own decisions, was taken north to live with his mother at Saighton Grange on Westminster's estate. Bend'or, now their greatest enemy, let it be known that anyone fraternizing with the Lygons would be dropped by him. With a final flourish, he wrote a curt letter: 'Dear Bugger-in-Law, You got what you deserved. Yours, Westminster.' The battle ground was set.

Sibell, who had become a worldly young woman, persuaded her lover, Lord Beaverbrook, to take action. The Canadian press baron controlled the Express newspaper group and had been Minister of Information during the First World War. As a masterful manipulator, he not only suppressed the story throughout 1931 in his own newspapers but ensured that it did not appear in rival ones. It was typical of Sibell's pugnaciousness to stand up to her uncle – she regarded it as one of her finest moments. Even in childhood, Dorothy remembered her as a 'rather stormy petrel – and a great wielder of the wooden spoon; if mischief was going to be made, she made it'. The children took a vow of silence regarding their father's affairs and, isolated from society, they closed ranks.

Over the early summer of 1931, before the visit of the Garter Knights, clandestine negotiations had been taking place between the University of London where William was Chancellor, the Prime Minister's office and Buckingham Palace. William knew that his brother-in-law was in pursuit and that it was only a matter of time before his sexual antics were exposed. The archives of the Senate House at London University throw some light on William's state of mind. In anticipation of his fall, he went to considerable lengths to extricate himself discreetly from his professional commitments. On 14 May 1931 a Harley Street specialist had written to the Principal of the University, Sir Edwin Deller, excusing the earl from 'work in every possible way, at least until the end of the session'. Soon afterwards, William took a cure at Bad Nauheim near Frankfurt. There is a handwritten though unattributed account of sub-sequent events in the Senate House Archive of London University. William signed an undertaking to 'depart from the Brit. Isles and to live o/s' though letters between him and the Vice-Chancellor throughout June and July suggested that he expected to return soon to his work. On 1 August he wrote to the Vice-Chancellor and the Principal, informing them that his cure at Bad Nauheim had been unsuccessful and consequently he 'must look forward to a less active life'.

Lloyd George also received a letter from William explaining that doctor's orders necessitated that he absent himself from public life for a while. Lloyd George's response gives us a measure of William's standing:

Your partial and temporary retirement from the very hard work you have done for us will be a real loss to the Party. We have come to rely so much upon your ready and very effective help in all our difficulties, that we shall miss it more than I can tell you . . . I dare not

> think what we should have done had your loyal service
> not been available to us during the last trying few years,
> but they [*sic*] will be needed as much, if not more than
> ever, in the coming months.

Almost four decades earlier Oscar Wilde had quipped to the manager of the St James' Theatre that 'everyone wants me to go abroad. I've just been abroad. One can't keep going abroad, unless one is a missionary, or, what comes to the same thing, a commercial traveller.' Now William followed in the footsteps of Wilde and other homosexual Englishmen – William Beckford, William Bankes, the Earl of Euston, Lord Arthur Somerset, Prince Albert Victor, Duke of Clarence and Avondale – into exile.

Inevitably, following his departure, rumours circulated in high circles that, contrary to the official explanation given by the press, the earl had not gone abroad for a 'cure' but had in fact fled the law. Among his acquaintances, as we have seen, his homosexuality had been suspected for some time. Perhaps Lloyd George himself was aware of it too. Surely Asquith, a close friend, who had nicknamed his Cabinet colleague 'Sweetheart' and had written to him and referred to him in this fashion, would have known. There is a thought-provoking entry – an old Scottish maxim – in a commonplace book at Madresfield, penned by Margot Asquith in 1909. It reads: 'They say – what say they? Let them say—'. It was not the fact of his homosexuality but his increasingly careless flaunting of it that had led to his downfall. Typically, amongst the upper classes, a blind eye was turned to 'eccentric' behaviour if conducted with discretion, but over the years William had become brazen, disregarding the law and perhaps even considering himself above it. Attitudes had hardened too. Quentin Crisp stated that by the thirties the police began to regard homosexuals 'as North American Indians thought of bison [and] cast about for a way of exterminating them in herds'.

Within days of his departure, contemporaries learned that the 'eccentric' Beauchamp had gone abroad 'to have mud baths', a popular euphemism for a Wildean exile. Anecdotes were exchanged with glee in drawing rooms up and down the land. How they tittered when they heard that, on having homosexuality explained to her, Lady Beauchamp referred to her husband as a 'bugler'! Closer to the truth, however, was James Lees-Milne's account in his diary. On driving with Lady Dorothy to Chatsworth one Christmas many years later he broached the subject of her father's homosexuality. Was Lady Beauchamp deeply shocked to learn of her husband's peccadilloes, he wondered? 'No,' Coote replied, her mother was extremely simple and never understood what homosexuality meant. There are, however, some curious entries in the countess's diaries that suggest she may have had some knowledge of her husband's sexual excursions. In fact, though innocent of the details, the countess had suspected her husband's desires 'ran contrary to what is natural'.

Wasn't it shocking that his daughters thought it best to advise their male guests at Madresfield to lock their bedroom doors at night for fear of their father's prowling? the gossips continued. How amusing, they hissed, that Beauchamp hired footmen according to their looks and that his guests were blinded by the sparkle of their rings and bracelets as they were served dinner. Yet in grand houses, footmen had always been the peacocks of the servants' world, ornamentally on hand in breeches and hose and in a livery reflecting their master's good taste. The Duchess of Portland was so fastidious that she insisted that her footmen took regular calisthenics classes to maintain pleasing calf muscles. The Schadenfreude is palpable in the diary entry of Sir Robert Bruce Lockhart, diplomat and banker:

A good story about the Baldwins, Lord Beauchamp and Lady Beauchamp. Lady Beauchamp has left him because of his homosexual habits. There was an almost open scandal lately. There was some ceremony at Madresfield, Malvern, lately – the enthronement of a bishop – and the Baldwins went there, staying with Lord Beauchamp. They received a letter of protest from Lady Shaftesbury (Lady Beauchamp's sister) and from the Duke of Westminster.

Both Bend'or and Lady Shaftesbury – nicknamed

'Cuckoo' – had written to remonstrate with the Baldwins for countenancing William. Baldwin, a decent man, stood by him. As Worcestershire neighbours (the Baldwins lived at Astley, a few miles from Madresfield) the two men had been friends for over a decade and Sibell counted Betty Baldwin her greatest friend. Though it seemed the one-time Prime Minister, a non-patrician Conservative, had little in common with the Liberal grandee, it was not so. Baldwin's aunt had married Edward Burne-Jones, the Pre-Raphaelite painter whose work was greatly admired by both Baldwin and William. As thoughtful men who pre-ferred conciliation to confrontation, and tolerance to invective, they shared a horror of war and sympathy for the working man. The kindly statesman-squire at home with his 'pigs, pipe and poetry' and the landed peer were both rooted in their county's soil. Indeed, in his speech entitled 'On England' in 1924, Baldwin made the oft-quoted observation that 'England is the country and the country is England.' Once the scandal had broken, Baldwin showed his neighbour kindness, being unusually alert to homophobia. His son Oliver was homosexual but, rather than cast the boy aside, he had continued to show him love, even welcoming Oliver's lover into the Baldwin family home.

Similarly, friends of William's children were less judgemental than his contemporaries. Virginia Woolf – though not typical of her generation – summed up the views of many of them when she commented on Lytton Strachey's death in her diary in 1932, 'Oh buggery's exploded – nobody could mind that now.' Diana Mosley, who was closer to the Beauchamps, observed the story unfolding and recalled a sharp contrast in attitudes between the generations. While William's homosexuality was known amongst many of her parents' generation, 'Lady Beauchamp preferred not to notice' and Diana Mosley's father refused even to discuss it. Nevertheless, 'all our generation was on the side of Lord Beauchamp – completely – but I would *not* say his own generation was. He was awfully off-putting. Lord Beauchamp would have evoked much more sympathy if he hadn't been so absurd in his pomposity. If someone poses as a hero of rectitude and then something like that happens, people are not as sympathetic as with someone more modest.' It was his insistence on ceremony and precedence which his children's contemporaries found risible.

The conventional façade of a family man, an upstanding peer of the realm, a servant of the state and a loyal courtier, contrasts strangely with his brazen behaviour. William had clearly been leading a double life. To some degree, bisexuality necessitated the assumption of a false persona in a society in which it was outlawed. William erected a pompous, formal exterior, breached only by those on intimate terms with him. Diana Mosley's set included a number of homosexuals; she commented that 'it was not accepted in Society . . . it was only by the time of the Wolfenden Report [1957] that things had changed quite a lot . . . But if one of our friends was queer we were all totally frank with one another, there was no more humbuggery.' She noticed that though the Lygon girls 'rose above' the scandal, they were deeply affected. What struck Diana Mosley most forcibly in the whole sorry tale was how his children 'supported him in every way. They loved him so much they were completely on his side – never wavered.'

But not everybody was broadminded. Sir William Dugdale, whose aunt had served with Mary Lygon as a lady-in-waiting, and who himself had served as William's page during George V's coronation, removed a photograph of the coronation from public display in the Dugdale home once the scandal broke.

Despite William's attempts, initially at least, to hide his homosexuality, his predisposition had been clear from an early age. It was known that his uncle, Henry, the fifth earl, had also taken 'cures' abroad as he struggled with his homosexual leanings, which at the time were seen as a capital offence if given in to. He died young, unmarried and childless. At English public schools homo-eroticism was often encouraged by the masters, many of whom were homosexual themselves. Soon after the Wilde case, William Stead wrote in his *Review of Reviews* that 'should everyone found guilty of Oscar Wilde's crimes be imprisoned, there would be a very surprising emigration from Eton, Harrow, Rugby and Winchester to the jails of Pentonville and Holloway.' While many made a successful attempt at what was known as 'reorientation' after school, William had recognized his true sexuality by the time he had reached Oxford – if not earlier – and it sat uncomfortably with his strictly Christian upbringing. During his adolescence and early twenties, he had suffered a series of mysterious breakdowns during which he left off his almost daily correspondence with his sister Mary, his closest confidante. He had escaped to Brighton and taken even longer trips abroad. In a letter to him, his sister Susan commented on his late return to Oxford after Christmas, adding 'it sounds a very curious sort of illness.' His accession to the title and its attendant dynastic responsibilities were a heavy responsibility; it is possible that his regular forays to the East End to work with the poor had served as a cover for his exploration of homosexual low-life in its Molly Houses.

Looking back at the splendid entertaining at Government House in New South Wales, it bore all the hallmarks of a homosexual aesthete – hallmarks that did not go unnoticed by Victor J. Daley of *The Australian Star*. He described an evening at Government House, in which 'the most striking feature of the vice-regal ménage is the youthfulness of its members. There may, perhaps, be an elderly retainer on the premises, but if so, I imagine that he works there in the daytime only, and goes somewhere else to sleep.' William's retinue instead was made up of 'rosy-cheeked footmen, clad in liveries of fawn, heavily ornamented in silver and red brocade, with many lanyards of the same hanging in festoons from their broad shoulders, [who] stood in the doorway, and bowed as we passed in . . . Lord Beauchamp deserves great credit for his taste in footmen.'

The scrapbooks, the Library and his friendships reveal the man. He pasted into his scrapbooks often homo-erotic images of athletes carved in marble, of near-naked young men taking exercise at an athletics college in Rheims, and of tattooed Maoris. The cuttings from *Studio* magazine show that William avidly followed C. R. Ashbee's refurbishment of the Grand Duke of Hesse-Darmstadt's palace. Hesse was a homo-sexual too, and had originally introduced the designer to the earl. Nor did Ashbee hide his predilections: he instantly recognized in his new client 'a touch more human tenderness', derived

> . . . from the homogeneric side of him for that side is there without doubt though I have not gone near enough to discuss it . . . His Lordship knows doubtless what a mighty solvent it is and caste is caste. But I chuckle to myself when I look into the eyes of a man whom I know to feel as I do, and think how if I chose to put forth the power of the word, I could make all the splendour and pomp pass away like smoke and leave only the bare soul of the man, naked as a *Quattrocentrist* might have drawn its progress to heaven or hell.

In his Library, alongside volumes on political thought and social policy, stood publications on the Aesthetic movement; writings by Whitman, Swinburne, Mallarmé and Verlaine; Oscar Wilde's *Salomé* and editions of *The Yellow Book*, published in volumes from 1894 to 1897, and featuring contributions by Aubrey

Beardsley, Walter Crane, Henry James, Sir Frederick Leighton and Edmund Gosse. It was reported that when Wilde was arrested he was carrying a volume of *The Yellow Book* (in fact it was a French novel with a yellow cover). This publication was seen, by some, as the epitome of the decadence into which the arts and literature had descended and the windows of the editorial offices were smashed by an angry horde during the Wilde scandal.

William had sought the company of similar-minded men in his political life. The office of the First Commissioner of Works certainly had its quota of employees who wished to project their taste – a camp taste – which had flourished under the fiefdom of Viscount Esher, and Loulou Harcourt, his predecessors there. The bisexual Harcourt regularly invited Beauchamp to his home on Brook Street – now the Savile Club – to compare their recent purchases of snuff boxes and portrait miniatures. Following a sexual scandal, Harcourt committed suicide there in 1922.

Similarly, the royal household had always attracted confirmed bachelors. Sir Edmund Gosse was, like William, a married man keen to mask his real sexuality. He described the predicament of the closet homosexual as being 'that of a man buried alive & conscious, but deprived of sleep'. It was said that during Robert Browning's funeral at Westminster Abbey, Gosse sat in a pew flicking through pictures of male nudes. Alive to the opportunities of social advancement, Gosse befriended the earl and came to stay at Madresfield on a regular basis between 1903 and 1914. Both men were brought up by religiously fervent fathers on a virtually literal reading of the scriptures at a time of fierce debate as to whether such a reading was sustainable in the light of evolutionary theory. Gosse masterfully chronicled his upbringing within the Plymouth Brethren in his frank, if unsympathetic, memoir *Father and Son*, published anonymously after his father's death, in 1907. There is a first edition at Madresfield.

The British consul Sir Roger Casement had been another of William's political allies. A remarkably good-looking man of 'courteous and seductive manners', he championed the Anti-Slavery cause, highlighting exploitation and human rights abuses on rubber plantations in the Belgian Congo and Colombia. Because of William's support of marginalized peoples in Australasia, Casement invited him to become President of the Congo Reform Association, and William had accepted. Despite this being a laudable campaign, Casement's reputation was ruined when his 'Black Diaries' of a depraved homosexual life came to light and were used against him in his subsequent trial for treason. Before being executed in 1916 for collusion with the Germans during the First World War, he was incarcerated in Beauchamp's Tower at the Tower of London. On the west side of Tower Green, this was the tower where Thomas Beauchamp, third Earl of Warwick, was imprisoned in 1397.

Repeating the decision made nearly three hundred

years earlier by Richard Ligon when he found himself on the wrong side at the end of the Civil War, William chose exile and commenced the life of a fugitive from justice at the end of June 1931. Following his stay at Wiesbaden, he was in Paris one week, the next in Venice, Rome or Sydney. He felt that the separation from his children was his greatest loss. On 28 July 1931, he wrote to Dorothy from Berlin wondering, 'Do you think there would be an awful row if I sent Dickie a snapshot of me? Does he ever write to you? Poor darling! How he would love to come to the [annual Madresfield Agricultural] Show.' A month later, in another letter written en route for Sydney, he complained about being followed by detectives – probably hired by Bend'or to provide more incriminating evidence – confiding that 'the detectives in Paris annoyed me a great deal. When will she [Lady Beauchamp] relax her hatred of us all?' Stopping over in the Hotel Europe in Singapore he explained to Dorothy on 22 November that 'My plans after Sydney remain vague. There seems to be no use in coming back if yr. mother is still implacable.'

On a lighter note he wrote to Hugh, his favourite son, referring to the strikes in Britain and hoping that Elmley had found a job – 'if not he may become Labour!' This was clearly a family joke as the stuffy Elmley was unlikely to follow his father's wishes and join what William believed to be the party of the future, the Labour Party.

Anxious about his children, William established a

schedule whereby he wrote to each one, in turn, every Sunday, beginning with Lettice. He requested that they share his letters with one another and, always sensitive to his children's needs, he added a coda that 'if there is anything private to say it will be slipped into the same envelope' but separately. He was glad that 'the servants are all very loyal and I was touched by their attitude.' The staff too had closed ranks. He ended the letter with the lament, 'What happiness your mother misses [away from home and family]! . . . I hope you will be happy together at Madresfield and I wish I could be with you!' The following summer, still hovering expectantly in exile, he returned to the northern hemisphere and wrote nostalgically: 'Imagine my excitement on seeing the Pont d'Avignon [in France] of wh. I had so often sung to the family one after another. So there [enclosed] is a picture for each of you.'

Eternally restless, William never stayed in one place for more than three weeks. A paragraph at the end of Wilde's *De Profundis* echoes this nomadic state. 'Society, as we have constituted it, will have no place for me, has none to offer; but Nature, whose sweet rains fall on unjust and just alike, will have clefts in the rocks where I may hide, and secret valleys in whose silence I may weep undisturbed.' Over the coming years, William would seek out the sweet rains of Paris, the clefts in the rocks of Sydney's Botany Bay, the secret valleys of San Francisco and the great waters of Venice, in an almost ceaseless passage between the four cities of the world reputed to tolerate the homosexual community. For hundreds of years, exiles seeking visual and physical pleasures were drawn to Venice where its inhabitants were known to turn a blind eye to homosexuality. Similarly, since the nineteenth century, Sydney had 'had bars, hotels and drag shows for homosexual men several years before there was firm evidence of such things in the United States'.

William also went to Rome, to stay with his old friend and fellow homosexual Gerald, the fourteenth Baron Berners. He was a colourful character whose home at Faringdon, some twenty-five miles from Madresfield, was known for its extravagant exotica, be it the turtle doves on the lawn dyed various sugar-almond shades, the white glass four-poster bed or the diamond necklaces hung round pets' throats. There William and he would discuss music and their common love of the medieval chronicles of Froissart which Berners had recently translated. His home in Rome was a terracotta-coloured stucco building at number 3 Foro Romano, a quiet, tree-lined street now distinguished by ambassadorial residences. On the first floor, three large arched windows overlook the spectacular ruins of the Colosseum. 'After the disaster we took it in turns to stay there with him in Rome. I think it was his love of Rome that made him seem so at home with Roman Catholics, unlike Mother!' Sibell reported. For each child who came to stay he prepared a diverting programme, be it sport, culture or, in Sibell's case, riding out with the Italian cavalry. 'It was so wonderful trotting through the streets of Rome with them. You can't imagine how smart it was!' she laughed. Too proud to contact old friends, he only saw those who took the initiative to find him, notably his children, his lawyer, Richard Elwes, the writer Stephen McKenna, the pearl-draped Ernest Thesiger and Berners and his lover, Robert Heber-Percy. But William was homesick: he composed a poem – undated – on the back of an envelope:

Thou muse of my manhood how oft have I stray'd
O'er thy lawns and thy meadows, in sun and in shade;
And though I no longer am domiciled here, –
To my heart will sweet Madresfield ever be dear.

And with joy through my life could wander about
Its gardens and shrubberies, its walks and its moat;
Till with aid of my fancy, loved nymph, I could feign
The days I so valued were with me again.

Wherever he went he took his embroidery. He had not only studied the history and techniques of embroidery, particularly English crewelwork, but he also found the craft itself a relaxing diversion for his tormented mind. He completed nearly two dozen *bargello* – Florentine flame-stitch – seat covers which he sent back for the dining chairs at Madresfield, each coloured thread tethering him closer – in his mind – to his home and his children. 'Every day I manage some embroidery but now cannot get on for want of the deeper yellow silk. However, I do hope it is on its way here by now.' The embroidery which 'helps fill his day' was taken up by his visiting children too as they sat by his side completing seat covers for home. On one sea journey with his father to Tahiti in July 1933, for example, Hugh reported to his siblings back in England that they were joined on deck by ladies with their own needlework. 'Soon we shall have a cosy little circle.'

If William settled anywhere, it was in Sydney where his 'friends remain constant which makes it very tempting to me to buy a house and live there with visits from you and others'. He did buy a house in Sydney and is reported to have said that 'I'm glad to find myself again in a democratic country, away from Europe, where the old, liberal philosophy, in which I was brought up, is suffering a serious decline . . . It is all the more pleasant to come back to a country where democracy rules unchecked.' Hugh, whose bankruptcy had recently been redeemed with a payment from his father, came out to Sydney to lick his wounds. Keenly aware of his son's unstable state, William believed that it 'never would have happened if I had known' and been close at hand. Hugh was his favourite: according to Rosalind Morrison, Hugh's niece, William intended to leave Madresfield to him and not to his first-born son, Elmley.

Father and son passed cheerful days side by side at Darling Point, Sydney, as recounted in a letter from William to Sibell in July 1933. They fell into a routine. William rose at six-thirty a.m. and swam in the pool. He then took the newspapers 'which I often read in Hugh's room' and then, having dressed and breakfasted, he went into Sydney for a massage and a drink at his club with friends before returning for 'luncheon (never alone) at one p.m'. In the afternoon, they surfed on Bondi Beach, played tennis or boxed before a six forty-five p.m. dinner 'if there is anything on in Sydney and if not at 7.45 p.m'. and bed by eleven. 'My dear, love letters are the greatest kindness to show me. Hugh appreciates the fact now! A sinner converted indeed! Your ever affectionate Daddy.' It was a 'pleasant, stupid existence' but quite a come-down for one who had been at the hub of national politics.

Despite distance, William did his best to continue to run the great house from abroad. Which wallpapers, he enquired, had been used in the Nursery and had its white bookshelves been properly arranged? Glad to hear that the Drawing Room was being used again, he suggested that the snuff boxes and other objets d'art be moved there from the Muniments Room under the Chapel because of the danger from the hot water pipes. He longed for news. Had the countess softened? Had his brother-in-law ceased his vendetta? According to Sibell, 'He never complained, never mentioned Bend'or again. He just bore it.' While he maintained relations with his children by post and anticipated their next visit, back in England Lady Beauchamp was even more isolated. Estranged from all her children, save for Dickie, she led a pitiful existence: alone, confused, ill and in thrall to her bullying brother. A poignant letter written to Dorothy on 21 April 1933, nearly two years after William's flight, gives some measure of her state of mind. Rosalind Morrison, her granddaughter, keeps it locked in a black leather writing box along with other precious and private family correspondence.

My Darling Dorothy, After the dreadful thing, of Daddy being obliged to leave England, I fear that you may feel that he was not treated kindly, whereas, the truth is [that] the greatest mercy and consideration were shown Him [*sic*] – far more, indeed, than any man guilty of similar conduct cd. expect. So I think that you should now be told by Me, just what seems right and necessary about the facts.

About two years ago, enquiries were made, tho' not by Me, or with My knowledge and most terrible things were discovered. These were laid before three of the greatest and wisest Barristers. They considered, most anxiously, the situation, not once or twice but many times. I myself saw them twice; and they advised the thing was so dreadful, that the best and kindest way was to give Daddy the opportunity to leave England, and sign a document, undertaking to remain abroad, and thus <u>avoid</u> any legal step being taken either by Me, or the authorities. But he would not avail himself of this, or sign the paper, until three friends of His, persuaded Him, at the last moment, to do so. Therefore, not by fault, a little Publicity, wh. <u>Might</u> have been avoided, was [unreadable] caused, by my having to file the petition, and his still staying here, even then.

Now you should know that for many years, I had strongly suspected that (with Daddy) all was not as it shld. be and that one side of his life and desires went contrary to everything that is Natural. It was for your sake, when you were all young, I deliberately refrained, thro' many years of anguish, from converting my suspicions into actual knowledge, but, as I once told Daddy, there were times when I welcomed the sufferings of illness, so as to escape from my great agony of mind.

So if you have not felt able to keep yr. love for me, I hope and pray, that you can now understand, some little part of what I have undergone and that the old love may yet be restored in its fullness, and even perhaps increased. For indeed you must believe me, nothing has been done without the greatest and gravest consideration, compassion, understanding and wisdom.

I also want you to realize all that this means for Richard's future – to keep him clear of all the ill that otherwise would doubtless have befallen him. All I can do is accept the inevitable and to trust Daddy to God's mercy, which never fails us when we turn to Him. The hardest part for me is not to be able to see Daddy.

On a new page she continues:

I began this letter 2 years ago but, in the sad circumstances, and owing to many misunderstandings, it was then thought wiser to keep it back, but now I am anxious for you to have it. Without my saying it, you know how much I like to see you, when and where the right times come along. This great sorrow which has

befallen us, I feel for you with all my heart and understanding, but out of it let us try to rise above earthly
things and thus enable it to be used for GOOD, in helping others. My love always, your ever loving, Mummy.

But Lady Beauchamp's children never made peace with
her. Three years after writing the letter she was dead.
She was only fifty-nine.

Six months after the letter had been sent, Sibell's rage
boiled over once again and she took another pot-shot
at Westminster, allegedly libelling him in a magazine
article. The *Oxford and Cambridge* magazine resembled
Tatler and in the mid-thirties was edited by the Earl of
Birkenhead. Sibell's fellow contributors included Peter
Quennell, Henry 'Chips' Channon and Evelyn Waugh.

Her column, entitled 'Messages from Mayfair', was
staccato, spiky and frank in style and tinged with regret,
if not bitterness. With her natural aristocratic hauteur
she made social observations about newly-weds, the
hunting fraternity and the *jeunesse dorée* who were
desperately competing for media coverage. At the end
of her column in December 1933 she wrote:

I am somewhat shocked, being patriotic, by the
behaviour of one, who although he is my uncle, should
know better, especially as he should set an example. I
refer to the Duke of Westminster. He is one of the
richest Englishmen. His money should do good in and
to England.

Instead of shouldering his responsibilities, he has

two houses in France, a pack of boar hounds, also in France, a yacht on which he spends a great deal of his time in foreign waters, and now I see that he is no longer going to have any race horses in England. He has sent his string over to France. [Unemployment had reached record heights at this time owing to the Depression.] Is this setting a good example? Dukes, I understand, are made to look up to. We are told they stand by their country. Where should we be if we copied them? Perhaps this behaviour is because His Grace has met with troubles in England but I think one should not shirk duty . . .

However, things are changing and one can take the attitude that England is better with those who really love her. She does not need the weak ones who leave her. Money and position are, in this case, hereditary. Can you blame socialists who think that money should go to those who would spend it well?

Noblesse oblige and the duties of the privileged were cornerstones of Sibell's upbringing, driven home to her by stories such as Charlotte Yonge's *The Little Duke* that her father had read to his daughters by the fire at Madresfield. Bend'or's behaviour was at odds with her understanding of an aristocrat's role.

Westminster threatened her with legal action in January 1934 and forced an apology from her. Sibell's diary for this year came to light as a result of a fire in 2006 just one year after she died. Throughout her life she insisted bravely that despite the scandal 'we coped, it was fine', but the entries reveal her anguish. She was drinking heavily: 'champagne all morning', 'black velvets in Matt's room at 11 a.m.', 'got jolly on three whiskies', 'got stinking tight'. She could no longer summon the courage to hunt with her customary bravery. She was rashly losing her temper and had to take large quantities of Sedachol to cope with insomnia. On 3 January 1934 she recorded: 'At dinner the Press Association rang me up in connection with the writ – it has got into the paper – was and am most worried.' On 22 January she admits that she 'thought a good deal about three years ago [when her father went into exile]'. Also according to these diaries, Bend'or had begun a campaign to besmirch her reputation. 'Benny said that he had a statement that I live with Speck and Foster – what a lie.' Hounded by Bend'or, unfulfilled in love and lonely, Sibell sought sanctuary at Madresfield. 'How I love the days here. They seem precious for the moment.' It was her 'paraclete' too.

Five months later at the annual Derby Day dinner hosted by the king at Buckingham Palace, Bend'or yelled at her across a crowded room, 'You little bitch! How dare you come here?' Lord Rosebery was so disgusted by this outburst that he protectively intervened, explaining to Sibell, 'He's very, very drunk,' as he guided her away. The duke was fast gaining a reputation for ruining many lives, including that of his one-time architect, Detmar Blow. 'If he wanted to persecute someone, he went to any length to do it,' according to Sibell, who was renowned for her short fuse. 'If I ever feel like that about someone, I just think of Bend'or, and stop!'

In the meantime her father's restless roaming continued. In 1934, he left Rome to winter once again in Australia but by February 1935 he was bound for Java aboard the SS *New Holland*, accompanied by Hugh and Elmley's old Oxford friend, Robert Byron. By the summer of 1936, he was back in Venice with Dorothy, his lawyer Richard Elwes and Elwes's wife. Here he learned of Lady Beauchamp's death. Elwes immediately travelled to London to determine whether William could attend her funeral. The decision rested with the Home Secretary, Sir John Simon, who had sat in Cabinet with William. The 'prim and passionless' Simon, who, according to Hugh Dalton, was 'the snakiest of the lot', refused to lift the warrant, submitting to Bend'or's unrelenting pressure. Elwes had to intercept William at Folkestone and prevent him from disembarking for fear of arrest. And so he turned back for Venice. Some time later, a contrite Simon visited Sibell. 'He felt terribly sorry', she recalled, 'and wondered what he had done. He was extremely upset but Bend'or was too strong for him – unstoppable!'

By the time of his mother's death, the thirty-one-year-old Hugh was an alcoholic wrestling with his own homosexuality. While Dorothy and Sibell always denied his sexual leanings – perhaps it was more than they could bear as they watched their father suffer – friends and more distant kinsmen knew otherwise. Since graduating from Oxford, he had struggled to find a role for himself and had sunk into melancholia. Preferring the gentler 'intimate content' of the country-side, surrounded by his horses and his two greyhounds, Luke and Dan, he had spurned London social life. After a brief interlude as a bank clerk in Paris he had returned to England and tried his hand as a horse trainer, an amateur jockey, a farmer – even an Arctic explorer. Hugh was in poor health. He had recently fallen from a horse and been punctured in the face by a stray pellet while out shooting. Overwrought after his mother's funeral, he took a motoring holiday through Germany with his friend the artist Henry Wynn. On a hot Sunday, 19 August 1936, having driven through the countryside in an open-topped car, they arrived at dusk in Rothenburg, in Bavaria. As Hugh stepped from the car he fell, overcome by heatstroke or drink. He fractured his skull on the kerb-stone.

Desperate to reach his ailing son, William chartered a plane and travelled with Dorothy and Sibell to his bedside. It was too late. Hugh never regained con-sciousness and within three days he was dead. William was beside himself with grief. He 'felt he had to bring the boy home . . . it had broken him up'. Despite the risk of imprisonment, he determined to return to Madresfield for the funeral. As a precaution, it was said that a Tiger Moth belonging to one of Hugh's friends lay in wait nearby in preparation for the earl's escape but such elaborate measures proved unnecessary. William was unaware that, once again, the feisty Sibell had intervened and, through Beaverbrook, she had prevailed upon Simon to lift the warrant for her father's arrest. Even the stony-hearted Simon felt moved to show Beauchamp mercy. The warrant was suspended and later annulled. On her arrival at Ostend alongside her father and sister, Sibell received a telegram from Beaverbrook which read 'Safe for your father to land'.

As evening fell on 24 August, three black limousines drew away from the dock at Dover, following the hearse that contained Hugh's body. His coffin was draped with the Beauchamp banner, a red dragon on a white ground, brought to the port by the devoted family butler, Bradford. At the funeral the crowd of mourners included Hugh's metropolitan friends, Patrick Balfour, Christopher Sykes, John Sutro, Robert Heber-Percy; and those with whom he had shared a quieter and simpler life in Worcestershire: members of the Barnard's Green Cricket Club whose floral bat and ball presentation lay on the Beauchamp banner; local farmers with whom he had worked and walked his dogs; huntsmen with whom he had ridden out. Hugh was laid to rest under the trees in the churchyard next to the old house.

The archive at Madresfield contains many letters of condolence addressed to Viscount Elmley but few to Beauchamp as only his close friends knew of his whereabouts. The earl's sister, Lady Susan Gilmour, wrote to her nephew Elmley: 'I am very glad your father was able to get to him as that will have been a great solace to him; but he will feel it terribly.' Another letter dated 21 August 1936 from James Wakefield holidaying in the

Tirol recalled Hugh as 'a most attractive boy and so promising', and added: 'Alas! That he did not fulfill that early promise – it has been a tragedy. May he find pardon and a new life.'

While the legal situation was still uncertain, William remained at Madresfield for just six days. The following spring, shortly after George VI's coronation, William's counsel, Sir Norman Birkett, wrote to the authorities. Since George V was now dead, perhaps his client could now officially return to England. If William was arrested, Birkett made clear, he would defend his client against homosexual charges and was confident that he would win. The charges were finally dropped. William's official return was recorded in the visitors' book under a black inked line by his signature and the date: 'Beauchamp 19.vii.37'. Still full of fury at his wife who had colluded with her brother and wrecked the family, within days of his return he had her image painted out with whitewash from the Chapel fresco which had originally been conceived as a celebration of their family life. Her marble bust was thrown into the moat.

There is a cine-film of William at this time. He is back in his Moat Garden. Dressed in blazer and white flannels with that distinctive Cap d'Antibes stance – one hip tilted, the flat palm of his right hand thrust into the pocket of his tight blazer – he looks a period piece. He is taking tea with his children. Though surrounded by five liveried footmen, it is he who 'plays mother': pouring the tea and passing the cake plate. He then steps to one side to watch his brood with palpable tenderness and pride. What he had not confided in them was that they would have little time together. He had been diagnosed with terminal cancer.

Before his disgrace and exile, every two years William, as head of the Lygon clan, had hosted a reunion of the Ligon [*sic*] Family and Kinsmen Association in America. Many, since his ancestor Richard Ligon's time, had settled in America. In the autumn of 1938 he set sail for New York City, accompanied by Mary, Dorothy and Dickie, to attend another reunion, a commitment which he took seriously and which his granddaughter continues today. He intended to travel on to Australia where, following the Munich crisis, he had been invited to broadcast on the situation in Europe, and then to pass the winter there with friends before returning to Madresfield in the spring. But in New York he fell gravely ill. Elmley just managed to get to New York in time and on 15 November 1938, in the Waldorf Astoria hotel, with Dorothy at his bedside, William died. His last words were: 'Must we dine with the Elmleys tonight?'

In a box in the Muniment Room lies a piece of paper on which is written in William's hand, 'Will of the seventh Earl Beauchamp, 5.vi.1938'. It reads:

To Elmley my wearable ring
To Lettice my pearl (coloured) studs
To Richard [Cotterell, Lettice's husband] my black pearl pin
To Sibell my gold box 17th century

To Mary my amethyst studs and link
To Dorothy my diamond studs 3
To Dicky my watch (repeater) and charm
To Bradford my big watch

He had signed his will on 19 August 1938 and it includes the statement: 'I give and bequeath all my Australian properties of whatsoever nature to the said David Smyth for his own use and benefit absolutely'. Smyth, his secretary, a loyal servant, had been his companion in exile. Sibell referred to Smyth as her father's 'bonne à tout faire but I don't think he was queer – I don't know.'

Beauchamp had, according to his granddaughter Rosalind Morrison, kept diaries throughout his life. After his death, she understands, the senior trustee, Leo Russell, arranged for them and other papers to be destroyed, but her aunt, Coote, believed that Elmley had destroyed them.

In the absence of diaries that might have given voice to the earl's deepest feelings, a poem by Sir Lewis Morris, which William pasted into the last volume of his scrapbooks, may be read as a plea for understanding and forgiveness from those he loved.

> *When I am dead and turned to dust*
> *Let men say what they will, I care not aught . . .*
> *But not that I betrayed a trust,*
> *Broke some girl's heart, and left her to shame;*
> *Sneered young souls out of faith, rose by deceit;*

Lifted by credulous mobs to wealth and fame;
Waxed fat while good men waned by lie and cheat;
Cringed to the throng; oppressed the poor and weak;
When men say this, may some find voice to speak
Though I am dust.

In the Long Gallery a small old bookcase stands by a window seat. It contains numerous hymnals and a volume entitled *Psychopathia Sexualis* by Dr R. V. Krafft-Ebing, originally published in German in 1886. The study catalogues personal accounts from Krafft-Ebing's homosexual and bisexual patients and includes the observation: 'The medical barrister finds out how sad the lack of knowledge is in the domain of sexuality when he is called upon to express an opinion as to the responsibility of the accused whose life, liberty and honour are at stake. He then begins to appreciate the efforts that have been made to bring light to darkness.' The work was not translated into English until 1892, the year after William's accession to the title. Perhaps the earl had been reading this edition, published in New York in 1938, in the months before he died.

Sibell, of all the Lygons the least squeamish about her father's homosexuality, outlived her other six siblings. Not long before her death, on being asked what she hoped for from a book about her family, and her father in particular, she replied, 'Just the truth. He was a very nice man and he did care so very much about his children. Mother was his greatest mistake and maybe because he was homosexual he made the wrong choice in marriage.' And what was her abiding memory of her father and what he had taught his children? 'Tolerance. Always tolerance.'

Today William's *bargello* chairs are placed in various rooms about the old house: half a dozen in the Smoking Room, a pair in the Library and a dozen in the Great Hall. Just outside the Great Hall, in the Ante-Room, stands the fruitwood table on which his red Cabinet boxes lie, including the one with the British Legion poppy inside. For the pacifist William the poppy had another and a secret relevance. Before it attained its symbolic role after the battles in the poppy fields of Flanders, the floppy scarlet poppy, *Papaver orientale*, had been associated in the late nineteenth century with homo-erotic passion, an association which lingered in the poetry of the First World War.

The old lead windows of the Ante-Room look out on to the Moat Garden where William loved to sit in the arc of his protective moat and from where he was beckoned by those three knights on that June evening in 1931. During his exile he commissioned a set of lead planters to distribute round the well. He had them inscribed with the plea: 'Every man has his own place and it's best to let him alone'.

Chapter Fifteen

THE SUNDIAL

A nother inscription at Madresfield brought solace to Maimie and her friend Evelyn Waugh. It is carved into the stone of an old sundial which stands in the herbaceous garden and it reads, 'That day is wasted on which we have not laughed'.

Often the two friends would walk in this garden before dinner, turning over the events that had rent apart her family. Waugh was alert to Maimie's suffering and, conscious of her devout – albeit High Anglican – upbringing, he urged her to turn to God. Did not the Chapel stand at the heart of her family home? Was not every day at Madresfield begun and ended with prayer? As they strolled back into the house, an 'illumination' painted by Henry Payne hung to the left of the front door. It is still there, set within a decorative border comprising vignettes of Madresfield – the moat, a medieval knight, St George, a pet dog. The script informs the household: 'Prayers 9 am & 8 pm. Meals 9.30 am, 1.30 & 8.15 pm'.

Turning right and passing through the Library, the two friends would have reached the Chapel.

> The whole interior had been gutted, elaborately refurnished and decorated in the arts-and-crafts style of the last decade of the nineteenth century. Angels in printed cotton smocks, rambler-roses, flower-spangled meadows, frisking lambs, texts in Celtic script, saints in armour, covered the walls in an intricate pattern of clear, bright colours. There was a triptych of pale oak, carved so as to give it the peculiar property of seeming to have been moulded in plasticine. The sanctuary lamp and all the metal furniture were of bronze, hand-beaten to the patina of a pock-marked skin. The altar steps had a carpet of grass-green, strewn with white and gold daisies.
>
> 'Golly,' I said.
>
> 'It was papa's wedding present to mama.'

This passage from *Brideshead Revisited* is an exact description of the Madresfield Chapel and it seems almost prescient that, of the paintings of William and Lettice Beauchamp's children, the fresco of Dickie, the youngest Lygon, is the only one that stands apart. It is painted on the wall of the organ loft and not with those of his siblings and parents in the main body of the Chapel; as if he were an afterthought, or excluded from the fold. Fifteen years after the fresco was completed it was he – and he alone – who was removed after the scandal from his father, siblings and Madresfield to accompany his mother to Saighton Grange on his uncle Bend'or's estate. After his mother died, his uncle barely spoke to him. He grew up ill at ease with the aristocracy, preferring to find friendship among the middle classes. He married a vicar's daughter. Many years later his daughter, Rosalind Morrison, was struck by the fact that he never mentioned his parents; the memories were too painful. Perhaps Waugh's novel had to suffice as an explanation.

Apart from Lettice Lygon, who prior to the scandal had married Sir Richard Cotterell, a Herefordshire landowner, those of her siblings who did marry all chose spouses outside their aristocratic social circle. Both Sibell and Rosalind are 'absolutely certain' that the young Lygons paid the price of their father's scandal. Sibell recalls, 'I expect they did shun us,' and that all her siblings 'had a very bad time'. Cut adrift from their familiar moorings in the aristocracy, some members of this generation, like the Flytes in *Brideshead Revisited*, drifted in unfamiliar reaches of society or, to avoid sinking, clung to unsatisfactory relationships and failed marriages. Sibell's diary for 1934 recalls a conversation with a girlfriend in which they concluded that 'we ought not to go out with jockeys'. Denied status and spurned by many of their peers, they drifted into their own Waste Land of recklessness anaesthetized by alcohol.

The girls had been abandoned at a vulnerable age: late adolescence. As young debutantes they had had little guidance from their mother. After the scandal they stumbled into social exile, no longer desirable marriage prospects, occasionally colliding with their peers. In *Brideshead Revisited*, the reckless beauty Julia Flyte is drawn to the suburban 'Metroland' that Waugh had parodied. Acutely aware of her family's compromised reputation, she marries an outsider, the Canadian tycoon Rex Mottram. It proves to be an unsuitable and unhappy match. Although it was Sibell who had the on-off affair with the Canadian press baron Max Beaverbrook, Julia closely resembles Maimie.

Maimie was so breathtakingly beautiful that on one occasion when she entered a ballroom, the band simply stopped playing. Before her father's fall, this flirtatious debutante served as lady-in-waiting to Princess Ingrid of Sweden – later the Queen of Denmark. At a party for the Royal Ascot races she met and was courted by the Prince of Wales's brother, the bisexual Prince George, fourth in line to the throne, who took up with Noël Coward some years later. Beauchamp's daughters, particularly Sibell and Coote, were furious when Coward was knighted in 1970. Why was he accepted by the establishment when their father was stripped of his honours and forced into exile? In just thirty years how attitudes had changed. Maimie and Prince George 'did have a fling but no engagement,' her sister Sibell recalled. Perhaps Maimie felt comfortable with a man of similar sensibilities to her father, whom Waugh referred to in letters to her as the 'pauper prince'. The relationship ended once the scandal broke. Estranged from her class and accompanied by her plainer sister, Coote, Maimie frequented hunting and racing circles. Even in the hedonistic world of the years between the wars in which young members of the upper class kicked off their shoes, 'discovered' sex and drugs and preempted much that we popularly associate with the sixties generation, these young women were lost souls. When Hugh died, Waugh was particularly concerned for the sisters' well-being, writing to Maimie, 'It is the saddest news I ever heard. I shall miss him bitterly . . . I know what a loss it will be to all of you and to Boom . . . I am having Mass said for him at Farm Street.' The Smoking Room bookcase holds a complete set of Waugh's novels. A first edition of *A Handful of Dust* includes an inscription on the title page. It reads: 'To Hughie to whom it should have been dedicated. Evelyn, September 3rd 1934'.

Eventually, in 1939, Maimie married a penniless White Russian, Prince Vsevolode, who would have been fifth in line to the Russian throne. He worked for a vintner and as an air warden. Friends observed their unhappiness. 'He spent all her money,' Diana Mosley explained, and they drank their way through a disastrous, impecunious marriage stroking their Pekinese dogs. Pots of boiling hot tea were flung at one another and, Waugh reported to Nancy Mitford, they 'follow the old, almost abeyant custom, of residing together without speaking. Difficult with servants.'

The publisher Christopher Sinclair-Stevenson remembers Maimie, who was a neighbour when he was growing up in London. 'She was quite wild – a

full-blown English rose with petals about to drop off!'
Flat broke and en route to her bank manager for a loan,
Maimie had come over one morning to seek his
mother's advice. She was dressed in a deep *décolleté* and
reeking of scent, as if she was intending to seduce the
bank manager. 'Mother suggested that the best advice
she could offer was to go right home and change.' On
another occasion, Mrs Sinclair-Stevenson was rung at
three a.m. by Vsevolode, saying that Maimie was so desperate that she was about to jump out of the bedroom
window. 'My mother refused to go round, reasoning
that it wasn't far to fall. Of course, nothing happened.
They lived on their uppers, drunk and rather broke.'

Evelyn Waugh stood by her. In 1939 he asked Maimie
to be a godmother to his son Auberon, writing to her, 'I
know you won't be able to come for christening on
account there's a war, but I could have a proxy for you.'
During the fifties he invited her to 'come and dine with
a cousin of Little Laura's [his wife] named Mrs. Fleming?
Her husband [the writer Ian Fleming] writes common
books but, as you would expect from a cousin of L.L.,
she is a lady of utmost refinement.' By 1956 Vsevolode
had abandoned Maimie and she descended further into
alcoholism. Waugh was concerned about Maimie's
mental condition and, conscious that he had not
managed to save his friend Hugh, he urged her to seek
peace and discipline within the Catholic Church. 'I
believe that everyone once in his (or her) life has the
moment when he is open to Divine Grace ... I don't
know, darling Blondie, whether that is your condition

now, but if it is, it's not a thing to dilly-dally about [and] I'd awfully like to pimp for you in that affair.' Deaf to advice, she continued drinking but all the while retained the mannerisms and the poise of a great beauty. Then one day at Madresfield she reported that she had given up alcohol 'because it tastes of iron filings'. She was dying of cancer. Coote devotedly nursed her to the end.

Sibell romped through many affairs, periodically being picked up and ditched by Max Beaverbrook and serving as the conduit through whom he dealt with other lovers. During the thirties, at a time when the polar opposites of Socialism and Fascism seemed to be the only alternatives, she took her father's political Liberalism one step further and became a Socialist. She was also courted by Aneurin Bevan. Her diary for 1934, one of the diaries found in 2006, throws light on her insecurity. She frequently registered surprise that acquaintances were 'decent to me' as she expected to be snubbed, for example, by her cousin Ursula Grosvenor at the Grand National. Week by week she confides her crushes – one day she likes 'Bunty', the next she is 'keen on John Corbett'. Knowing that her love for Beaverbrook was doomed, she nevertheless took her 'courage in both hands and spoke to Max on the telephone. I love him so much that I can't let go and I have no hope that it might be right again. I ought to realise that it won't Ever be. His love (if such it be) here and gone. My love for him is sapping my vitality.'

Her own liaisons were almost as notorious as those of her father. Finally, a year after his death, in 1939, she became engaged to Michael Rowley, an aircraft designer who was eight years her junior. It was a strange co-incidence that his stepmother, Violet Cripps, married Sibell's uncle, Bend'or. Several dates were set for Sibell's marriage. Initially it was planned for January but Rowley's father scathingly announced that he had never heard of Lady Sibell. A plan to marry later that month at the Oratory in London was also postponed and it was not until the following month that they finally did so. However, within weeks Rowley admitted that he was a bigamist: the previous year he had married a German girl after a drunken lunch in Mexico.

During the war, Rowley served as a fighter pilot in 601 Squadron but in 1940 was diagnosed with a brain tumour. When Rowley's German wife, Eleonore, made enquiries about him in 1941, Sibell – for fear of losing him – claimed that he was dead. Eleanor sued for damages and was awarded £814. The bona fide marriage was dissolved, leaving Rowley to marry Sibell for a second time in 1949. By his side, she adopted some of his Midlands expressions and pronunciations which sat incongruously with her extreme upper-class intonations. She nursed him until he died, in September 1952. Sibell was childless.

Alone again, she took to the field and hunted – for many years side-saddle – until well into her eighties and was appointed Master of the Ledbury Hunt. Though she pursued various liaisons, such as with Lord Rosebery, Sibell never married again. Constant rows with friends and family kept her sparky; there was always a feud on the go, though they never lasted long. She died aged ninety-eight in a Gloucestershire nursing home, feisty to the end.

In the nursing home she passed the time reading the memoirs, diaries and biographies of her peer group in an attempt to keep up with the families that, by birth, she would – had her father not fallen from grace – have counted among her circle. When asked about the effect her father's exile had had on her family, she always stoically replied, 'We coped.' However, in the last months of her life she was asked again. She hung her head. One tear fell into her tweed lap. 'It was very difficult really.'

Waugh's dear friend Coote, who partly informed the character of Cordelia Flyte, was kind, spinsterly and plain. She variously worked in the Women's Auxiliary Air Force as a photographic interpreter during the war, as secretary to the British ambassador in Greece, as a governess in Istanbul where she slept under a table, as a farmer, a social secretary and an archivist for Christie's auction house in London. One of her young colleagues there, Simon Dickinson, observed that this fastidious, clever and 'very old-fashioned-looking woman' set up a perfect cataloguing system 'never bettered' and was adored by the young because of her forthrightness and sense of fun. Members of her family have speculated that her cleverness was deployed in espionage – as her ancestor Richard Ligon's had been during the Civil War – but she never confirmed it. Her exceptional height, enormous feet, Joyce Grenfell lop-sided gait and thick

Maimie, Coote, a friend and Evelyn Waugh, 1939.

spectacles certainly meant she was noticed in a crowd but perhaps that larger-than-life quality was a perfect foil to a secret life.

For decades Coote lived in a poky prefabricated bungalow, surrounded by Craxton paintings and first editions of Waugh's books presented and inscribed to her by him. She was an inveterate traveller, impervious to discomfort and delighted by people. In her late eighties she saw nothing strange about driving halfway across England to attend two weddings in one day. A deft cook, she would entertain friends of all ages and walks of life at the drop of a hat. Her bungalow was situated outside the gates of Faringdon Manor, the home of her father's loyal friend Lord Berners and his lover, Robert Heber-Percy. Coote, their unofficial châtelaine, placed herself at their beck and call but was dropped when her presence was considered inconvenient. After Berners' death, astonishingly, aged seventy-three, she married the elderly and sick 'widow' Heber-Percy. Sibell was shocked. 'Why did she do it? Just to say she'd been married? She'd sit there admiring the ring on her finger.' Waugh's biographer, Selina Hastings, who knew her, speculates that Heber-Percy's friends prevailed upon him to take pity on Coote and offer her a secure future by marrying her in old age, all the while assuming that she knew the score – it would be a lavender marriage. Sadly, Coote did not want to see it that way. 'When Robert came up the aisle Laura [Duchess of] Marlborough was entwined round him with another lady entwined on the other side. And there was Coote just following along behind with a doctor carrying a huge hypodermic syringe just in case Robert needed an injection. He was quite ill. I cried. I was horrified by her wedding. And I *know* Robert did it just to annoy Laura. I think Laura and Robert had a bash [affair].'

The marriage was a sham. On the first night of their honeymoon at Positano on the Amalfi coast, which Coote organized entirely, the newly married couple checked in to the hotel and were given the keys to the bridal suite. 'Are you mad?' Heber-Percy roared at Coote. 'The bridal suite! Just look at yourself. Do you think I'm going to share a bedroom – never mind a bridal bed – with you?' Coote spent her honeymoon alone in the only available accommodation remaining: a maid's room. On returning to Faringdon, now her marital home, the possessive Polish cook tossed Coote's withering bouquet and wedding dress on to the floor and handed in her notice. It was typical of Coote's generous spirit that only a year later she made it up with Heber-Percy and they remained friends until his death. She had always valued the friendship of avowed homosexuals and perhaps she, like Maimie, hoped to replicate the closeness she had shared with her father.

Brave and greatly liked – Laura Waugh described her to Evelyn as 'the nicest of all your friends' – Coote was one of the few women in England who continued to ride side-saddle. Since she disapproved of the woman her brother Elmley – who became the eighth Earl Beauchamp – married, she refused to return to

Madresfield until the countess died in 1989. The coast was finally clear. Coote rushed back to her childhood home and the first room she visited was the Nursery. It had not changed a bit. Passionate about Madresfield to her dying day, in her will she requested that all her possessions – including the morocco-bound prayer book her father had given to her as a child – be returned to her family home.

Brideshead Revisited is popularly, but mistakenly, read as a book with a sad ending. Some readers focus on the worldly facts: that the Flyte children walk away from earthly happiness and a dynasty expires. Waugh, by contrast, intended it – 'his most vulnerable book' – as a tale of redemption. At the beginning of the story, he describes a skull sitting on a bowl of roses in Charles Ryder's Oxford rooms. The Latin motto, *Et in Arcadia Ego*, is inscribed across its forehead. The classical translation is 'Death is even in Arcadia' or that mortality menaces this present happiness, an interpretation from classical literature that was revived in medieval times and used in art, often in conjunction with a death head or skeleton, as a morbid admonition, a *memento mori*. But did Waugh mean the reader to think of the more modern mistranslation, which owes its origins to Nicholas Poussin's paintings: 'I, too, was born, or lived, in Arcadia'? This suggests a retrospective idyll of unsurpassed beauty which is now unattainable but still resides in the memory. Had the Flyte/Lygon family indeed inhabited an Arcadia for nearly a thousand years? The Flytes, like the Lygons, were all flawed characters; Waugh gave them good, if not in worldly terms easy, lives; God's will had triumphed over their own. Perhaps Sebastian, Julia, Cordelia and Bridey would themselves ascend to the eternal Arcadia of heaven. This redemption is symbolized at the end of the novel by the familiar Christian icon of light . . .

> a small red flame – a beaten-copper lamp of deplorable design relit before the beaten-copper doors of a tabernacle; the flame which the old knights saw from their tombs, which they saw put out; that flame burns again for other soldiers, far from home, farther, in heart, than Acre or Jerusalem.

Brideshead Revisited, enjoyed by so many and on numerous levels, was selected by the Book Society as choice of the season, and was an immediate success in Britain. When published in America in 1946, it sold over half a million copies. To the Americans it provided vicarious tourism to an England which was not easily reached during the early post-war years; an older and gentler world of high-born living steeped in history. Ironically, its publication coincided with the very era in Britain's history when hundreds of grand country houses were being abandoned or pulled down; either surrendered by families who could no longer afford either the staff or funds to run them or deemed in the post-war world to be redundant symbols of privilege. It seemed that William Beauchamp's campaign to save the great houses and parks of England had been in vain.

As early as July 1940 *The Times* reported that the 'new order ... cannot be based on the preservation of privilege, whether the privilege be that of a country, of a class, or of an individual'. But, though Waugh was writing against his times, for a significant minority his old-fashioned sympathies were pleasing and nostalgic. He had written himself out of debt and into affluence and fame.

Television helped to create one of the great mis-understandings about the novel, a misunderstanding which has been repeated in the new film. When Charles Sturridge made his sympathetic and popular 1980s television adaptation of the novel, the Lygons, par-ticularly Coote, who shunned publicity, would not entertain the idea of film cameras at Madresfield. So it was filmed at the Howards' home in the North Riding of Yorkshire. Castle Howard became the popular visualization of Brideshead Castle. Set in a vast park and looking out over an ornate fountain, Castle Howard is a Whig palace boasting baroque grandeur. The Howards' and the Lygons' homes stand at opposite ends of the spectrum of English country house living: one, the extrovert, was designed to project to the world; the other, the introvert, to withdraw from it. Castle Howard, as its name suggests, is a self-consciously dynastic house built for the politically ambitious Charles Howard, third Earl of Carlisle. Its architect, Sir John Vanbrugh, created for him a show house designed to secure the Howards' place in history. When it was built (1699–1712), it was the finest private palace in

England. Carlisle nearly bankrupted himself with the project and it is said that because he could not afford a fitting dowry his third daughter was condemned to remain a spinster. The whole ensemble calls to mind Lady Frederick Cavendish's lament: 'When one lives in Paradise, how hard it must be to ascend in heart and mind to heaven.' Howard's final conceit was his mausoleum, designed by Nicholas Hawksmoor and costing £38,000. The Lygons of Madresfield on the other hand chose to be buried under trees with only a carved headstone or, in the seventh earl's case, a simple cross marking his grave. It is Madresfield and *not* Castle Howard that contains the true spirit, as well as the actual inspiration, for *Brideshead*.

In spite of the eventual fate of the family, for Waugh, at a low point in his life and 'homesick for nursery morality', Madresfield and the Lygons had brought him laughter and repose. Just before the outbreak of war, Maimie and Waugh stopped beside the sundial and she turned to him and said, 'Well, you and I haven't wasted a day, have we?'

EPILOGUE

A ditch, approximately four metres wide, scars a field on the south-east corner of the estate. Archaeologists have recently determined that it is over eight hundred years old and probably marked the original boundary of the manor because it is fringed with rare and ancient wild service or 'chequer' trees which have spread their suckers along the excavation. These trees are confined to primary woodland which has never been ploughed or disturbed. The ditch is similar to, and may indeed be, the very one that Robert de Braci's serfs dug out to define and defend the family lands in the twelfth century. Nearly nine hundred years later, this plot saved Madresfield for de Braci's descendants, the Lygons.

On his father's death in 1938, Lord Elmley became the eighth and last Earl Beauchamp. Together with his wife he lived at Madresfield but his sisters – particularly Coote – preferred to stay away. They had little in common with their sister-in-law, who was, according to Sibell, a 'frightful snob'. The eighth earl led a quiet life, unburdened by children or distinction. After his death in 1979, his widow, Else de la Cour, who had one child from a previous marriage, remained at Madresfield until she too died ten years later. Upon her death, the trustees invited Rosalind Morrison, Dickie's daughter, the eighth earl's niece, to live at Madresfield with her husband, Sir Charles Morrison. In order to address death duties, 150 acres of land including the field into which the original ditch had been dug were put up for sale. A commercial developer built a business park, housing and a supermarket on this land. Today, the stagnant, rubbish-strewn waters in the medieval ditch contain an abandoned supermarket trolley.

One of the abiding impressions of visitors to Madresfield is that, no matter the season, the house is invariably shrouded in either a dense morning mist or an 'implacable' – almost Dickensian – fog. Fog creeps up the old bricks to explore the gabled roof. Fog drifts down into the recesses of the moat, concealing the heads of all but the tallest swans as they glide largely unseen. Beyond, in the park, bare branches claw the fog into tatters which trail across the meadows. Cattle move slowly, now visible, now veiled, down the Gloucester Drive. Dogs snatch at the fog-rags being pulled by the wind back towards the house. At daybreak, fog often shrouds the house; some days it is burned away by the weak English sun, but on others it lingers over the Lygon lands.

As a child, Rosalind Morrison often visited Madresfield. On her first night as its châtelaine, she walked along the Staircase Hall, up the rock crystal staircase and stopped in front of the William Ranken portrait of her grandfather, the exiled seventh earl. She touched the canvas and said, 'It's all right, Grandpa, we're back.' There was work to be done. Madresfield needed to be made cosy and welcoming. Being more familiar with the proportions of a farmhouse than a stately home, the couple initially settled into the little rooms at the far corners of the house, avoiding the large and formal ones until they were made homely. When repairs to the moat necessitated dredging it, the workmen found the marble bust of the Countess Beauchamp which Rosalind's grandfather had tossed into it on return from exile. Rather than replacing the bust on the original plinth next to her husband in the Staircase Hall, Rosalind respected their estrangement and had her placed in the Entrance Hall. The countess's image, which had been angrily whitewashed from the Chapel wall, was also restored.

The recent repairs are virtually unnoticeable. Returning from one week to the next, for example, the visitor may believe nothing has changed until he sinks into a sofa and realizes that it has been reupholstered in a cloth that looks as if it has been there since the twenties. Frayed Arts and Crafts curtains have been strengthened by adding thick nutmeg-brown velvet borders and rehung. Walking down the flag-stoned Kitchen corridor along which those wicker hampers of produce have passed over the centuries, the visitor may peek round one of the doors which lead into what was once the Creamery. On the floor stand a dozen rows of flowerpots planted in staggered sequence with pelargonium and amaryllis lilies to be brought out into the main rooms week by week as they come into bloom. The old house is run with precision and attention to tradition.

As a foil to Madresfield's riot of architectural features, the sixty acres of pleasure gardens have been simplified by clarifying the concentric circles around the house. From the outer circle inwards, the progress towards the house commences with neatly clipped, ten-foot-high yew hedges which stand like a crenellated stockade beyond the moat. One step nearer is a perimeter formed by the stewes which have yielded Lenten fish over the centuries. Standing quietly by, one may see a heron banking over the yew to dive for his quarry or the turquoise flash of a stooping kingfisher. Nearer still, the moat walls are planted with a fringe of *Senecio saracenicus* or Saracen's comfrey, used as a poultice on wounds since the time of the Crusades. Inside the circle of the moat stands the Victorian Moat Garden, a conversation of grey foliage, grey stone and grey lead planters, punctuated with lavender, which is slowly unveiled in the morning as the mist or fog pulls away. By the door which leads into the Library stands a four-foot-high shard of Welsh slate which has recently been carved with the same evocative inscription as on the old sundial: 'That day is wasted on which we have not laughed'.

Madresfield has cast aside its social garb. There have been few house parties, shooting parties, balls or political gatherings. It has withdrawn into a restorative period of repairing, sorting out, archiving and, in a sense, lying fallow. When the next generation of Lygons and their children come to live here, they will take the family's association with the house into a second millennium.

NOTES

All letters quoted from in the book, unless otherwise indicated, are held in the Muniment Room at Madresfield Court, as are the Lygon family's scrapbooks and diaries. All quotations from Lady Sibell Rowley, *née* Lygon, are taken from conversations with the author, 2003–5. All quotations from Diana, Lady Mosley, are taken from conversations with the author, 2003.

Epigraph: Muthesius, cultural and technical attaché at the German Embassy in London 1896–1903, published his magisterial survey of the English house, *Das englische Haus*, in 1904. The quotation is from a letter to his patron, Grand Duke Carl Alexander of Saxe-Weimar, written in 1909.

Prologue
23: ' "I had been there before" ': *Brideshead Revisited*, Evelyn Waugh, Chapman & Hall, 1945.
23: 'the home of the Lygons': The surname Lygon is variously spelt through the ages, for example Liggon, Ligon.

24: '"I loved buildings"': Charles Ryder in *Brideshead*, Waugh.

25: 'four tree-lined avenues': Elm, so prolific in the county that it was known as 'Worcestershire weeds', originally made up the fourth drive but it was lost to Dutch elm disease in the 1970s.

30: '*Portrait of Clare*': The dedication from Francis Brett Young in this book reads, 'To Countess Beauchamp because of her love of Worcestershire and mine of Madresfield', 1927.

30: 'Few landed families have survived': In an article which appeared in the *Field*, February 1994, a list was compiled of a handful of families who could claim such unbroken longevity in one place: the Fulfords of Fulford, Devon (since before 1200); the Gordon-Duff-Penningtons of Muncaster, Cumbria (1208); the Hoghtons of Hoghton, Lancashire (since the beginning of the thirteenth century); the Giffards of Chillington, Staffordshire (since William the Conqueror).

30: 'eighth and last Earl Beauchamp': The earldom died out with him in 1979.

33: '"blue remembered hills"':

> Into my heart an air that kills
> From yon far country blows:
> What are those blue remembered hills,
> What spires, what farms are those?

A Shropshire Lad, A. E. Housman, 1896.

33: '"those curious bubblings up"': *Rural Rides*, William Cobbett, 1830.

34: '*maeðeresfeld* for "Mower's Field"': *The Concise Oxford Dictionary of English Place-Names*, Eilert Ekwall, Oxford, 1960. It has also been suggested that the name derives from the madder plant, *Rubia tinctorum*, which has grown in England since at least Anglo-Saxon times. The roots of the plant give a rosy-pink dye much loved by the Arts and Crafts movement of the late nineteenth century.

1 The Nursery Window

38: ' "slowly and reluctantly" ': 'Madresfield and Brideshead', Lady Dorothy Lygon, in *Evelyn Waugh and His World*, edited by David Pryce-Jones, Weidenfeld & Nicolson, 1973.

41: ' "Dearest Lady Dorothy" ': Letter in Rosalind Morrison's private collection.

41: 'two intense homosexual friendships': 'I went to Oxford and visited my first homosexual love, Richard Pares,' Waugh noted in his diary of 1954. His homosexual affairs are also referred to in his letters to Nancy Mitford.

41: ' "that low door in the wall" ': *Brideshead Revisited*, Evelyn Waugh, Chapman & Hall, 1945. It is, of course, an echo of Alice's entry into Wonderland.

41: ' "preference for the well-born" ': Lord Deedes in conversation with the author, 2003.

43: ' "always just missing the happiness" ': *A Little Learning*, Evelyn Waugh, Methuen, 1964.

44: ' "sharp disturbance in my private life" ': *Vile Bodies*, Evelyn Waugh, Chapman & Hall, 1930.

44: ' "How he howled" ': Harold Acton, interview in the *Observer*, 1973.

44: ' "unintelligible . . ." ': *Evelyn Waugh: The Early Years 1903–1939*, Martin Stannard, Dent, 1986.

45: ' "never spoke" ': 'Waugh the Catholic', Ian Ker, *The Tablet*, 18 October 2003.

45: ' "no possessions" ': *When the Going Was Good*, Evelyn Waugh, Duckworth, 1946.

47: 'his "paraclete" ': In the sense of a consolation or

sanctuary, derived from the Christian concept of the Holy Spirit as a comforter.

48: ' "the best which he couldn't really finance" ': Lord Deedes in conversation with the author, 2003.

51: ' "Well, I am living with" ': Waugh to Mary and Dorothy, from the Ritz Hotel, London, 1932 (?). His letters to the Lygons starkly contrast to those addressed to Katharine Asquith who, like Waugh, was a recent convert. She lived at Mells Manor, near Frome in Somerset, another country house where he used to stay regularly, though here with Jesuits, scholars and politicians, not socialites. The letters addressed to Katharine were appropriately serious-minded.

51: ' "the time is coming" ': Sibell's obituary in the *Daily Telegraph*, 16 November 2005.

52: ' "pure jealousy" ': Bill Deedes, Waugh's journalistic companion in Abyssinia, observed that 'Waugh could be very cruel and he knew that. He was fully aware that we are all sinners and he resorted to his religion for help.' Lord Deedes in conversation with the author, 2003.

53: ' "the famous man-about-town" ': Letters in Rosalind Morrison's private collection.

53: 'Oxford University Arctic Expedition': Their maps and intelligence later proved vital during the Second World War.

54: ' "which proved to be as cold" ': 'The First Time I Went North', Evelyn Waugh, in *The First Time I . . .*, edited by Thelma Benson, Chapman & Hall, 1935.

55: ' "the size of a *wagon-lit* . . ." ': Ibid.

56: ' "tell Hughie to hurry up" ': Waugh to Mary and Dorothy from Chagford, Devon, October 1934.

56: ' "la vie de château" ': *Evelyn Waugh*, Christopher Sykes, Collins, 1975.

57: ' "have been adapted . . . twenty electric light bulbs" ':

A Handful of Dust, Evelyn Waugh, Chapman & Hall, 1934.

58: 'During 1944 . . .': Waugh was probably unaware of the fact that Madresfield, for the second time in its history, had been reserved for royal occupation pending a successful Nazi invasion. The palace sent crates of canned food down to await the royal family's possible arrival.

59: 'a springtime delicacy enjoyed . . . by the landed classes': When Waugh was a young boy, his cousin Edmund Gosse sent Waugh's father some plover's eggs for Easter. Arthur Waugh was so struck by the very unusual gift that he penned a ditty of thanks to Gosse for the lordly fare rarely found on suburban dining tables.

> But lo! A cousin's heart that beats
> With tender and harmonious chords
> Wafts to our poor suburban streets
> The menu of the House of Lords.

62: '"suggested to Evelyn"': *A Year to Remember: A Reminiscence of 1931*, Alec Waugh, W. H. Allen, 1975.

62: '"I am writing . . . Mad"': Waugh to Dorothy, letter HW53, from Chagford, Devon, 23 March 1944.

63: '"as appreciative of porphyry"': Letter from Waugh to Mary, August 1960.

64: '"sits at Madresfield"': Letter from Waugh to his wife Laura, 11 November 1940.

64: 'Details in the novel': David Gilmour, a kinsman of the Lygons, in conversation with the author.

65: '"Sebastian gives me such pangs"': Dorothy to Waugh, 30 May 1945.

65: 'it had, indeed, been based on them': In 1945, Waugh attempted a prequel to the story, entitled *Charles Ryder's Schooldays*. Though he wrote only twenty-three pages and then abandoned it, they are revealing. Charles's school is called 'Spierpoint College'. Lady Emily

Pierrepont was the maiden name of the Lygons' grand-mother. He described the building as a product of 'the Oxford Movement and the Gothic revival'. The sixth Earl Beauchamp had commissioned the neo-Gothic extension to Madresfield and had been an important figure in the Oxford Movement. The schoolboy was given a love of Gothic architecture and the breviaries.

2 The Ditch

67: 'Anxious to define . . . the extent of his land': We know that the Shire Ditch at nearby Hanley Castle, for example, was cut and recut by Gilbert de Clare in 1287, following a dispute over hunting grounds with the Bishop of Hereford. Today the line of Robert de Braci's ditch can still be made out in places. *Cartulary of Worcester Cathedral Priory*, R. R. Darlington, Pipe Roll Society, 1968.

68: ' "gelded and gouged" ': *Worcestershire Relics*, J. Noake, Longman & Co., 1887.

68: 'As sheriff, he was known': *Biographical Illustrations of Worcestershire*, John Chambers, 1820.

71: 'the rank of gentleman': *Origins of the English Gentleman*, Maurice Keen, Tempus, 2002. It was not until 1414 that this term was first used and then in the case of an 'ungentlemanly' act: murder. The plaintiff, Robert Stafford, required in court to declare his name, place and 'mystery or degree' – his occupation or station in life – described himself as 'a gentleman'.

71: 'half a dozen servants': Typically, a steward for the master of the household, a maid of the chamber for his wife, a bailiff or reeve to manage the estate and two or three serfs to work the farm and the kitchen and the pleasure gardens.

72: 'The young Robert was knighted': We know this because

in 1319 he is recorded as Sir Robert, a witness to a charter of Edmund de la Mare of Hanley Castle, the headquarters of Malvern Chase. Three years later Roger de Hanley holds the posts of Constable and Keeper of Hanley Castle. Hanley's role as chief forester is handed on to Sir Robert de Braci, *dominus* of Madresfield. *Victoria County History: Worcs*, vol. 4.

72: 'described as being Keeper': Ibid.

73: 'Robertus de Braci ... returned to Parliament': *Parliaments of England, 1213–1702*, London, 1873.

74: 'the king's escheator': An escheator was an important medieval officer with power and responsibility. Under feudal law, a fief reverted to the lord and ultimately to the Crown when the tenant died without an heir. The county escheator was required to record this change of status with the Exchequer, a fundamental duty given the significance of land in medieval England.

74: ' "the mad priest of Kent" ': *Chronicles*, Jean Froissart, 1395.

75: ' "beyond the memory of man" ': Witness statement of Geoffrey Chaucer in 1385, when the claims of Sir Richard Scrope and Sir Robert Grosvenor to bear arms were heard in the Court of Chivalry.

80: ' "wise and sound administrators" ': *The Treasure of the City of Ladies or the Book of the Three Virtues*, Christine de Pisan, 1405.

80: ' "complementary and overlapping roles" ': ' "How ladies ... who live on their manors ought to manage their households and estates": 'Women as Landholders and Administrators in the Later Middle Ages', Rowena E. Archer, in *Women in Medieval English Society*, edited by P. J. P. Goldberg, Stroud: Sutton Publishing, 1997.

81: 'In 1294 ... the cost of just cleaning': Westminster Abbey Muniments, 27694. Christopher Dyer, in

Medieval Fish, Fisheries and Fish Ponds in England, edited by M. Aston, British Archaeological Reports, British Series 182, 1989.

82: 'nature's "sweets"': *Flora Britannica*, Richard Mabey, Chatto & Windus, 1996.

84: '"moost troublouseust season"': Public Record Office, E404/68/103.

85: 'Aleanor Denys': Denys is sometimes spelt Dennys or Dennis.

3 The Portrait

87: 'Federigo Zuccaro': A contemporary painter from Florence who was a friend of Vasari.

89: 'Farnando': Variously spelt Ferdinando, Ferdinand, etc.

90: 'entered the service of Nicholas Heath': *The Madresfield Muniments: An Account of the Family and Estates*, Charles Lethbridge Kingsford, the Echo Office, Worcester, 1929.

90: 'enough to make him change sides': Ibid.

91: '"false books, ballets"': Calendar of State Papers, Domestic I, 82.

92: '"For many consecutive days"': Ven. Cal., vol. vi. Letter dated 17 March 1556. *The History of Mary of England*, J. M. Stone, Sands & Co., 1901.

93: '"relished the scheme"': According to Simon Renard, Spanish ambassador to London, who wrote to the Spanish king on 14 September 1556.

93: 'He had been brought up': It was common at the time for members of the gentry to be sent to a great man's household to be educated in the finer aspects of scholarship and courtly etiquette.

94: '"able to bring a great part"': According to the confession of fellow-conspirator Sir Thomas White, Calendar of State Papers, Domestic.

95: 'Cardinal Pole, Mary's loyal Archbishop': The Lygons

were in correspondence with the cardinal. The Madresfield Muniments include a letter to William Lygon, dated 30 June 1556, from Cardinal Pole allowing for the renunciation of his executorship under the will of a William Pynnock.

96: ' "Item – to speak for" ': Memoranda of one of the confessors, Calendar of State Papers, Domestic II.

97: ' "so general as to be scarcely disreputable" ': G. M. Trevelyan, quoted in *Jolly Roger: The Story of the Great Age of Piracy*, Patrick Pringle, London Museum Press, 1953.

98: 'As the Killigrew family': Piracy ran in Killigrew's blood. His mother was the daughter of a Suffolk pirate and, as an old woman, was arrested with two of her servants for boarding a ship that had gone aground and helping herself to the spoils. Allegedly, a secret passage led from the Killigrews' family home, Arwennack, down to the sea. It was along this passage that booty was transported up to the house and pirates passed along it to dine at the Vice-Admiral's table. *Elizabethan Privateering*, Kenneth R. Andrews, Cambridge University Press, 1964.

99: ' "Corsarios Luteranos" ': *Blood and Silver: A History of Piracy in the Caribbean and Central America*, Kris Lane, Signed Books, Oxford, 1999.

99: 'Foxe's *Book of Martyrs*': A contemporary edition of Foxe's *Martyrs* can be found in the Madresfield Library.

100: ' "the Father of Colonization . . ." ': *Some Early Barbadian History*, P. F. Campbell, 1993.

101: 'Nicknamed "William the Wastrel" ': Five successive generations of Lygon sons bore the Christian name 'William' and so, to avoid confusion, their descendants gave them sobriquets, such as William the Correspondent and William the Wastrel.

104: 'the Wastrel had received a knighthood': At the beginning of the sixteenth century one in ten villages in

England had a member of the upper class living in them. By 1560 some 4,000–5,000 men had been knighted and 1,800 could style themselves esquire. *Houses of the Gentry*, Nicholas Cooper, Yale, 1999.

106   'great housekeeping': Letter of William the Correspondent, the Wastrel's great-grandson.

4 The Herbs

109: 'thyme': It was known as shepherd's thyme in Worcestershire and apart from flavouring food was used to cure headaches and giddiness.

109: 'tansy': 'Let those Women that desire Children love this Herb,' wrote Nicholas Culpeper in his *Complete Herbal*, 1653, 'tis their best companion, their Husband excepted.' It was said its crushed leaves applied to the abdomen could stave off miscarriages while its oil, if drunk, would induce an abortion.

109: 'A *True* & Exact. . .': Its full title is *A True & Exact History of the Island of Barbadoes: Illustrated with a map of the island, as also the principal trees and plants there; together with an ingenio that makes the sugar with the plots of several houses, rooms and other places, that were used in the whole process of sugar-making; viz the Grinding-room, the Boyling-room, the Filling-room, the Curing-room, Still-house, and Furnaces.*

111: 'probably page to': A deduction made because he makes several references to the queen in his book describing her habits, dress and demeanour in some detail.

111: 'at a cost of £3,000': *Feast: A History of Good Eating*, Roy Strong, Cape, 2002.

116: ' "a stranger in my own country"': Unless otherwise indicated, all quotations in this chapter come from Richard Ligon's book.

119: 'Six thousand would die . . . perpetuated the cycle of

death': *John Winthrop's History of New England 1630–1649* (abridged), edited by Richard S. Dunn and Laetitia Yeandle, Harvard University Press, 1997.

122: 'this business, the most pre-eminently profitable': Discounting a third of the island as unsuitable for cane, Richard estimated that the rest 'may be laid to sugarworks'. Ideally a plantation should stretch across 500 to 700 acres and over the growing cycle, an acre of cane would yield, on average, 3,000 pounds in weight of sugar which would fetch 3*d*. per pound in Bridgetown. After 22 months and having been shipped to London, white lump-sugar would fetch, conservatively, 12*d*. per pound. There was also the ancillary trading in molasses, muscovado brown sugar and rum to be considered. Being such a stable and transportable cargo, sugar almost guaranteed high profits. In 1650, Richard valued one harvest for the whole island at just over three million pounds.

5 The Hamper

All letters from William the Correspondent are to be found in the Correspondence of William Lygon 1688–1721 in the Madresfield Muniments.

134: 'Bridge of Sighs': Il Ponte dei Sospiri or the Bridge of Sighs is a sixteenth-century white limestone bridge connecting the old prisons to the interrogation rooms in the Doge's Palace in Venice. Byron coined the famous phrase, recalling the passage of prisoners as they took their last view of the city. The sixth Earl Beauchamp erected a replica, in white-painted wood, between the back of the house and the far side of the moat.

134: 'the Lygon, Stanhope': Many bedrooms at Madresfield are named after the various families into which the Lygons have married.

135: ' "my dear father's" ': William the Correspondent to Isaac Tullie, 18 May 1717.

136: 'It was not unusual': By Queen Anne's reign, according to the traveller De Saussure writing in 1727, 'commerce is not looked down upon as being derogatory, as it is in France and Germany. Here men of good family and even rank may become merchants without losing caste. I have heard of younger sons of peers, whose families have been reduced to poverty through the habits of extravagance and dissipation of an elder son, retrieve the fallen fortunes of their house by becoming merchants.' *Foreign View of England in the Reigns of George I and George II: The letters of Monsieur César de Saussure to His Family*, translated and edited by Mme Van Muyden, 1902; *The Gentleman's Daughter: Women's Lives in Georgian England*, Amanda Vickery, Yale, 1998.

137: 'the Grocers soon became': The Livery Company controlled the weights and measures at the Port of London until the Great Fire of London, after which it was handed over to HM Customs & Excise.

139: '£83,00 at today's value': www.measuringworth.com

139: ' "another enemy" ': *Selections from Clarendon's The History of the Rebellion and Civil Wars and The Life by Himself*, Edward Hyde, First Earl of Clarendon, originally published 1702; OUP, 1955.

140: ' "on the grounds" ': *The Greatest Benefit to Mankind: A Medical History of Humanity from Antiquity to the Present*, Roy Porter, HarperCollins, 1997.

140: ' "The destruction of the Hall" ': Quoted in *The Worshipful Company of Grocers: An Historical Retrospect, 1345–1923*, J. Aubrey Rees, Chapman & Dodd, London, 1923.

141: ' "an estate's a pond" ': *The Complete English Tradesman*, Daniel Defoe, 1726.

141: 'Frequently a grocer was elected': Between 1351 and 1901 sixty-eight members of the Grocers' Livery Company were elected Lord Mayor of London.

141: 'As a member of the Grocers' Guild': The Correspondent and his son William, but not Corbyn, became Freemen of the Company. *Index to Apprentices 1600–1720* and *Index to Freemen 1600–1750* at the Grocers' Hall.

141: 'this pageantry': *The Worshipful Company*, Rees.

142: 'Considerable annuities . . . to his sisters': It was not until these women died that William the Correspondent's income climbed to £900 a year.

142: 'Margaret': Margaret married Reginald Pyndar of Kempley, Gloucester-shire. It was to prove a hugely significant liaison for the Lygons half a century later.

143: 'land values rose rapidly': Between 1600 and 1640 land prices rose by 500 per cent. *A Monarchy Transformed: Britain 1603–1714*, Mark Kishlansky, Allen Lane, The Penguin Press, 1996.

144: '"the golden age of quackery"': *The Greatest Benefit*, Porter.

144: 'his share of quacks': Perhaps the term comes from the Dutch 'quacksalver', meaning a doctor who used mercury to treat syphilis.

144: '"I was glad to hear"': Letter 273.

147: 'both were plain': Unfortunately, there are no portraits of father or sons.

148: '"after the discharge of some sighs"': *Birth, Marriage and Death: Ritual, Religion, and the Life-Cycle in Tudor and Stuart England*, David Cressy, OUP, 1997.

149: 'wide adoption of strict settlement': *Marriage Settlements 1601–1740: The Adoption of Strict Settlement*, Lloyd Bonfield, CUP, 1983.

149: 'males were not replacing themselves': *The Demography of the British Peerage 1603–1938*, Supplement to

Population Studies, XVIII, T. H. Hollingsworth, 1964.

149–150: ' "I am now so farr . . . this letter" ': Letter 520a.

150: ' "The Honour your Lordship . . . expect for it" ': Letter 523, 2 September 1713.

150: ' six daughters to marry off': In the end all six girls died young.

150: ' could not "give one of them" ': Letter 525, 6 September 1713.

151: ' "the now usual settlements" ': Letter 529, October 1713.

151: ' "till shee could enjoy" ': Letter 532, n.d.

151: ' "I would only beg" ': Letter 537, n.d.

151: ' "My Lord. Your eldest Daughter's" ': Letter 570, 22 May 1714.

152: ' "when you are pleas'd" ': Letter 597, 25 July 1714.

152: ' "settle for present maintenance" ': Letter 604, [?] mid-August 1714.

152: ' "my integrity is all" ': Letter 635, late October 1714.

153: ' "I cannot upon any account" ': Letter 642, 19 November 1714.

153: ' "or at least a very low Churchman" ': William the Correspondent to Mrs K. Wylde, 3 December 1714.

153: ' "I have during my whole life" ': William the Correspondent to M. Cotterell, letter 650, 4 December 1714.

153: ' Miss Esther Jennens': She married William Hanmer, and was the mother of Susanna Hanmer, who married Reginald Lygon in 1739. An important tale, told in the next chapter, hangs on that marriage.

154: ' "A Coach etc" ': William the Correspondent to his son William, letter 675, June 1716.

154: ' "very much marked . . . her marriage portion" ': Mrs K. Wylde, the go-between, to William the Correspondent, letter 701, 16 April 1717.

155: 'Tangles of mistletoe . . .': The current occupant of Madresfield, Rosalind Morrison, suggests that so high a price does mistletoe now fetch in the Christmas markets of England's cities that, should the need arise, she could harvest the estate's mistletoe rather than sell the family silver.

155: 'Since earliest . . .': *The Golden Bough: A Study in Myth and Religion*, Sir James Frazer, 1922.

6 The Red Heels

156: 'The fashion spread': *Dressed to Rule*, Philip Mansel, Yale, 2005.

158: 'Pyndars': Variously spelt Pyndar, Pindar, Pynder.

160: ' "the beauty of intimacy" ': *Analysis of Beauty*, William Hogarth, 1753.

161: 'Ottoman costume': Fashionable interpretations of *Turquérie* were taken up by European ladies, particularly once the Swiss artist Jean-Étienne Liotard had popularized them. He affected to dress like a Turk having stayed in Constantinople from 1738 to 1743, and brought the fashions from 'terra incognita' back to the ballrooms of Northern Europe. Society 'fatimas' and 'sultanas' seized upon the look but preferred to wrap light silks and muslins across bodices and under Turkish-style coats. Hogarth was sceptical about the style, opining that 'Eastern dresses are very rich and have one sort of dignity, but it is a mock dignity in comparison of [*sic*] the simplicity of the antique.'

162: 'Jennens': The surname is variously spelt.

162: 'The richest commoner in England': William Beckford (1760–1844) of Fonthill Abbey was perhaps equally rich (*The Rise of the Nouveaux Riches*, J. M. Crook, John Murray, 1999). Henry Cavendish (1731–1810), who at the age of thirty-nine inherited a personal estate of one million pounds, was the first millionaire but clearly Jennens's assets were even more considerable.

162: 'two million pounds': This is equivalent to £100 million at today's value.

164: 'the aristocracy's high-stakes gamblers': Gamblers were so desperate to remain at the tables rather than break for a meal that the Earl of Sandwich asked for two slices of bread to be stuffed with beef and brought to him. The sandwich was born. The obsession with betting became so heightened that it was reported that when a man's body was found on the doorstep of White's some members wagered each other whether he was dead or had simply passed out, but would not help him for fear that it would alter the outcome of the wager.

164: 'Rumours circulated': *The Claimants to the Estates of William Jennens, Late of Acton Hall, Near Long Melford, Suffolk*, Messrs Harriman & Willis, Sheffield, 1879.

165: ' "the dividends on most of his stocks" ': 'The Great Jennens Inheritance', a document dated 1876 and held in the Madresfield Muniments.

165: 'short distance from his house': *Handel's Messiah: A Touchstone of Taste*, Robert Manson Myers, Macmillan, 1948.

166: ' "more full of maggots than ever" ': Ibid.

167: 'long avenues radiating out': *Man and the Natural World*, Keith Thomas, Penguin, 1991.

167: ' "a whole country" ': *The Prose Works of William Wordsworth*, ed. Alexander B. Grosart, 1876.

168: 'Pitt received three letters': Writing to her brother, William, Earl Beauchamp, in 1892, Lady Mary Lygon was amused to report that while reading through three volumes of applications and requests made to William Pitt 'while he was in office, for preferments, peerages, offices, money and every sort of thing, I discovered 3 from "Mr. Lyggon" asking for a Peerage!' Interestingly, Pitt's niece Lady Mary Stanhope married that 'Mr. Lyggon's' grandson, Frederick, the sixth Earl Beauchamp.

170: 'from the seventeenth-century dowries': *A Monarchy Transformed: Britain 1603–1714*, Mark Kishlansky, Allen Lane, The Penguin Press, 1996.

172: ' "£10,000 for getting her husband advanced"': Diary of Thomas Creevey, 10 February 1827; *The Creevey Papers*, ed. Sir Herbert Maxwell, 1903; John Murray, 1933.

172: 'ancient and illustrious title': The connection to the great medieval family of Beauchamp was a long and tenuous one through the female line. Despite Catherine's persistent manoeuvrings, no new registration was made at the College of Arms by which the baronial supporters to their shield were upgraded to the comital supporters of an earl. It was only later in the century that the supporters of a muzzled bear and a collared and coroneted swan were added. The bear stood as testament to Anne Beauchamp being a kinswoman of the earls of Warwick. We can conjecture that the swan supporter was assumed in reference to the fact that Beauchamp was a firm ally of the House of Lancaster, whose device was a swan.

173: 'Napoleonic Wars': During these wars Madresfield was reserved for royal occupation should Napoleon launch an invasion of Britain. It was thought to be sufficiently remote and defendable to provide a refuge for the royal family.

173: 'Certainly the French . . .': *Paris Between the Wars, 1814–1852*, Philip Mansel, John Murray, 2001, and in conversation with the author, 2006.

179: 'Two wooden truncheons': One truncheon, black-lacquered and with the royal crest in gold, reads:

'Tewkesbury, March 1857. Close of Poll – Lygon 200; Martin 169; Brown 127; Cox 25. Lygon majority 73.'

179: 'the Jennens Inheritance': The author is grateful to Professor Patrick Holden of Brunel University for his work on the Jennens Inheritance.

179: ' "considerable sums of money" ': According to 'The Jennens Case', a document dated 1874 and held in the Madresfield Muniments.

182: 'the claims kept coming': On 29 January 1886 *The Times* reported Lord Justice Fry's comment when summing up the Willis v. Beauchamp case: 'An action brought after this lapse of time was almost *prima facie* frivolous and vexatious.'

182: 'Isaac Martin, to bankruptcy': Martin v. Beauchamp (Frederick, the sixth earl), 1884.

185: 'an article published . . .': The *Atlanta Journal Sunday Magazine*, 25 July 1943.

186: ' "The one great principle . . . insupportable injustice" ': Article published in *Household Words*, 1851.

187: ' "inertia of an antiquated jurisprudence" ': *The Times*, 1 January 1852.

7 The Breviary

190: 'Jonathan Martin': The brother of John Martin (1789–1854), an artist renowned for apocalyptic paintings such as *Great Day of His Wrath*.

191: 'Maynooth': In 1845, Peel's Conservative administration introduced a bill to raise the government's annual grant to Maynooth College, County Kildare, from £10,000 to over £26,000. The intention was to stem the flow of Catholic seminarians to France. However, anti-Irish and anti-Catholic sentiments provoked an outcry; critics argued that it was inappropriate – indeed, hazardous – to bolster Catholicism. Gladstone, a member of Peel's

Cabinet, while supporting the bill, felt honour-bound to resign for fear that he would be accused of compromising his principles to retain office. Gladstone's deliberations led Peel to comment in exasperation, 'I really have great difficulty sometimes in exactly comprehending what he means.'

192: 'ancient vicar of Bloxham': *Confessio Viatoris*, Paul C. Kegan, 1891.

192: 'such misfits': They were known as the 'port wine faction'. *The Spirit of the Oxford Movement: Tractarian Essays*, Owen Chadwick, CUP, 1990.

193: '"dishonouring to Christianity"': *Gladstone: Church, State and Tractarianism, A Study of His Religious Ideas and Attitudes 1809–1859*, Percy Butler, Clarendon Press, 1982.

193: '"did for the Church of England"': *Essays Critical and Historical*, John Henry Newman, 1871.

194: '"crippling narrowness"': *God's Funeral*, A. N. Wilson, John Murray, 1999.

195: 'A photograph of him': The National Portrait Gallery, London, photograph dated *c*.1866–68, by John Watkins.

196: '"He hated anything 'fancy' . . ."': Obituary pasted into one of the scrapbooks belonging to his son, the seventh Earl Beauchamp.

198: '"a deficit which Beauchamp himself"': Letter from Halifax to Stanhope, 30 August 1892.

198: '"could not help putting"': The Archbishop of Canterbury to Frederick, 30 December 1858.

198: '"had a good deal of the martinet"': Letter of condolence on the death of William the seventh earl's father from I. A. Shaw-Stewart, an undergraduate with Frederick at Christ Church, Oxford, and a life-long friend, March 1891.

201: 'Oxford Union Society': In 1873, the year of the Union's fiftieth anniversary, Gladstone's Cabinet could boast seven one-time Presidents of the Oxford Union.

201: 'Charles Pakenham . . . had converted to Catholicism': Pakenham had sold his commission in the Guards, donated his money and possessions to charity and entered the novitiate of the Passionist Order at Broadway in Worcestershire under a new name, Father Paul Mary. His family disowned him, even deleting his name from the Longford entry in *Debrett's*. The local Worcestershire paper summed up establishment disdain when it referred to 'The Honourable Charles Reginald Pakenham who has . . . degraded himself by carrying the cross' in public down Broadway's main street. Father Paul Mary returned to Dublin, where he was born, founded the first house of his order in Ireland, known as Mount Argus, and devoted himself to charity. On his deathbed less than a year later, when questioned about his sternness towards the English, he replied, 'Ireland has nothing to thank England for.' He was mourned by the local people who regarded him as a saint and prayed for his beatification. Thirty-seven years later, his coffin was opened and his official biographer recorded that 'the body [was] then found perfectly intact and incorrupt, and the face wore a most lifelike expression as of one who lay in a peaceful slumber.' In ancient times, such unaided preservation would have signified a person of exceptional holiness.

201: 'in the company of Monsignor Edward Howard': Other priests in Rome were also involved, including Gilbert Talbot at the Accademia Ecclesiastica, who wrote to Frederick on 7 April 1856: 'If you go to Birmingham one of the fathers of The Oratory who is here tells me that you would be received there with all hospitality – you would be quiet, have books, and Oxford and Cambridge men to solve your difficulties.'

202: 'physical expression of the script': For instance, Howard to Frederick, 12 April 1856: 'I have offered up the Holy Sacrifice to you every day since last Sunday and will continue to do so. I need not tell you your leaving [probably in a heated moment] grieved me very much but I feel and accept, as I firmly hope you did, you acted from what you deemed your duty, that grace and strength will be given you in proper time to your needs and your weakness . . . I will not add more nor will I write to you a controversial letter, I will only beg of you to keep *clearly* before your mind, the *Visible Unity, Catholicity, Apostolicity* and *Sanctity* of the True Church of Christ.'

203: 'first edition of his *Day Hours*': Within Frederick's lifetime five editions of *The Day Hours* were published (each edition running to 5,000 copies) and a sixth edition of 7,000 was produced just before his death. All of these were heavily subsidized by Frederick.

203: 'Gathorne-Hardy': Gathorne Gathorne-Hardy, first earl of Cranbrook, a prominent Conservative politician, Home Secretary 1867–8 and Secretary of State for War 1874–8.

203: 'an historical event': Disraeli to Frederick, July 1865.

203: ' "a very smart, bright man" ': Archbishop Benson in *The Complete Peerage*, ed. G. E. Cockayne *et al.*, Alan Sutton, 2000.

204: ' "Mr Lygon" ': *The Times*, retrospective look at the decade in Parliament, 1869.

204: 'Disraeli should publish these': The result was published in 1865 and entitled *Church and Queen: Five speeches delivered by the Rt. Hon. B. Disraeli, M.P., 1860–1864*, edited by Frederick, sixth Earl Beauchamp.

204: ' "No one but you" ': Disraeli to Frederick, 1864.

205: ' "The American hotels"': Henry Lygon to Frederick, 1853.

208: ' "I notice that"': *The Crown of Wild Olive*, John Ruskin, 1866, a first edition of which can be found in the Library at Madresfield along with all his other works.

209: ' "the young Hardwick"': *The Buildings of England: Worcestershire*, Nikolaus Pevsner, Penguin, 1968.

209: 'Hardwick later completed': During the Victorian era two other notable architects were commissioned to work at Madresfield. Norman Shaw, best known for designing Scotland Yard, added North Lodge to the estate in 1872 and C. F. A. Voysey created a pair of cottage gatehouses in 1901.

210: 'his house . . . Chevening': Now leased by the government and used by the Foreign Secretary as his official country residence.

211: 'the Duke of Beaufort held': *The Great Landowners of Great Britain and Ireland*, John Bateman, Harrison and Sons, 1878.

211: 'one-third of the senior administrative': *Making Aristocracy Work*, Andrew Adonis, Clarendon Press, Oxford, 1993.

212: ' "It is impossible"': Letter from Disraeli to Queen Victoria, 12 April 1878, Hughenden Papers.

215: ' "counteract Rugby and Balliol"': Letter from Frederick, Earl Beauchamp to Liddon, 9 April 1869.

217: ' "that new place near the Parks"': Unattributed newspaper cutting in Frederick, Earl Beauchamp's scrapbook.

217: ' "droning sameness"': *The Times*, 26 April 1876.

217: ' "rumours of evolution . . . running into debt"': *Daily News*, 26 April 1876.

218: ' "It was designed as a protest"': *The World*, 3 May 1876.

219: 'original Norman church': The twelfth-century church was bequeathed by Anne Beauchamp. It was knocked down in 1852 and August Pugin designed a replacement. When he went mad, his seventeen-year-old son Edmund built the church but, according to the rector, the Reverend G. S. Munn, he set it 'absolutely on the surface' – without foundations – so that within twelve years it was collapsing. The sixth earl commissioned Frederick Preedy to design a new church on a site further west, using as many artefacts as possible from the old church.

219: ' "the tablets to the Earls Beauchamp" ': *The Buildings of England: Worcestershire*, Pevsner.

8 The Illumination

223: ' "I owe in good measure" ': *The Roxburghe Club: Its History and Its Members, 1812–1927*, Lt-Col the Hon. Clive Bigham, OUP, 1928.

224: ' "champions . . . clad in complete steel" ': *The Bibliographical Decameron*, Thomas F. Dibdin, 1817.

225: 'An inventory of 1899': This was privately printed by William, seventh Earl Beauchamp.

232: ' "a rare simplicity of character" ': *The Times*, December 1979.

232: 'The Roxburghe Club members': James Stourton, a recently elected member of the Roxburghe Club, in conversation with the author, 2003.

9 The Tuning Fork

236: 'an Indian jade hookah': The hookah pipe was reputedly owned by Tippoo Sahib and was part of the plunder at the taking of Seringapatam by Sir David Baird in 1799. Later it was bought by the collector William Beckford of Fonthill Abbey, who sold it in 1823 to the first Countess Beauchamp.

238: ' "most miserable-looking lad" ': *Forgotten Worcestershire*,

Hubert Leicester, Ebenezer Baylis, 1930.

239: ' "turning a grindstone . . ." ': *Edward Elgar: A Creative Life*, Jerrold Northrop Moore, OUP, 1984.

239: 'In the Victorian home the piano . . .': Thanks both to hire purchase and mass manufacture, by 1890 there were twice as many being manufactured in England as in 1850.

242: 'Perhaps they reminded Elgar': Twenty-five years later, he wrote music to celebrate the Indian coronation ceremony of George V, his 1912 masque *The Crown of India*.

242: 'a proposal . . . from Lord Digby': Lady Mary's ancestor, William the Correspondent, had attempted during Queen Anne's reign to marry his son and heir, William junior, to one of Lord Digby's daughters, to no avail.

244: ' "the [German] Empress" ': Lady Mary to the Duchess of Teck, 22 April 1896, the Royal Archives.

247: ' "In country districts" ': Lady Mary to Elgar, 17 May 1903. Archive of the Elgar Birthplace Museum, Broadheath, Worcestershire.

248: ' "Dear Lady Mary Lygon, The whole of" ': Transcript of letters at Lady Mary's house in Cornwall.

250: ' "We only sing . . . upon us" ': Lady Mary to Elgar from York House, St James's Palace, 17 October 1898. Elgar Birthplace Museum.

253–4: ' "no mean . . . excellent tempo" ': *Sydney Bulletin*, 3 July 1899.

254: ' "Every girl with a voice" ': *Sydney Daily Telegraph*, July 1899.

254: ' "This will" another journalist predicted': Unattributed Sydney newspaper cutting in William, Earl Beauchamp's New South Wales scrapbook.

255: ' "An additional interest here . . ." ': 'The Voyage of H.M.S. *Ophir* – a 7½ month Journey', Part 2, by Lady

Mary Lygon in *Madresfield Agricultural Club's Quarterly*, 1902.

255: ' "Dear Lady Mary Lygon, We are . . . progress" ': Transcript by Dr John Buttrey of letter at Lady Mary's house in Cornwall, given to author via Jerrold Northrop Moore.

256: ' "My dearest William, I" ': Lady Mary to William, Earl Beauchamp, 22 February 1899.

257: ' "My Sweet Mary" ': Elgar revealed this also in a letter to August Jaeger in May 1899.

257: ' "1880 is usually given" ': Gustav Holst lecture notes, 'England and Her Music', in *Heirs and Rebels*, Ralph Vaughan-Williams and Gustav Holst, OUP, 1959. The 'Enigma' Variations were brought to another generation when, in 1968, Sir Frederick Ashton devised a ballet for the score. To this day, the *Variations* remain part of the canon of English music.

258: ' "from his very *soul*" ': Letter from Alice Elgar to Mrs Nicholas Kilburn, 3 August 1900.

260: 'it won recognition': Richard Strauss at the Lower Rhine Festival, 1902, declared Elgar to be 'the first English progressivist'.

260: ' "How splendid *Gerontius*" ': Letter from Lady Mary to Elgar, 15 June 1903. Elgar Birthplace Museum.

262: ' "your marsh [Longdon Marsh]" ': Ibid., 5 September 1903.

264: 'Her stepmother was shocked': Sibell to author.

265: ' "heavenly . . . Lady M. is as of old . . ." ': Letter from Elgar to Leo Francis 'Frank' Schuster, July 1910. Elgar Birthplace Museum.

10 The Wedding Present

270: 'facts of life': Sibell to author.

270: ' "Dearest Beauchamp came" ': Lettice's diaries were

rescued from a fire in 2006 and are now in the Madresfield Muniments.

274: 'William Robinson ... a "wild garden"': A copy of *The Wild Garden or the Naturalization and Natural Grouping of Hardy Exotic plants with a chapter on the Garden of British Wild Flowers*, William Robinson, John Murray, 1894, is in the Library at Madresfield.

278: 'the average workman's wage': Figure supplied by the National Office of Statistics for 1900. In decimal currency £1 8s. is £1.40.

278: ' "I looked in and saw the dove"': 11 August 1902.

11 The Tree of Life

283: '*repoussé*' : Relief decoration on metal produced by hammering from the underside so that the decoration projects. It is the opposite of chasing. In this case the pewter was beaten by hand with a tiny hammer.

283: 'Shocked by a report': 'The Bitter Cry of Outcast London: An Inquiry into the Condition of the Abject Poor', Charles Booth, 1883.

286: ' "Mudfog"': *Bleak House*, Charles Dickens, 1852–3.

288: ' "My men and boy friends"': Ashbee to Janet Forbes, 2 September 1897.

289: ' "leave Babylon"': *Memoirs: Vol. I, The Guild Idea*, C. R. Ashbee; letter dated 18 December 1901. Archive of King's College, Cambridge.

289–90: 'These Cockneys ... "Camelot"': *From Whitechapel to Camelot*, C. R. Ashbee, Essex House Press, 1892. It is a Cautionary Fairytale.

290: 'equally incomprehensible': *Alec Miller: Guildsman and Sculptor in Chipping Campden*, Jane Wilgress, Campden and District Historical and Archaeological Society, 1987.

291: 'One homesick guildsman': Ibid.

291: ' "a new imaginative life ... or the sixteenth?"':

C. R. Ashbee: Architect, Designer and Romantic Socialist, Alan Crawford, Yale, 1985.

292: ' "I have just finished reading" ': Miller to Ashbee. Archive of King's College, Cambridge.

292: ' "There was the same rustling . . . human tenderness" ': Ashbee's journal. Archive of King's College, Cambridge.

293: 'development of the panels': The Guild of Handicrafts' bill for the carving of the Library bookcase ends and door panels was £200, excluding Ashbee's design fee.

293: ' "Lord Beauchamp came down" ': Hart to Ashbee, 3 March 1905. Archive of King's College, Cambridge.

294: ' "How swift is time" ': *The New Inn*, Ben Jonson, 1629.

294: ' "Faust the Doctor" ': Ashbee to the seventh earl, 7 April 1902. Archive of King's College, Cambridge.

295: 'Like Ashbee, William was a committed pacifist': Ashbee's press printed the *Manifesto of the Central Organisation for a Durable Peace* (1915), and he travelled the United States of America lecturing on the merits of pacifism. In August 1917 Ashbee published the *American League to Enforce Peace: An English Interpretation*, which included an introduction by his King's College friend Goldsworthy Lowes Dickinson.

295: 'The dreaming architect': In 1952, long after Ashbee's death, Phoebe Haydon wrote to Alec Miller: 'I have read hundreds of letters from young people (now grown old) thanking him for the way he influenced their lives and opened their eyes to the beauty of things. Many of these letters were from people who I know hated and feared him in their youth but in later years realized how much they owed to him, simply by living near or working for or with him.' 27 January 1952.

12 The Red Boxes

297: ' "a strong influence on" ': *The Return to Camelot: Chivalry and the English Gentleman*, Mark Girouard, Yale, 1981.

299: ' "cool, grey-clad . . . Liberty tie . . . Peck' quad . . . Socialist peers"': *Isis*, June 1893, written by F. E. Smith, later a leading Conservative statesman, ally of Winston Churchill and raised to the peerage as the first Earl of Birkenhead. Liberty & Co. in Regent Street, London, were the fashionable purveyors of Arts and Crafts fabrics. Peckwater is a quadrangle in Christ Church, Oxford.

299: ' "display . . . Papa . . . the most strait-laced . . . moderate understanding"': Vincent, 159; Liverpool Records Office, the Earl of Derby diary, 21 February 1891.

300: ' "I do so trust "': March 1891.

300: ' "his delivery is smooth"': Newspaper cutting in William, Earl Beauchamp's scrapbook, probably *The Times*, 1891.

301: ' "ornamental mayor"': *The Decline and Fall of the British Aristocracy*, David Cannadine, Yale, 1990.

302: 'Joseph Chamberlain': He held the parliamentary seat of West Birmingham.

302: ' "scarcely knew where was"': *Australian Dictionary of National Biography*.

302: ' "with ideas of his own"': Undated cutting from the *Westminster Gazette*.

303: '£292 for the transportation . . . £400 for objets d'art': This amounts to £22,590 and £30,947 respectively in today's value. It is little wonder that only wealthy grandees could afford to take on such offices of state. Letter from William, Earl Beauchamp to the Rt Hon. G. H. Reid, Prime Minister of New South Wales. State Papers at the National Archive: Colonial Office 201/625.

306: ' "Sydney is getting ready"': The Woman's Letter column in *The Bulletin*, 20 October 1900.

307: ' "as a deliberative assembly"': *Making Aristocracy Work*, Andrew Adonis, Clarendon Press, Oxford, 1993.

309: ' "Lord and Lady Beauchamp shook hands"': Undated and unattributed newspaper cutting in a scrapbook.

310: ' "We shall 'ave Hindia . . ."': *C.B.: A Life of Sir Henry Campbell-Bannerman*, J. Wilson, 1973.

312: ' "as anxious today"': *Hansard*, vol. 13, cols 704–12, 29 January 1913.

315: 'of all people . . . 1914/15': *Asquith*, Roy Jenkins, Collins, 1988.

315: ' "much plain speaking . . . 'Sweetheart' . . . mellifluous"': Ibid.

316: ' "peace party"': Asquith papers, 25.170, Bodleian Library.

316: ' "I have seldom felt"': Memorandum, *The Papers of John Morley*, ed. Samuel S. Hyde, Bodleian Library, 2003.

316: ' "he [Asquith] is the chief figure"': William, Earl Beauchamp to Morley, 5 August 1914.

317: ' "It is very difficult to sit down"': Paper in the Madresfield Muniments.

318: ' "There are a great many people . . ."': *Hansard*, vol. 27, cols 529–537, 14 December 1917.

319: ' "A good deal of courage"': Diary of Sir Charles Hobhouse, 23 March 1915. *Inside Asquith's Cabinet*, edited by Edward David, John Murray, 1977.

319: ' "This is a good moment"': Gosse to William, Earl Beauchamp.

320: ' finding "the weekly change"': Asquith to William, Earl Beauchamp, 1916.

320: ' "Be an angel and ask"': Asquith to William, Earl Beauchamp, 26 May 1915.

320: ' "light grey Biarritz"': Undated and unattributed newspaper cutting in a scrapbook.

322: ' "of a normal civil character . . . for punishment"': Letter from the Work Centre, Princetown, Devon.

322: '*The Economist*': Hirst to William, Earl Beauchamp, 22 June 1916.

323: ' "the Prussianism which is besetting us" ': Lord Courtney of Penwith to William, Earl Beauchamp, 18 August 1917.

324: ' "a large number of these men" ': William, Earl Beauchamp kept a copy of this letter.

328: 'escalation of land sales': *The Decline and Fall . . .*, Cannadine.

329: ' "The upkeep of a large country house" ': *The Fall and Rise of the Stately Home*, Peter Mandler, Yale, 1993.

330: ' "Lord Beauchamp's robust Liberalism" ': Undated and unattributed newspaper cutting in one of William, Earl Beauchamp's scrapbooks.

330: ' "He supported Lloyd George" ': Dorothy to author.

330: ' "All Englishmen" ': Lloyd George, 23 December 1923. *War Memoirs*, David Lloyd George, Odhams Press, 1938.

13 The Scrap of Paper

333: 'Charlotte M. Yonge, a Tractarian . . .': She had been present, along with Beauchamp's father, at the opening ceremony of Keble College, Oxford, on 23 June 1870.

338: ' "very un-Victorian . . . private parts" ': Sibell to author.

339: 'cubhunting': The killing of young foxes early in the hunting season.

339: ' "She didn't even like . . . very political" ': Dorothy to Dr Tania Rose, Madresfield Muniments.

340: ' "in case I have to hire a train" ': Sibell to author.

345: ' "Are you aware . . ." ': *The Autobiography of G. K. Chesterton*, Ignatius Press, 2006.

346: ' "simply thrown in the deep end" ': Sibell to author.

348: ' "a way of getting rid . . ." ': Sibell to author.

348: ' "If they had their hair" ': Sibell to author.

349: 'Princess Louise Augusta and Princess Patricia': Her Highness Marie-Louise of Schleswig-Holstein, granddaughter of Queen Victoria, daughter of Prince Albert of Saxe-Coburg, and Princess Patricia of Connaught, granddaughter of Queen Victoria and later Crown Princess of Sweden.

349: ' "cabbage, mince" ': Sibell to author.

349: ' "insipid" ': article in the local paper, Mr Crump, n.d.

352: ' "telling her about the curse!" ': Sibell to author.

355: 'Augustus J. C. Hare': He had been a friend of the sixth Earl Beauchamp and came to stay at Madresfield.

356: ' "Mrs Strong's enthusiasm" ': Mrs Strong's identity is not known.

359: ' "no one, not even myself" ': Byron to William, eighth Earl Beauchamp, 1940.

362: ' "There was this enormous warmth . . ." ': 'Baby' Jungman in conversation with the author, 2003.

366: ' "intimate content" ': Robert Byron, quoted in *A Choice of Ornaments*, Nicholas Bentley, André Deutsch, London, 1959.

14 The Embroidery

369: 'two Garter Knights and one peer of the realm': Stanmore was the grandson of the fourth Earl of Aberdeen and had worked with Beauchamp at the palace as a former lord-in-waiting to George V. He was Chief Liberal Whip in the House of Lords. Though we have no record of who accompanied him, looking at the short list of Garter Knights at that time it is probable that they were his fellow Liberal Cabinet minister and friend the Marquis of Crewe, who had also served as Leader of the Liberal peers, had held office as Secretary of State for the Colonies, Lord Privy Seal and Lord President of the Council, and the Earl of Athlone, Prince Alexander of Teck, who was Queen Mary's brother. Beauchamp's sister, Lady Mary, had served as lady-in-waiting to Queen Mary and knew the family well. An outside possibility is the elderly Viscount Grey of Falloden, who as Sir Edward Grey had served as Foreign Secretary in Asquith's Cabinet alongside Beauchamp.

369: 'criminal acts of indecency': An amendment to the 1885 Criminal Law Amendment Act stated that 'Any male person who in public or private commits or is party to the commission, or attempts to procure the commission by any male person, of any act of gross indecency with another male person, shall be guilty of this mis-demeanour.' The punishment was two years' imprisonment.

370: ' "I thought men like that shot themselves"': *King George V*, Kenneth Rose, Weidenfeld & Nicolson, 1983.

372: 'rota began as the older children . . .': In June 1931 William's children ranged from fourteen to twenty-seven years of age.

372: 'stories had circulated': In 1927 Lord Lee of Fareham 'was painfully cognisant of Beauchamp's unsavoury moral reputation' and protested when he presented the prizes at a school speech day. *A Good Innings: the private papers of Viscount Lee of Fareham*, ed. A. Clark, 1974. And Hugh Walpole, when he visited 'the Baths at the Elephant & Castle . . . saw Ld Carisbrooke naked: saw Ld Beauchamp in the act with a boy'. *Diaries of Virginia Woolf*, ed. A. O. Bell and A. McNeillie, 5 (1984).

372: ' "He explained . . . wrist was sprained': *A Wiser Woman?*, Christabel Aberconway, Hutchinson, 1966.

373: 'His hosts asked Bernays . . .': Bernays related this story to Harold Nicolson who recorded it in his diary though it was expurgated from the published version.

373: 'never liked William': Diana Mosley to author.

374: ' "nothing but . . . aging playboy"': *Evelyn Waugh*, Christopher Sykes, Collins, 1975.

374: 'Edward died of peritonitis': This tragedy was captured in Evelyn Waugh's novel *A Handful of Dust* (Chapman &

Hall, 1934). Westminster never produced another heir and the title passed to cousins.

374: ' "As far as women were concerned" ': *Bendor, The Golden Duke of Westminster*, Leslie Field, Weidenfeld & Nicolson, 1983.

376: 'hardly a glittering career': On Bend'or's death, Chips Channon wrote: 'He lived for pleasure – and women . . . he was restless, spoilt, irritable, and rather splendid in a very English way . . . yet his life was an empty failure; he did few kindnesses, leaves no monument.' *Chips: The Diaries of Sir Henry Channon*, Weidenfeld & Nicolson, 1962.

376: ' "moral indignation . . . a halo" ': *The Wife of Sir Isaac Harman*, H. G. Wells, 1914.

378: 'her lover, Lord Beaverbrook': The short, lascivious Beaverbrook, described by Clementine Churchill as a 'bottle imp', embracing the six-foot-two-tall Sibell conjures up a comic image.

378: ' "rather stormy petrel . . ." ': Obituary of Lady Sibell Rowley, *Daily Telegraph*, 16 November 2005.

379: ' "work in every possible way . . . depart from the Brit. Isles . . . must look forward to . . ." ': London University, Senate House Archive, VP 14.

381: 'by the thirties': Later in the twentieth century, two other prominent men, the Liberal politician Jeremy Thorpe and Lord Montagu of Beaulieu, would shock their peers because of homosexual liaisons in which they too had consorted with members of the working classes. During Thorpe's trial at the Old Bailey in 1979 references were made in the press to the Beauchamp Affair in which the Duke of Westminster was cast as a hypocrite and the villain of the piece.

381: ' "as North American Indians" ': *The Naked Civil Servant*, Quentin Crisp, Cape, 1968.

381: ' "eccentric . . . mud baths" ': *A Wiser Woman?*, Aberconway.

381: 'James Lees-Milne's account in his diary': *Ceaseless Turmoil: Diaries 1988–1992*, John Murray, 2004.

382: ' "ran contrary to what is natural" ': See letter from Lady Beauchamp to Dorothy, pages 397.

382: ' "A good story" ': Entry for 8 August 1932 from the *Diaries of Sir Robert Bruce Lockhart, 1915–1938*, edited by Kenneth Young, Macmillan, 1973. The Baldwins' visit took place shortly before the earl's fall from grace, when rumours were already circulating.

383: ' "pigs, pipe and poetry" ': *Beaverbrook*, Peter Howard, Hutchinson, 1964.

384: 'Wolfenden Report': Sir John Wolfenden headed a Committee on Homosexual Offences, a British Government study, which was published in 1957 and recommended that the law on homosexuality should be relaxed.

385: 'often encouraged by the masters': *The Worm in the Bud: The World of Victorian Sexuality*, Ronald Pearsall, Weidenfeld & Nicolson, 1969.

386: ' "it sounds a very curious sort of illness" ': Lady Susan Lygon, later Lady Susan Gilmour, to William, Earl Beauchamp, September 1892.

386: 'Molly Houses': Discreet venues known to homosexuals where they could meet one another and hire rent boys.

386: ' "rosy-cheeked footmen" ': 'An Evening at Government House' by Victor J. Daley of the *Australian Star*. Cutting in William, Earl Beauchamp's scrapbook.

387: 'He pasted into his scrapbook often homo-erotic': Scrapbook 32.

387: ' "from the homogeneric side of him" ': C. R. Ashbee's journal for March 1902. Ashbee and Beauchamp shared a keen interest in the writer Edward Carpenter who had been praised by his friend E. M. Forster for 'his courage and candour about sex, particularly about homosexuality'.

388: 'The office of the First Commissioner of Works': Philip Mansel to author, 2006, and Michael Bloch to author, 2005.

388: ' "that of a man buried alive" ': Gosse to John Addington Symonds, *Strangers: Homosexual Love in the Nineteenth Century*, Graham Robb, Picador, 2003.

389: ' "courteous and seductive manners" ': *Homosexuals in History*, A. L. Rowse, Weidenfeld & Nicolson, 1977.

390: 'followed by detectives': A number of letters written by homosexuals in exile describe the unnerving shadow of detectives stalking them, probably hired by enemies, kinsmen or spouses to provide incriminating evidence. In 1889, Charles Hammond, for example, had fled from the Cleveland Street Scandal and wrote to his sister-in-law describing the Scotland Yard men who were tailing him: 'One of the two men that followed in from France has gone away, and a Belgium [*sic*] man has come in his place. If we only go across the road from the hotel they follow us. If I ask any questions they go and ask the people what I said to them. It makes me feel so ill I can scarcely eat any meals.' *The Worm in the Bud*, Pearsall.

390: ' "if not he may become Labour!" ': William, Earl Beauchamp to Hugh from 7, rue Anatole de la Forge, Paris, 31 August 1931.

391: ' "if there is anything private . . . the servants are all very loyal . . . What happiness . . . I wish I could be with you!" ': William, Earl Beauchamp aboard MS *Baloeran*, off the coast of Portugal, 27 October 1931.

391: ' "imagine my excitement" ': Letter from William, Earl Beauchamp from the Hôtel Splendide, Marseilles, 25 September 1932.

391: ' "Society, as we have constituted it" ': *De Profundis*, Oscar Wilde, 1905.

392: ' "had bars, hotels and drag shows . . . States" ': *Strangers: Homosexual Love in the Nineteenth Century*, Graham Robb, Picador, 2003.

393: ' "Thou muse of my manhood" ': Envelope in the Madresfield Muniments.

393: ' "Every day I manage" ': William, Earl Beauchamp to Dorothy, December 1932.

393: ' "helps fill his day" ': Hugh to Dorothy, April 1933.

394: ' "Soon we shall have" ': Hugh to his siblings. Letters were shared and this one is undated.

394: ' "friends remain constant . . ." ': William, Earl Beauchamp to Dorothy from the Astor Hotel, Sydney, 24 April 1932.

394: ' "I'm glad to find myself" ': Beauchamp's obituary in the *Sydney Morning Herald*.

394: ' "never would have happened" ': Sibell to author.

395: 'Which wallpapers, he enquired': These domestic obsessions call to mind William Bankes, a Victorian MP who, on being caught in August 1841 with a guardsman in Green Park, had fled to Venice to avoid the gallows. Bankes, like Beauchamp, moved every three to four weeks in an agitated migration, gathering consignments of treasures and shipping them back to Kingston Lacey in Dorset with detailed instructions on how they should be displayed. Bankes's taste had been greatly influenced at Cambridge by the aesthete William Beckford and in a curious echo Beckford's jewel-encrusted Middle Eastern hookah pipe sits in a display cabinet in the Drawing Room at Madresfield. The pipe was one of the most sentimentally valuable items stolen in a burglary in 2003.

396: ' "my having to file the petition" ': Lady Beauchamp

probably countersigned the petition of her brother, the Duke of Westminster.

400: ' "champagne all morning" ': 26 March 1934; ' "black velvets in Matt's room" ': 3 January 1934, Matt's identity is unknown; ' "got jolly on three whiskies" ': 5 January 1934; ' "got stinking tight" ': 14 January 1934; ' "Benny said that he had a statement" ': 25 January 1934 – all quotations from Sibell's diary.

400: ' "in connection with the writ" ': Bend'or took out a writ suing Sibell for libel over her article in the *Oxford and Cambridge* magazine.

400: 'her "paraclete" ': See the note to p. 47.

400: 'Five months later . . . guided her away': Sibell to author.

402: ' "felt he had to bring the boy home" ': This account was reported in the *Daily Express*.

404: ' "a most attractive boy . . . a new life" ': James Wakefield to Elmley, 21 August 1936.

404: 'her marble bust': Carved by Charles Rutland 1909–11.

406: 'David Smyth': Sibell to author.

407: '*Psychopathia Sexualis*': At the end of the nineteenth century there was a great interest in the phenomenon of homosexuality. Ronald Pearsall calculated that in the ten years between 1898 and 1908 more than one thousand works on the subject were published.

15 The Sundial

410: ' "The whole interior" ': *Brideshead Revisited*, Evelyn Waugh, Chapman & Hall, 1945.

411: ' "absolutely certain" ': Rosalind Morrison to author, 2003.

411: ' "we ought not to go out with jockeys" ': Sibell's diary, 9 February 1934.

412: ' "Metroland" ': A disparaging reference to the suburban world that Waugh parodied in *Decline and Fall*.

412: ' "a fling but no engagement" ': Sibell went on: 'We had great thoughts that it might [result in an engagement].' Prince George later married Princess Marina of Greece.

412: ' "pauper prince" ': Waugh to Mary, February 1934.

413: ' "It is the saddest news" ': Waugh to Mary, from Mells Manor, the Astor house, date uncertain, probably 12 September 1936.

413: ' "they follow the old" ': Waugh to Nancy Mitford, June 1952.

413: ' "She was quite wild" ': Christopher Sinclair-Stevenson to author, 2003.

414: ' "Mother suggested . . . rather broke" ': Ibid.

414: ' "I believe that everyone" ': Waugh to Mary from Combe Florey, 'Monday before Ascension', 4 May 1959.

415: ' "because it tastes of iron filings" ': Rosalind Morrison to author.

415: 'found in 2006': The fire was at the home of Rosalind Morrison's mother and sister fifteen miles from Madresfield, near Pershore.

415: ' "decent to me" ': Sibell's diary, 6 January 1934.

415: ' "keen on John Corbett" ': Ibid., 3 January 1934.

415: ' "courage in both hands . . . sapping my vitality" ': Ibid., 31 January 1934.

417: 'Christie's auction house': Originally Dorothy was hired as 'a grand stenographer with lots of those well-born ladies in the St James's Square office' but her skills were soon put to better use. Philip Hooke to author, 2007.

417: ' "very old-fashioned-looking . . . never bettered" ': Simon Dickinson to author, 2005.

419: ' "When Robert came up the aisle" ': Waugh's biographer Selina Hastings to author, 2004. Like many of Coote's friends, she believes that Coote was deeply in love with Robert and quietly from the sidelines always had been.

420: ' "Are you mad? . . . with you" ': Ibid.

420: ' "the nicest of all your friends" ': Obituary of Lady Dorothy Heber-Percy, *Independent*, 20 November 2001.

421: ' "his most vulnerable book" ': John Mortimer, BBC interview.

421: 'retrospective idyll': The real Arcadia was the land of Pan where he played his syrinx on Mount Maenalus and its denizens of ancient lineage were famous for their musical skills, rugged virtue and hospitality.

424: ' "When one lives in Paradise" ': Lady Frederick Cavendish, 1863, referring to Cliveden in Buckinghamshire.

424: ' "homesick for nursery morality" ': Charles Ryder in *Brideshead*, Waugh.

Select Bibliography

Adonis, Andrew, *Making Aristocracy Work*, Clarendon Press, Oxford, 1993

Amory, Mark (ed.), *The Letters of Evelyn Waugh*, Weidenfeld & Nicolson, London, 1980

Anderson, Robert, *Elgar*, J. M. Dent, London, 1993

Andrews, Kenneth R., *Elizabethan Privateering*, Cambridge University Press, 1964

Ashbee, C. R., *An Endeavour Towards Teaching of John Ruskin and William Morris*, Essex House Press, London, 1901

Ashbee, C. R., *From Whitechapel to Camelot*, Essex House Press, London, 1892

Aslet, Clive, *The Last Country Houses*, Yale University Press, 1982

Balston, Thomas, *John Martin: His Life and Works, 1789–1854*, Duckworth, London, 1949

Battiscombe, Georgina, *John Keble*, Constable, London, 1963

Begent, Peter J., and Chesshyre, Hubert, *The Most Noble Order of the Garter, 650 Years*, Spink, London, 1999

Bennett, H. S., *The Pastons and Their England*, Cambridge University Press, 1922

Bigham, Lieutenant Colonel The Hon. Clive, *The Roxburghe Club: Its History and Its Members, 1812–1927*, Oxford University Press, 1928

Briggs, Asa, and Macartney, Anne, *Toynbee Hall, The First Hundred Years*, Routledge & Kegan Paul, London, 1984

Cannadine, David, *Aspects of Aristocracy*, Yale University Press, 2004

Cannadine, David, *The Decline and Fall of the British Aristocracy*, Yale University Press, 1990

Cannadine, David, *Ornamentalism: How the British Saw Their Empire*, Allen Lane, London, 2001

Carter, John, *Taste and Technique in Book Collecting*, London Private Libraries Association, 1970

Chadwick, Owen (ed.), *The Mind of the Oxford Movement*, Adam & Charles Black, London, 1960

Clark, Kenneth, *The Gothic Revival*, Constable, London, 1928

Cobbett, William, *Rural Rides*, Reeves & Turner, London, 1885

Colley, Linda, *Britons*, Yale University Press, 1992

Coss, Peter, *The Lady in Medieval England, 1100–1500*, Sutton, Stroud, 1998

Crawford, Alan, *C. R. Ashbee: Architect, Designer and Romantic Socialist*, Yale University Press, 1985

Cressy, David, *Birth, Marriage and Death: Ritual, Religion, and the Life-Cycle in Tudor and Stuart England*, Oxford University Press, 1997

Dyer, Christopher, 'Jardins et Vergers en Angleterre au moyen âge' (Gardens and Orchards in Medieval England), in *Jardins et Vergers en l'Europe occidental*, Centre Culturel de l'Abbaye de Flaran, 9e Journées internationales d'histoire, 1989

Dyer, Christopher, *Making a Living in the Middle Ages: The People of Britain 850–1520*, Yale University Press, 2002

Dyer, Christopher, article in *Medieval Fish, Fisheries and Fish Ponds in England*, editor, M. Aston, British Archaeological Reports, British Series 182, Oxford, 1989

Fussell, Paul, *Abroad: British Literary Travelling between the Wars*, Oxford University Press, 1980

Fussell, Paul, *The Great War and Modern Memory*, Oxford University Press, 1975

Gragg, Larry, *Englishmen Transplanted: The English Colonization of Barbados, 1627–1700*, Oxford University Press, 2003

Green, Roger Lancelyn, *Mrs Molesworth*, Bodley Head, London, 1961

Habakkuk, John, *Marriage, Death and the Estates System*, Clarendon Press, Oxford, 1994

Halifax, Edward F. L. Wood, *John Keble*, London and Oxford, 1909 and 1932

Heath, Baron, John Benjamin, *The Worshipful Company of Grocers*, privately printed, 1869

Herlihy, David, *The Black Death and the Transformation of the West*, Harvard University Press, 1997

Hobson, J. A., *The Crisis in Liberalism: New Issues of Democracy*, P. S. King & Son, London, 1909

Holdsworth, W. F., *Dickens as a Legal Historian*, Yale University Press, 1929

Hollis, Christopher, *Oxford in the Twenties: Recollection of Five Friends*, Heinemann, London, 1976

Hoskins, W. G., *The Making of the English Landscape*, Hodder & Stoughton, London, 1955

Hutchinson, William G., *The Oxford Movement*, Walter Scott Publishing, 1906

Ingram, Kenneth, *John Keble*, P. Allan, London, 1933

Jewell, Helen, *Women in Medieval England*, Manchester University Press, 1996

Keen, Maurice, *Chivalry*, Yale University Press, 2005

Keen, Maurice, *Origins of the English Gentleman*, Tempus, London, 2002

Kennedy, G. M. S., *Portrait of Elgar*, Oxford University Press, 1968

Loades, David, *Intrigue and Treason: The Tudor Court 1547–1558*, Pearson Longman, London, 2004

MacCarthy, Fiona, *The Simple Life: C. R. Ashbee in the Cotswolds*, Lionel Humphries, London, 1981

Manson Myers, Robert, *Handel's Messiah: A Touchstone of Taste*, Macmillan, London, 1948

Martin, Jonathan, *Life of Jonathan Martin: Tanner*, 1826

Meacham, Standish, *Toynbee Hall and Social Reform, 1880–1914: The Search for Community*, Yale University Press, 1987

Muthesius, Hermann, *The English House*, Frances Lincoln, 2007; *Das englische Haus*, first published in Berlin, 1904–5

Nash's Worcestershire, Worcester Historical Society, James Parker & Co., Oxford, 1894

Nicolson, Harold, *George V: His Life and Reign*, Constable & Co., London, 1952

Noake, J., *Worcestershire Relics*, Longman & Co., London, 1887

Norman, Edward, *The House of God: Church Architecture, Style and History*, Thames & Hudson, London, 1990

Northrop Moore, Jerrold, *Edward Elgar: A Creative Life*, Oxford University Press, 1984

Northrop Moore, Jerrold, *Elgar: Child of Dreams*, Faber and Faber, London, 2004

Northrop Moore, Jerrold, *Spirit of England: Elgar and His World*, Heinemann, London, 1984

Noy, Michael de la, *Elgar the Man*, Allen Lane, London, 1983

O'Dwyer, E. J., *Thomas Frognal Dibdin: Bibliographer and Bibliomaniac Extraordinary, 1776–1847*, Pinner Private Libraries Association, 1967

Pearce, Joseph, *Literary Converts*, HarperCollins, London, 1999

Porter, Roy, *The Greatest Benefit to Mankind: A Medical History of Humanity from Antiquity to the Present*, HarperCollins, London, 1997

Pringle, Patrick, *Jolly Roger: The Story of the Great Age of Piracy*, Museum Press, London, 1953

Rackham, Oliver, *Trees and Woodland in the British Landscape*, J. M. Dent, London, 1976

Robb, Graham, *Strangers: Homosexual Love in the Nineteenth Century*, Picador, London, 2003

Rowell, Geoffrey, *The Vision Glorious*, Oxford University Press, 1983

Ruskin, John, *The Crown of Wild Olives: Three Lectures on Work, Traffic and War*, Hurst & Co., 1910

Rutland, John the Fifth Duke and the Duchess of, *Journal of a Trip to Paris, July 1814*, privately published

Schama, Simon, *Landscape and Modern Memory*, HarperCollins, London, 1995

Seba, Anne, *The Exiled Collector: William Bankes and the Making of an English Country House*, John Murray, London, 2004

Stannard, Martin, *Evelyn Waugh: The Early Years, 1903–1939*, J. M. Dent, London, 1986

Sutherland, John, *Inside Bleak House*, Duckworth, London, 2005

Thomas, Keith, *Man and the Natural World: Changing Attitudes in England 1500–1800*, Penguin, London, 1984

Thurston, R., *Moated Houses of England*, Country Life Ltd, London, 1935

Uglow, Jenny, *A Little History of British Gardening*, Chatto & Windus, London, 2004

War, Jennifer C., *English Noblewomen in the Late Middle Ages*, Longman, London, 1992

Waugh, Evelyn, *The First Time I . . .*, edited by Thelma Benson, Chapman & Hall, London, 1935

Waugh, Evelyn, *A Little Learning*, Methuen, London, 1964

Wilgress, Jane, *Alec Miller: Guildsman and Sculptor in Chipping*

Campden, Chipping Campden and District Historical and Archaeological Society, 1987

Wilson, A. N., *God's Funeral*, John Murray, London, 1999

Wilson, Richard, and Mackley, Alan, *Creating Paradise: The Building of the English Country House*, Hambledon, London, 2000

Woolgar, C. M., *The Great Household in Late Medieval England*, Yale University Press, 1999

Woolgar, C. M., *The Senses in Late Medieval England*, Yale University Press, 2006

Ziegler, Philip, *The Black Death*, Collins, London, 1969

ILLUSTRATION CREDITS

INDEX

Lygons with the same forename are listed in chronological order. Women's names: female members of the Lygon family are all indexed under Lygon. Lygon wives and Beauchamp wives are indexed under their maiden names. See the Family Tree for further guidance.

Figures in **bold** refer to pages with illustrations.